G000045295

Robin Bryans was born in Belfast i̶n̶ and in Enniskillen, County Fermana a cabin boy on a dredger in Belfast medical missionary. He left Belfast South Wales Bible College and he w Canada and Venezuela. He took up diamond prospecting in Canada and South America and his hunting and trapping with the Blackfoot and Stony Indians began a long interest in American Indians who feature in his many travel books which were published in the 1960s.

Under the name Robert Harbinson he has published a four-part autobiography: *No Surrender*; *Song of Erne*; *Up Spake the Cabin Boy* and *The Protégé*. In addition to these and his travel books he has also published *Tattoo Lily and Other Ulster Stories*, the novel *Lucio*, and his collection of poems *Songs Out of Oriel*.

In more recent years he has become involved in music, concentrating on his work as an opera librettist from his London home/music studio.

ULSTER

A Journey through the Six Counties

ROBIN BRYANS

THE
BLACKSTAFF
PRESS

BELFAST

First published in 1964 by
Faber and Faber Limited
This Blackstaff Press edition is a photolithographic facsimile of the text
of the first edition printed by W. and J. Mackay and Company Limited

This edition published in 1989 by
The Blackstaff Press Limited
3 Galway Park, Dundonald, Belfast BT16 0AN, Northern Ireland
with the assistance of
The Arts Council of Northern Ireland

Printed by The Guernsey Press Company Limited

British Library Cataloguing in Publication Data
Bryans, Robin, 1928–
Ulster: a journey through the six counties.
1. Northern Ireland. Description & travel
I. Title
914.16'04824

ISBN 0-85640-421-7

For
ERIC EWENS
who has also dropped Ulster
hayseeds in London streets

Contents

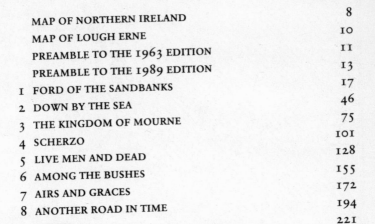

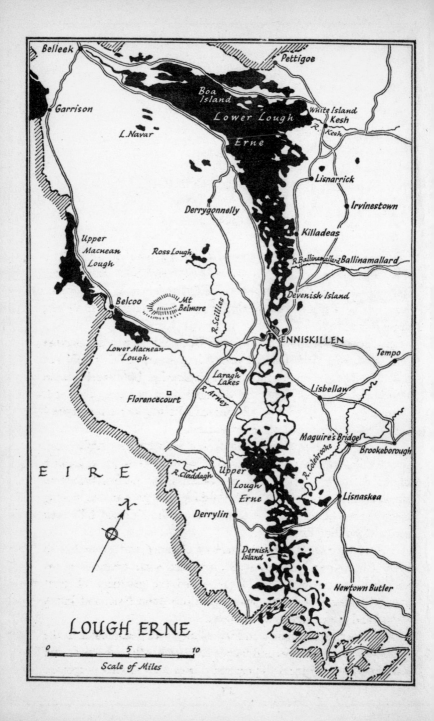

Belleek

Pettigoe

Garrison

Boa
Island

White Island
Kesh

Lower Lough

L. Navar

R. Kesh

Erne

Lisnarrick

Irvinestown

Derrygonnelly

Killadeas

Upper
Macnean
Lough

Ross Lough

R. Ballinamallard Ballinamallard

Devenish Island

Belcoo

Mt
Belmore

R. Scillies

ENNISKILLEN

Tempo

Lower Macnean
Lough

Laragh
Lakes

Lisbellaw

Florencecourt

R. Arney

Maguire's Bridge

Brookeborough

E I R E

R. Claddagh

Upper
Lough
Erne

R. Colebrooke

N

Lisnaskea

Derrylin

Dernish
Island

Newtown Butler

LOUGH ERNE

0   5   10

Scale of Miles

Preamble
to the 1963 edition

There is no place like home—or at any rate not *quite* like it. And this was as good a reason as any for a book about Ulster. Being born in Ulster makes it difficult to be dispassionate—but then who *wants* to be dispassionate about the lyrical loveliness of these six, sea-girt counties?

But because I had lived away from Ulster for many years, making only spasmodic visits home, I planned a journey which would not only embrace the six counties topographically, but which would also show me how Ulster has changed since my own boyhood. Covering the whole area in one tour would also give me the impression strangers have on coming to this land.

My summer journey revealed things I never knew before and reminded me of others I had forgotten, such as the empty splendour of the miles-long, gold and sandy beaches, the perfect beauty of streams and rivers and the thrill of fishing they give, or the moving magnificence of the Mourne mountains or the Donegal hills seen across a sparkling River Foyle.

I discovered the Georgian legacy of elegance and order left to every Ulster town and village. I discovered some treasures of art and architecture in Belfast. I discovered the grandeur of great country houses and estates, masterpieces by John Nash and James Wyatt, and even a garden by Le Nôtre.

I saw for the first time a striking affinity with Scandinavia in the blond hair and blue eyes and loughs like fjords where sea birds and waterfowl teem, where seals play and whales come in after porpoises.

PREAMBLE

To my special joy, I discovered that old bitternesses are waning and that the beauty of Ulster is no longer scarred by old terrors. The province of Ulster proper has nine of Ireland's counties, and it is six of these which make up Northern Ireland. Yet though the beauty melts the borders I had to be stern with myself and stay within the six.

The best way to list the people who helped my journey of discovery would be to quote almost the whole of the Post Office directory—everybody helped, with cars or food or smiles or songs. But particularly I must mention Robert Frizzell and his staff of the Northern Ireland Tourist Board who arranged most of the photographs, Richard Whittington-Egan for facts and figures about Sir Hamilton Harty, and Elizabeth Nicholas, who thought a book of this kind necessary and suggested that I should do it.

I have done it, and here it is.

ROBIN BRYANS

London,
1963

Preamble
to the 1989 edition

In 1944 I left Belfast for Wales as a student, yet Christmas of that year found me already back again at Granshagh Little Farm in County Fermanagh with the old brother and sister, Christy and Maggie, with whom I had been billeted as a wartime evacuee. Until 1970 I made frequent visits to the beautiful Erne valley in the west, feeling especially delighted when asked to return and write this book in 1963. The time seemed opportune. On both sides of the border and the religious divide men and women of goodwill had every reason to be optimistic that sectarian struggles had come to an end. In the 1963 edition's Preamble I wrote: 'the beauty of Ulster is no longer scarred by old terrors'. Many believed it and many more wanted to. Then, all too soon, the peace lay shattered, and ancient enmities returned with fearsome new ferocity. Nights of curfew and days of burning houses brought the long nightmare back again.

As a boy in Fermanagh I had seen both Catholics and Protestants lift the latch of the lonely Granshagh farm to share 'a bit in the hand' around the turf fire, an experience I related in *Song of Erne*. That this song had not outlived its singing, I discovered in 1988, when invited to join in celebrations of the tenth anniversary of Enniskillen's library. The Fermanagh people decided in that year to work 'together' for the restoration of its live-and-let-live atmosphere that had so enraptured me as a twelve-year-old evacuee. After nearly fifty years I had little difficulty in recognising George Cathcart whose outwintering bullocks always seemed to be crossing the Battery Hill at twilight as Maggie and I went to draw last water from the spring well divined by her father in the last century; Joan Trimble the composer, now editor of the family newspaper, sat next to that other lady of Irish art-and-letters, Mary Lappin, whose uncle I remember as the Whitehill parish priest with a moustache-cup kept specially for

13

use by his friend Hugh MacManaway, for long the Protestant rector of Errigle Keerogue; generations of Browns turned up although they had outlived the under-gardener's cottage at Ballycassidy where I stayed for six months as an evacuee; May Reihill, daughter of Old Pat and sister of Young Pat, came and persuaded me to sing her mother's favourite song. I was happy to meet these people again with their neighbours in the Enniskillen library, for they were anxious, like James Stephens had been, to regard 'remembered goodness as a benediction'.

Another old friend, Larry Hall, had died but his son David kindly drove me to my next lecture in Armagh which has seen so much strife in recent years. But here too the library audience concerned itself with Irish characters and books, including Paddy Kavanagh, the shoe-maker/ploughboy who became a poet in the 1930s. The armoured cars patrolled outside, but the people of Armagh at my hotel sang all the old Irish songs until long after midnight.

In this book I call the author Forrest Reid 'a familiar sight' in the Belfast of my boyhood. Unlike some writers, I would not call Reid a misogynist who would only talk to women through his letter box, because two favourite visitors to his home were the sisters Grace and Jean Hamilton. In 1917 Reid became 'honorary assistant editor' on *Kenneth's Magazine,* started by the schoolboy Kenneth Hamilton with help from his sister Grace. Over seventy years later in her London flat Grace Hamilton was asking me whereabouts in Belfast my 1988 lecture would be given. At mention of the Linen Hall Library we instantly thought of Forrest Reid's words: 'curled up in a low deep seat, I would sit gazing out between the trees. . .' This venerable institution, founded in 1788, is one of Europe's oldest subscription libraries but, even more importantly, it is a unique literary club, where members from all walks of life come together to curl up in window seats and sample its famous collection of Irish books. John Gray, the librarian, kindly asked me to talk to its members. The UTV crew who recorded this lecture included some who had been present in the goodwill era of the 1960s when that epitome of goodwill, James Boyce, had interviewed me and the old Fermanagh farmer Christy and his sister Maggie in their farm kitchen. Since then a younger generation of authors and poets have given Ulster literature a new international dimension, and they too share the same 'togetherness' of the Fermanagh farmers and the poets of my day: Robert Greacen, whose aunt kept our paper shop; and George Buchanan who went bargain-hunting with Forrest Reid in the second-hand bookshops of Belfast's Smithfield Market.

The wonder of my Belfast childhood, second only to the Bog Meadows with their gypsy camps, was Smithfield's warren of booths selling every imaginable and unimaginable item under the great glass roof. But the sheet-music specialists and suppliers of lapel buttons and collarettes for Orangemen, Freemasons, Blackmen and Hibernians have all disappeared under steel and concrete, like the nine marshes and four lakes of the Bog Meadows. Over the years I have been grateful to Belfast neighbours in Donegail Avenue where I spent the first twelve years of my life, who have written to me about old friends and their animals. Joseph Connor wrote on 24 July 1987, recalling what had lived in the farmyard between the gable walls of 184 and 186 Donegall Avenue: 'As well as the forty pigs, there were six cows, a calf, a milking goat, several horses, geese, ducks and hens which had free grazing on The Bogs.'

Opposite our house lived the beautiful Mary Neill, whose husband kept the breadserver's horse which luckily kicked none of us boys when we ran under its belly to prove to each other we were not 'cissies'. I express my thanks to Mrs Neill's grandson, John Keyes, the Newry Arts Director, who researched my life on the Bog Meadows for the BBC and took me around old haunts. Thanks also to Paul Yates of UTV whose family lived next door to us and were most tolerant of my father's crowded pigeon loft and of my backyard jungle's rampant ivy which threatened to engulf their outdoor lavatory.

Louis MacNeice and Mary Wimbush had planned to spend part of 1963 with me revisiting mutual friends in 'The North'. Before dying that year Louis wrote: 'Maybe, if I look back, I shall find that my life is not just mine, that it mirrors the lives of the others – or shall I say the Life of the Other?'

ROBIN BRYANS

London,
1989

1

Ford of the Sandbanks

Belfast Lough, running in between the green coasts of Down and the massive cliffs of Antrim, has always seen the passing up and down of ships beneath its wide, windy skies. And long before the *Titanic* sailed out, or the grain clippers before it, or the high-pooped merchantmen and wooden men-o'-war before them, long before the city of Belfast arose on the lough marshes, men of learning sailed from these shores, missionaries of the light which extinguished the Dark Ages.

There may not have been apes and peacocks, sandalwood and sweet white wine among the lough's cargoes, but there were men of zeal and passion. Seven such young men sailed down the lough from Belfast in 1898 on their way to preach among the pyramids of the Nile. They left a lawyer, William Fulton, behind them who was to stay in Belfast and organize the newly-founded Egypt General Mission.

Fifty years later William Fulton was still alive and put another young missionary on board ship. It was a troopship, for this was near D-Day in the Second World War. The young missionary was only 16, and had, in fact, still to do his training. In his own mind, however, he already *was* a missionary and filled with the quite presumptuous belief that Timbuctoo and Tokyo could not possibly do without him.

After valedictory prayers in William Fulton's house off the Lisburn Road he went abroad, feeling rather special. Because of impending D-Day civilians were still banned from crossing to England. But for this young man, William Fulton had used his influence. And so, following the line of many before him, the young would-be missionary set sail with a boatload of soldiers.

That, however, was about as far as the young man got with missionizing. He discovered, luckily in time, that though Timbuctoo and Tokyo could very well do without him, *he* could not do without *them*. The next time he appeared in the Lisburn Road, near William Fulton's house, was after a lecture to the Royal Society of Ulster Architects about his travels in Brazil. In the intervening twenty years the young man had travelled in many parts of the world, for better or for worse, without hawking any spiritual wares.

The erstwhile missionary, later traveller, and lecturer to the Ulster Architects, was myself. And I had a curious mixture of feelings when I slipped out for a moment from the architects' celebration dinner and wandered along the Lisburn Road I had known under such different circumstances long before.

Had I changed so much or had Belfast?

The Lisburn Road certainly had. Although William Fulton's home still stood, others of the big Victorian houses I once knew had gone to make way for student hostels. And next day I found many other things I once knew had gone too. I had written about my childhood and the colourful but poverty-stricken Belfast of the 1930s in my book *No Surrender*. The day after the lecture to the architects, I went with some staff of the *Belfast Telegraph* to re-visit the old places. Many had gone. The *Telegraph* photographer wanted my picture against one of the slogans 'No Surrender' which, with other political maxims, used to be painted on our gables and backyard walls. But though we hunted in many streets we could not find one in a good enough condition to photograph.

'No Surrender' and our fierce Protestant beliefs were once life and death to us. Now it looked as if the fervour was declining. It was this and other changes I saw in 1962 which made me determine to see what else had happened, not only in Belfast but elsewhere in Northern Ireland. I had returned occasionally for longer or shorter visits to Ulster, in the twenty years after William Fulton put me on the troopship. But until last summer my picture of the province was fragmentary, and the changes were seen piecemeal. So I spread a map of the Six Counties on the floor of my London flat and pored over it, planning my journey.

Strangely, any journey through geographical Ireland becomes a historical journey also, for every part has some powerful link with bygone ages. Bangor Abbey, for instance, a few miles down the coast from Belfast, is such a place. From here Gallus went out to become Switzerland's patron saint. Columbanus was another monk from Bangor who crossed Europe and established the famous monastery of Bobbio, 'the light of northern Italy'. Every part of western Europe knew the missionaries from Ulster with their odd clothes and strange Celtic tonsure.

These men, who had great learning and a knowledge of architecture, took their skill in music on their travels to the delight of Frank, Gaul and Goth. Something of the beauty created by these sixth-century men from Bangor Abbey can still be seen today in the Ambrosian Library at Milan. Amongst the canticles and anthems once used at Bangor is the lovely Eucharistic hymn, *Sancti venite Christi corpus sumite*.

Unlike those early and earnest missionaries, I went back to my native land with no mission other than to see it, if possible, with new eyes. Belfast is the inevitable place to begin looking at Ulster, for the boats from Heysham and Liverpool go there and the airport is at Aldergrove, fourteen miles from the city. However, Belfast, like most capital cities, is not typical of the country as a whole. The city, though highly individual, is a hybrid of Ulster life and English life, this English contribution being largely in the form of industry and nineteenth-century architecture.

The marshes, extending each side of the long lough opening from the North Channel, had originally given Belfast its name—*Bel*, an entrance or ford, and *Fearsad* meaning a sandbank. The reclaiming went on throughout the centuries, though the modern city occupies a much larger area than in previous times.

The sloblands must have discouraged extensive city building for many years. Even as late as 1660 Belfast consisted of nothing more than a hundred and fifty houses grouped in six streets and five lanes. Nothing at all remains of this Restoration town and even the later, elegant Georgian Belfast is remembered only by a few, scattered buildings. Belfast is really a child of the nineteenth century.

Georgian street architecture has survived at Chichester Street in a short terrace of chocolate-coloured brick houses whose gracefulness is comparable with Georgian urban building anywhere. In the basement of one of the houses I saw an exhibition of work by Dürer. This was in the fine little gallery run by the Arts Council. Another Georgian survival is the beautiful First Presbyterian Church of 1783, an oval building whose plain façade is adorned by the Ionic order—which order seems later to have become Belfast's architectural signature tune. The streets graced by Georgian buildings are few and far between and, for better or worse, Belfast is a two-faced city—Victorian Grandoise on one hand and Victorian Grisly on the other. The city's saving grace is the omnipresent countryside of County Down and the Antrim mountains, and its justifiably famed Attic light.

Ever since I left Belfast as a boy-missionary of God-knows-what, my return visits home have been punctuated by points of awareness. One of these points of awareness was reached when the *Belfast Telegraph* took me on the hunt of my childhood haunts. Another had been when I wrote *No Surrender* and realized how fantastic my 1930's childhood had been. In those days, I had known only one of Belfast's faces—Victorian Grisly.

Because I was born and reared in the city's meaner streets my interest in them is perhaps understandable. Although they are, architecturally at least, Victorian Grisly they draw me each time I visit Belfast. In the years since I left them, these streets had changed little. The people were still as neighbourly. Much of the dire poverty, though not all, had gone. Children still swung on the lamp-posts outside the brightly painted houses with whitened doorsteps. They still sang skipping rhymes, though different from those my sisters knew:

> *Charlie Chaplin went to France*
> *To teach the cannibals how to dance*
> *With your heel and your toe and a birly-i-o*
> *Touch the rope and out you go.*

The most noticeable change was that cars now lined the streets, some of the bigger American models being longer than the width of the houses they were parked by. Windows and doors still had yellow brickwork, but the colour of flags and bunting and decoration in celebration of the great Twelfth of July had lost the wild enthusiasm they had. But the decline of the fiercer kind of loyalties has not taken away some of the older habits. In the backyards the elaborate paintings of King William III crossing the Boyne are missing, but today's youths still busy themselves in the elaborate wooden pigeon lofts, and their fathers, scarves knotted round their necks, still take their muscled, nervous greyhounds out for exercise. But of the black peasant shawl I remembered so well, I saw nothing.

Like its industrial city counterparts elsewhere in Britain, Belfast had embarked on an ambitious re-housing programme. But such things come slowly in a democracy, and I saw that most of the city's people still lived in the rows of narrow, terrace houses. Many of the streets lie near the docks and the River Lagan which winds its way through the city. Originally this was marshland and the houses were built on screw-piles invented by Alexander Mitchell, a local engineer. Another Belfast resident was so inconvenienced by the alleyway cobbles he rode over on his bicycle that he invented the pneumatic tyre. This was John Boyd Dunlop, whose flowing, flying beard used to be a familiar sight in old Belfast.

With notable exceptions, both the rich and the poor Victorian accepted his station in life as ordained of God. 'The rich man in his castle, the poor man at his gate, God made them, high or lowly, And order'd their estate,' wrote Mrs. Alexander, wife of the Irish primate, in her famous hymn, *All things bright and beautiful*. Thus, while row upon indistinguishable row of back-to-back housing was considered adequate for the poor, the houses of the rich had accordingly to be more castle-like, and Belfast had its quota of rich men's castles. The Malone Road became known for its grand residences, even having a discreetly hedge-screened house designed by Voysey.

Belfast also had its share of castles which the Victorians built to express their awareness of civic corporateness. Churches and chapels leave the visitor in no doubt that Belfast is a pattern book of Gothic Revival. St. Anne's, the Protestant cathedral, is the exception on the grounds that it was designed in the manner of Romanesque Revival, and indeed, Romanesque Survival, for the apse, which looks like a stage-set for *Hamlet*, was only recently completed.

Though Revivals of any sort are distasteful to many people, I thought St. Anne's worth visiting, because the new stone apse was magnificent and the whole church gained a spacious grandeur in no way disturbed by the borrowed style and decoration. Part of the decoration included carved portraits of famous men. Archimedes was there and Lord Kelvin also, a Belfast man whose electrical inventions gave the world the galvanometer and transatlantic cable—3,700 miles of it to be exact, a fact I knew in my boyhood and pondered upon instead of listening to sermons during Church Lads' Brigade services in the cathedral.

Perhaps the worst aspect of modern cathedrals, in whatever style, is that they no longer represent the greatest skill and brains of their age. In Belfast, the city's true cathedral spires were the shipyard gantries, the real vaulting was in the huge, curving sides and ribs of half-finished ships. The shipyards reveal the truth about the city in ways which a myth in stone about a make-believe world of romantic art could never do.

I discussed St. Anne's new Norman-cum-Romanesque apse with Robert McKinstry, a Belfast architect whom I had met the previous year at my lecture. His wife Cherith unfortunately was not there, but an exhibition of her work was taking place at the Arts Council Gallery. She is a painter and sculptor who has mined a rich vein of colour which reminded me of Rubens's fiery passages of reds and rich oranges merging through yellows and browns to red again. Cherith McKinstry had allied her sense of voluptuous, almost monochrome colour to superb draughtsmanship. Colour and line together served to express her sensitive ideas. Most of her pictures were figurative, many being of religious subjects. She seemed to be as fluent with tragedy, as in her monumental *Ecce Homo* for instance, as with domestic calm, shown by the recumbent figure in *Mary at Bethlehem* or her own *Baby in the Pram*. But Cherith McKinstry's art was not sentimental and her figures had a kind of heroic scale that few painters today are capable of creating. Belfast is fortunate in having an artist of this calibre working in the city.

Belfast is full of contradictions and, perhaps in this way more than any other, it is most Irish. It is an industrial city, yet is paradoxically under the influence of rural Ulster. The modern Ulster poet W. R. Rodgers put his finger on this when he said, 'As far as Belfastmen go, every one has hayseeds in the turn-up of his pants.'

I saw a young man in washed-out jeans and open shirt flying bareback on a huge shaggy mare down Georgian Chichester Street. His horse only had a rope halter, but in spite of this he went full gallop through the traffic, ignoring the red double-decker buses, scorning the shiny this-year's cars. He was the nearest thing I had ever seen in real life to that most beautiful of all equestrian sculptures, Anne-Marie Nielsen's memorial in Copenhagen to her composer husband.

Later, I saw other horses in Chichester Street and discovered something I never knew in all my boyhood years: a blacksmith's forge right in the heart of the city. Following the horses and then my nose—for a forge's acrid smell of burning is unmistakable—I found the blacksmith wreathed in yellow smoke in a yard. Right beside the Ministry of Commerce, foals were suckled as their mothers waited to be shod. To the rhythmic clang of the anvil and the gasp of bellows, tinkers and draymen waited with their carts and in the yard geese tried to drive off some dignified and offended-looking Pekinese bantam cocks in their feathered trousers.

Hayseeds and the hills, ships and the sea, meet in Belfast, and encroach at every street's end. Not only after church or chapel on Sunday, but after a day in the shipyard or on the loom the men and women of Belfast can take their greyhounds or their lovers out to the Black Mountain, Cave Hill, McArt's Fort, Squire's Hill, and out to the alluring groves of Carr's Glen and Shaw's Bridge, and on up to the majestic sweep of Divis—the Mountain of Tears. Here, on this highest of the Belfast Hills, they have the city and its lough before them as though in the palm of their hand. Up there, nearly sixteen hundred feet above the sea, the Storm God of the ancient Druids was said to have his throne. And there too the pagan priests called on their gods to defend them from the new Christians whose symbol of power was impudently nothing more than two bits of a rough tree trunk fashioned into a cross.

The pagan priests and gods did not have much luck in the Lagan Valley, and though neither the Druids nor the early monks, who might have stood on Divis, could possibly have dreamed what the marshland settlement below them would become by the twentieth century, the city never forsook a stern sense of conscience.

This conscience is, perhaps, too stern and too unyielding in a weak and yielding world. Judged by the faces of the statues, set on high pedestals about the city and concentrated especially in the City Hall's gardens, Belfast's city fathers of the last century must have been stern indeed. As I walked on the lawns there, fearful of treading on the importuning pigeons, I thought I saw disapproval registered in their bronze and stone features—disapproval of the sensuous way that the office and shop girls were taking advantage of the humid, scorching July lunch time to sprawl in sleeveless and low-cut summer dresses on the grass. I thought I read disapproval also of the youths in tight American jeans, tee-shirts and black leather jackets who looked with undisguised longing at the blue-eyed, freckled-faced blonde and auburn-haired girls, the soft-skinned, sweet-smiled girls who, basking coquettishly, were not unnoticed by the city's summer visitors—Fiji soldiers on leave, Scandinavian sailors from the docks, German hitch-hikers with tanned faces and muscled legs and impossibly heavy rucksacks.

Only the statues seemed to frown. Pigeons were bad enough staining the bronze robes of office with an impudent white. But worse for the city fathers was to have their civic plinths used for sitting on, as though the City Hall's precincts were no more than a slave market. Yet this sternness, this uncomfortable obsession with morality which the founders of modern Belfast undoubtedly had, produced at least one admirable result. In whatever way the city had been crippled by religious intolerance, whatever poverty had built its civic architecture, the same intolerance had made those men set their faces against slave markets.

Well may their monuments have disapproved of so much sweet flesh turning amber in the sun being displayed in the centre of their city, for they opposed the slave trade in human flesh so rigorously that not only did they wage a righteous war against slavery as such, but refused to let the slavers' ships dock at Belfast. While Liverpool, only a few miles across the water, waxed wealthy on the slave trade, as Bristol did also, Belfast stood firm in its belief, preferring a clear conscience to the gains made from the evils of slaving from which English ports profited. No slaver ever sailed in or out of Belfast Lough.

Not many roads in Belfast lead to Rome but most lead in some way to the City Hall where some of the august statues stand in their various attitudes of indignant piety. Chief among their company is the figure of Queen Victoria who looks, as she does in most statues ever made of her, like a film actress dressed up for the part. The Queen Empress, however, is graced in Belfast by some beautiful bronze figures done in that sentimental but sometimes appealing manner that was the last breathing of the old, pre-1914 War order of things.

In so far as Belfast has a centre, the City Hall standing in the wide Donegall Square is it. Sir Bramwell Thomas was the architect and although such plagiaristic architecture is now almost beyond belief, his building bears all the attributes that could reasonably be expected of a city hall. John Betjeman, the champion of so much down-trodden and despised Victorian architecture, wrote to me about my visit to Belfast and bade me take due note of Thomas's 'Baroque Extravaganza'.

I duly took note of this encyclopaedic Classical building, a structure as rhetorical as the statues on its lawns, a council house in which all the elements seemed to be making speeches and declaiming, as the carved figures in its central pediment were.

Taste is every man's own affair, and John Betjeman would be the first to agree, since he is so anxious to convert others to his own taste. But whatever may be said about the City Hall, there can be no denying that Bramwell Thomas knew his Baroque pattern book thoroughly. The building is almost an A to Z dictionary of Baroque features, including saucer domes and Baroque turrets, rustication and Baroque scrolls round the main central dome. The parapets have Baroque pinnacle pots, stone garlands—although strangely, this is a swagless building.

Despite a tarnish of green moss on parts of the stonework and a liberal pigeon whitewash on others, the building generally succeeds in its role of being grandly civic. The City Hall is large, square on plan and squat in proportion and domed with the light-bright green of weathered copper. Surprisingly, the principal order is Ionic and not Corinthian.

Inside, beyond Queen Victoria and the *porte cochère*, the architect had made surprises too. The main entrance hall was opened up right through to the underside of the main dome. The effect, despite a certain vulgarity, was most magnificent. There is marble everywhere, chunks and slabs and blocks of it, carved without the slightest sign of embarrassment or self-consciousness. In the Council Chamber itself the Baroque dictionary goes through G for Grinling Gibbons, in its carved woodwork and W for Wren in its plaster pendentives and saucer domes.

Paintings in the corridors and rooms record events and visits of royalty and other important guests. My favourite story about the City Hall's V.I.P. visitors concerns Lady Lavery, the legendary London hostess of the 1920s. Her husband was the Belfast-born Sir John Lavery whose paintings were one of the Royal Academy's main attractions at Burlington House for many years. Belfast always fêted the Laverys, although Hazel lent her extraordinary beauty as model for the colleen on the Irish Free State banknotes and was a close friend of Michael Collins. On her first visit to Belfast after her husband's knighthood a civic banquet was given in their honour. She swept up the marble stairs. At the top landing before the banqueting room, she paused.

'Lady Lavery,' she said proudly to the lackey announcing names.

Embarrassed, he whispered in her ear, 'Second door on the right, by the Lady Mayoress's retiring room.'

I had heard a similar story of Hazel Lavery in connection with the famous staircase at Londonderry House in London. The circulation of the story so amused her that for the rest of her life she readily accepted the title of Lady Lavatory. She was famous for her 'Gay 20s' sense of humour. 'How we laughed,' she once quoted at dinner, 'when the Grand Duchess tripped up and fell flat in the herbaceous border, and His Majesty instantly observed "There's no place like loam!"'

Recent dictionaries of art and artists have dropped Sir John Lavery's name and this is a pity, for though, like the architect of the City Hall, he practised in a manner now unfashionable, he was an undoubted master. Belfast has kept his work alive, however, and in the Ulster Museum and Art Gallery I found a number of his canvases stored carefully away in one of the attics, temporarily making room for a fine exhibition of Irish country houses, shown by paintings, mostly done in the eighteenth century.

Here, in the city again, the hayseeds were in the turn-ups—though this time the sophisticated hayseeds of the great estates, the Ulster of hills and trout streams and neatly husbanded fields, and southern landscaped parks with temples and Classical bridges and, in the middle of all, the great Georgian houses. Although so many bitter episodes lie embedded in the history of the contact between England and Ireland, it was, nevertheless, English eighteenth-century taste which moulded Irish towns, country estates and many of the great mansions.

Looking at those paintings with their benign, conventional skies and serene trees caught in perpetual summer, echoes of a romantic past were woken in me. In recent years social historians have laid bare the horrors of the Age of Elegance. Hogarth's drawings of gin and Bedlam, and accounts of brutality in Newgate or the Navy have all but obscured the fact that such a life went on in the midst of most beautifully designed surroundings. The landscapes in that Belfast exhibition reminded me of other truths about the eighteenth century, for unlike the photographer, the painter tends to record accurately. Also, the Irish landscape has not been scarred and marred like the English one. Many of the houses and their grounds remain unviolated to this day. My two years as an evacuee in County Fermanagh brought me a taste of that spacious world, unchanged in so many respects, which has long gone from England—the country of its origin.

The exhibition catalogue quoted a letter of 1737 written by Lord Orrery to Tom Southern of Dublin. The words make plain the secret behind so much of Ireland's unique beauty; 'There is indeed a great Difference in the Complexion of the two Islands. Nature has been profusely beneficent to Ireland, and Art has been as much so to England. Here, we are beholden to nothing but the Creation; there, you are indebted to extensive Gardners and costly Architects.'

There were more than hayseeds, however, in the turn-ups of the

Ulster Art Gallery. I was discovering that Belfast was so oddly and so awkwardly and so mysteriously a microcosm of Ulster's country life which begins so abruptly beyond the last street of the last suburb, and which even invades the grand downtown areas, for even there the Antrim mountains are always in sight.

A member of the Art Gallery staff let me loose among the stacked canvases in the attics. At once I saw a painting by Sir John Lavery, a masterly portrait of Michael Cardinal Logue. Lavery's chocolate-box manner, lavished on so many pictures of his wife, would not do for the Cardinal. Here was force both of art and character, the churchman defying world, flesh and Devil and presumably Lavery as well with a personality which the Cardinal's famous ugliness could not conceal. Something of Augustus John's deep and vivid perception had guided the Lavery skill, as I confirmed by next finding a John portrait, *Vivienne*.

Also hidden away up there was an early Graham Sutherland *Miner probing a drill-hole*, the miner entombed, a massive masculine figure curiously like Henry Moore's drawings, full of timeless monumentality which Moore alone of all modern sculptors has mastered. I found also an interesting period piece *Field of corn at Pont-Aven*. Roderic O'Conor painted it in 1892, only four years after Gauguin met Émile Bernard at Pont-Aven. Here were the brilliant passages of colour of Impressionism, still an outrage at that time, and a brush technique which told that O'Conor admired Van Gogh even if he did not actually meet him. One of the most impressive canvases in the store was the violently coloured and violently designed *Les Routiers* by William Roberts, a dynamic picture of racing cyclists and their machines, a tangle of muscular limbs, handlebars, saddles and wheels wrought into a taut and sinuous symbol of physical effort.

Best of all, the gallery's store contained some of Stanley Spencer's work. *Daphne* was his Belfast niece and he had painted her with that scrupulous line and loving observation which made him a draughtsman first and a colourist after. *Daphne* was lucid, pale and yet alive, painted as though he was afraid the colour might obscure some truth about her beauty. Stanley Spencer rose to fame, and his posthumous fame rests on his reputation as a seer. He is known as a weird prophet of resurrection, who saw the problems, without attempting to solve them, of what would happen when fat wives and their moustached husbands in braces came out of their graves as though death had not interrupted their lives. But the picture of *Daphne* showed Spencer's supreme competence at the plain business of drawing and portrayal. The gallery store also had a figure composition by him and one of his religious pictures, *The Betrayal*, a dark canvas full of dark symbolic figures, going about their dark deeds against a background of brick walls and swooping roofs, the whole being reminiscent of a seventeenth-century Dutch domestic painting.

Stanley Spencer had many connections with Belfast and he was fond of the city. His musician brother Harold lived there and Stanley often visited the family. The city's streets did not seem mean to the painter. His acute eyes saw beauty in the endless rows of bricks and the neat painted doors and windows. Empathy stirred in him when he looked at the gaunt faces of men at the bus-stops waiting to cross over to Queen's Island shipyards.

During his visits to the city Stanley Spencer loved to stay with two extraordinary artists who still live in Belfast—George MacCann and his wife Mercy Hunter. They had both been pupils of Stanley's other brother, Gilbert Spencer.

For many years the door-key on a bootlace hung inside the Mac-Canns' letterbox has been the free welcome for architects, painters, sculptors and writers into the MacCanns' home. When Stanley stayed there he got up at six every morning. This was to talk undisturbed with Mercy about art and to hear her stories of the trans-Siberian journeys she undertook to her girlhood home in China, where her Russian mother and Ulster father were missionaries. Then, when Mercy left the house for the school where she taught, Stanley would follow, talking to the children and helping them with their drawing. The children called him simply Stanley, an affectionate use which he would not hear of being changed when he became a celebrity and a knight.

I knew Stanley Spencer off and on for years at Cookham, long before he was snapped up by wealthy patrons. It pleased me immensely on going home to Belfast again to find others who also knew him for what he really was: a gentle, small man, haunted by religious notions interested in little more than the plainest of life's plain things.

Stanley Spencer had no idea of self-defence at all and consequently people could misrepresent him without a demur from the painter. He never wanted to be noticed. Possibly the only drawing of himself he ever requested was from Mercy Hunter herself whom he much admired and respected. She drew him in pencil, revealing the little man's bespectacled, elfin face, pursed and cautious with the tension of the scientist who wants to *know* rather than the artist who wishes to *express*. But in this drawing Mercy Hunter also showed her own considerable ability as a draughtsman.

It would have been good if her husband George MacCann had done a sculpture of Stanley, though perhaps the little painter from Cookham would not have had patience to sit for the making of a bust. George MacCann would no doubt have done Stanley as much justice as Mercy did in her pencil sketch. Although George MacCann is mainly known as a teacher, as his wife is known as a B.B.C. art critic, he is a sculptor capable of infusing form with life and vitality. I liked his two horsemen from a London exhibition of 1953. The horses and riders were stripped of superficialities, full of lithe movement and strength.

Looking round the big living-room at the MacCanns' I saw a Dan O'Neill, which artist, with John Luke and Colin Middleton, makes up a very diverse trinity of Ulster painters. As I was sitting in the room where Stanley Spencer had his shakedown, it was only natural that I should hear about his introduction to Dan O'Neill. Waking up in the night to somebody breaking in through a window Stanley seized a bayonet, normally used for poking the fire, and advanced to deal with the intruder. Fortunately, George MacCann arrived to prevent the shedding of Dan O'Neill's blood. Dan, perched on top of a builder's ladder taken from a yard next door, explained that he was merely rather late and was climbing in to pay his respects to the great English painter. When Stanley later saw O'Neill's paintings he said, 'Crikey! I'm glad I didn't stick that bayonet through him.'

Stanley Spencer must at some time or another have found his way to Smithfield Market, that part of Belfast which looks permanently like one of the painter's resurrections. Housed under one glass roof, the market is an eruption of books and pictures and records and musical instruments, some new, mostly old and all going for less than a song. All through the day the second-hand bookshops have customers ranging from university dons to shipyard journeymen all foraging through the immense piles and pyramids and solid walls of books. The record shops too do a roaring trade—literally when their speakers are turned on full volume so that the alleys between the lock-up stalls echo and rumble to whatever beat and whatever voice is new. The Belfast teenager is not so very different from his counterpart elsewhere. At least if he is mad it's bound to be music-mad, for Northern Ireland, like its twenty-six sister counties across the border, has music and dancing in its very air. After the Twelfth of July celebrations and processions I met an old friend from Enniskillen.

'How was the Twelfth?' I asked.

'Och!' he answered, 'It was grand. We had over a hundred bands.'

As I was wandering through Smithfield waiting for a summer shower to hold up, one of the music shops began to play a Kathleen Ferrier song, *Down by the Salley Gardens*. I wondered how many people idling under Smithfield's glass roof, or how many of the millions the world over who love the singing of Kathleen Ferrier and Mary O'Hara and John McCormack, realized that much of their repertoire would not exist but for the work of a Belfast man, Herbert Hughes born in 1882.

With a quite peculiar genius, and an unflagging persistence, Hughes collected old Irish airs and ballads. He had no time for folky arty-craftiness and no interest in trying to live in the past. All he wanted was to extract the musical juice from what he heard. Much folk music falls hideously on the sophisticated musical ear, yet Herbert Hughes was able to turn many old airs into immortal music, saving many beautiful melodies from oblivion, as Cecil Sharp, Vaughan Williams and others did in England. Hughes had no need to write symphonies and concertos with four volumes of *Irish Country Songs* to his credit. With his charming *Rhymes* and *Parodies* he had no need to bother with sonata form and fugues—though perhaps his son Spike Hughes thought otherwise.

Herbert Hughes's special skill lay in weaving a firm and lyrical line of melody from the original material and devising an accompaniment to enhance the melody's beauty. He made hundreds of such arrangements, Mary O'Hara's *Spanish Lady* and Kathleen Ferrier's *The Lover's Curse* being among them.

None is more lovely for me than *The Salley Gardens*, once known as *The Maids of Mourne Shore*. This is not only because of the tune but also because of the haunting words W. B. Yeats wrote for this haunting air:

> *In a field by the river my love and I did stand,*
> *And on my leaning shoulder she laid her snow-white hand*
> *She bid me take life easy, as the grass grows on the weirs;*
> *But I was young and foolish, and now am full of tears.*

A cursory visit might give the impression that Smithfield Market was nothing more than a junk-yard, even though a fascinating one. For me, it will always be a treasure island, where, at any time, treasure trove can be discovered. When I started my working life as a 14-year-old cabin-boy on the dredger in Belfast Lough, I used to go ashore shopping for the crew. My errands included messages for sailors on the larger ships for this was during the war and men of many nationalities were working aboard. In Smithfield Market I often picked up French novels or essays on Kierkegaard or Polish-English dictionaries. And for myself, while rummaging there, I went straight to the portfolios which then, as still today, were crammed full of prints and drawings and engravings and lithographs. And it was from there that I rescued a red conté crayon drawing which, many years later, turned out to be extraordinary. When I bought this framed drawing of a child's head I was only fascinated by the appealing eyes, the loose tumble of hair about the little girl's head and the curious, silky softness of the skin suggested by reflected lights about the cheeks and forehead. The artist's initials in the corner, M.M.McD., meant nothing to me. And it was not until years later that the Red Cross stamp on the back showed that the drawing had been sold at Christie's in a 1918 society sale to raise funds for the First World War soldiers, and that the artist was Margaret McDonald.

Although this picture fetched a high price in 1918 I bought it for 5s. in Smithfield. I have often wondered since if Sir John Lavery bought it at Christie's and took it home with him to

Belfast, for he belonged to the Glasgow art movement in which Margaret McDonald and her husband Charles Rennie Mackintosh were so influential. For years Lavery was an active member of the Glasgow School. He began life earning 7s. 6d. a week in Glasgow's Railway Mineral Department—an ironical comment on his later fame which included the commission to paint Queen Victoria's visit to the Glasgow Exhibition, the first of many such royal commissions.

The Glasgow School had few followers in England. Its most powerful influence was on the Continent. Charles Mackintosh was the first British architect and designer since the Adam brothers whose name became a household word on the Continent. Yet though the effect of the Glasgow School was perhaps a cleansing and purifying one, the actual style itself, like the more widespread *Art Nouveau* of which Margaret and Charles Mackintosh were pioneers, did not survive. Perhaps it was too rarefied to last in the harsh atmosphere the 1914 War ushered in. However, I am extremely fond of my drawing from Smithfield, especially as it is one of Margaret McDonald's rare life drawings done as a straightforward study, not in the highly stylized mannerism of the Glasgow School.

Long before *Art Nouveau* or the Glasgow School took root and flourished, there were odd indications, hints and rumours that the whole art world was about to be stripped of much affectation and frippery, its styles and conventions made to correspond with the vigour of life's truths rather than with what polite society dictated. By 1880 the French Impressionists were scorching the fashionable salons with their sunshine.

Yet it seems strange that in architecture, imitation Gothic was still in vogue. Even then, however, a veering of interest away from the purely imitative could be seen. William Butterfield was prominent amongst the architects who, if not attempting to break away like Charles Mackintosh, at least hammered the Gothic style on their own anvil.

In 1878, a year between two of the Impressionist exhibitions in Paris and five years before Lavery, the former Ulster farm labourer, went to live with the Impressionists at Grès-sur-Loigne, Butterfield began the building of St. Mark's Church at Dundela in Belfast. The church stands on a ridge overlooking the lough and the shipyard hulls and gantries, and is not the least among Butterfield's works. St. Mark's is a sugar rock candy mountain of pink and yellow stone arranged in the Sienna-like horizontal stripes of which Butterfield was so fond. But Belfast is the richer for the architect's sense of noble space and proportion. The nave is wide and high, and the interior's most striking feature and a masterstroke of design is the baptistery, boldly divided from the nave by two high, tracery-filled arches supported on a free-standing column. The chancel could only be Butterfield with its blind wall arcading filled with the savoury mess of wall tiling and mosaics such as Butterfield loved.

Complying with a practice not uncommon in his day, Butterfield went into his half-completed buildings and himself drew on the walls profiles for mason and carpenter to work by. I do not know whether he actually visited Belfast, though what he would have thought of the literature on display when I visited the church I cannot imagine. It was the same kind of literature to be found in Butterfield's not dissimilar church of St. Alban's in Holborn. The pamphlets at St. Mark's were much more in line with the Church of England than that of Ireland. I am sure that not many Belfast Protestants would wish to purchase the S.P.C.K. *Retreats* or a *Letter to a Homosexual* which were on sale.

From St. Mark's the visitor may look across to the shipyards. The network of steel webs is spun high in the air, changing its gossamer patterns as the great gantries travel slowly up and down the hulls of unfinished ships. The hulls lie dark and huge like mountains where, now and again, the will-o'-the-wisp of welders' torches sparks.

I walked downhill from the church, going immediately amongst the anonymity of terraced houses, down the steps to Strandburn Drive, passing by Miss A. Jordan's, the agent for 'Thomas Johnston's Complete Funeral Service' where I wondered what an incomplete funeral might be. And so on down to Victoria Park shadowed by the gantries and ringed by the green, slimy banks of the Connswater.

Here the children played, chasing each other or swinging on the swings or coming from the swimming pool with their hair hanging in rats' tails. It was their long summer holiday and even if they had been taught so in school they would not now care to remember that the Connswater was named after the magnificent King of Connaught

—Conn the Hundred Fighter—who took Northern Ireland in A.D. 200 setting up a dynasty which made Tara its capital and themselves High Kings.

But that was hundreds of years before shipbuilding came to Belfast in the eighteenth century. The city had to wait until the middle of the nineteenth century before its gigantic yards came into being through G. W. Wolff of Hamburg joining up with Edward Harland in the yard he bought in 1858, so pushing the quiet Georgian city into the iron claws of the Industrial Revolution.

The children in Victoria Park may not have been history-conscious but at least they knew what was going on in 'The Island'—as the shipyards are known. I talked with some young boys who were rolling on the grass. They told me what each hull was destined to be, who it was being built for and where its future voyages would likely be.

One of the boys told me proudly that his 'gran'da' had worked on the *Titanic* when the doomed liner had been built in the same yard. But the boys could not remain serious for long and began to wrestle again, unperturbed by the jet planes from Short and Harland's which swooped so low over the park that the poplar trees trembled. The old park attendants shouted above the din trying to keep performing dogs and toddlers from the rose-beds.

That day was Belfast's annual 'Butcher's Holiday' and several lads, dressed in Sunday best, were playing a kind of whist called 'Scotch' on the grass, recklessly losing their savings and wolf-calling at women pushing prams in the afternoon heat. An attendant blew his whistle and waved a stick at two small boys riding tricycles on holy ground. Some bold hussies came from the swimming pool and waved their wet costumes at sleeping lorry drivers who, drugged by the sun and humid atmosphere, lay in provocative attitudes.

But the people in Victoria Park and the people living round about were not strangers to me for their blood was my blood—I was born there within sight and sound of the shipyards. This was Ballymacarrett, in olden days the weavers' district. This too was the Belfast of St. John Ervine, and more recently, another Irish playwright, Sam Thompson.

When I was cabin-boy on the dredger out in the lough I used to throw slop buckets over the side, always, after one disaster, on the leeward side, but even then not always to the pleasure of the bargees working alongside at a lower level. Three men were also at work giving the old dredger a new coat of paint. And just as Stanley Spencer was glad not to have run Dan O'Neill through with the bayonet, so I am glad not to have emptied my slop bucket over the three painters for one of them was Sam Thompson.

Not until he was 39, with twenty-five years in the shipyards already behind him did Sam decide to become an actor. The reason was simple enough. He became infuriated with the false and emasculated dialogue passed off in films and plays about the shipyards as the real thing. For years he had heard his mother say 'Take a tram and go over the bridge', and the first play he wrote himself was called just that, *Over the Bridge*.

In this play and his second one *The Evangelist*, Sam Thompson has caught Belfast with its breeches down. There is no accounting for taste, least of all the taste of London audiences. The poor reception in the West End of plays which have packed the Irish theatres may simply be because John Bull is totally unaware of life in what remains of his other island.

I walked up Dee Street, where gantries peered like steeples over the gables of houses. Slogans had been painted on the gables— 'Mickeys keep out' and 'No Pope here'. I wondered how many Catholic children still today believe that the *Titanic* went down because such slogans had been scrawled on its sides in the shipyard— as I, when a boy living in the Protestant district, believed that the liner struck the iceberg because God willed so, in retribution for similar rude slogans, though against the British Crown.

Dee Street held many childhood memories for me. They came crowding back as I went to look for the last of my family who lived there. But my cousin Davie had been taken away to a home some months previously and so had gone one of Ballymacarrett's saddest sights. For forty years Davie had hopped through those streets, able only to make inarticulate noises. He was deaf and partly blind. When he was a teenage boy Davie's arms and legs and face had been mangled in an accident in Belfast's other great industry at the end of Dee Street, the rope-works—'the biggest in the world' they still tell you.

I walked sadly away from the little house which had been more like a prison than home to him, the past coming vividly back again when some boys asked 'Give us a penny, mister.' A penny! I looked at them, roguish and dusty from rolling like dumplings in the sandy soil in the waste lands around the Unionist Association Hall. I hoped a penny was not as important to them as it had been to me thirty years before, when I made the same request of passers-by.

Now, as then, the children knew what it meant to see the steel skeletons of ships rising starkly among the Island's gantries. They had a special interest to learn the names of the new tankers and cargo boats, for when there were no skeletons and no keels being laid and no riveters' hammers stuttering, they knew also that their fathers would be hanging listless and defeated about the street corners while once again unemployment stalked the streets of Bally-macarrett.

The boys of Ballymacarrett will be boys whether the cupboard at home is bare or not. I watched them throwing stones at the wire-meshed windows of the Special Care School. I saw their little sisters go peeping and pushing and giggling into the temptingly open door at a Sisterhood meeting going on in the Salvation Army hall on the corner of Pansy Street. Some children stood to watch the unfailing mysteries of the knife-grinder who sat pedalling furiously at his marvellous contraption, a combination of bicycle and sewing machine, sending a stream of sparks flying, more homely and not less bright sparks than those of the welders' torches which flashed from the shipyards.

I turned into the Vulcan Arms to drown the thirst made worse by the close, summer heat of the streets. With a pint of porter in front of me, I almost felt as if I belonged to Ballymacarrett and had never been away. The Vulcan Arms's only concession to the affluent age was a television set with, of course, at that time of the afternoon, horse racing. I watched the old men lighting their pipes at the thin gas jet burning on the counter. Behind the bar an official notice had been pinned up, worded in a curiously antique way. It sounded like 1846 though the date was in fact 1946—'Notice is hereby given that seats are provided in this shop in the proportion of at least one seat to every three persons employed as Shop Assistants, and that these Assistants are intended to make use of the seats whenever the use thereof does not interfere with their work.'

There were none of your smart, easy-to-clean plastic table-tops at the Vulcan, none of your imitation this and imitation that finished off in chromium plate or aluminium trim. The Vulcan Arms was good, honest hardwood mellowed by beer and elbow-grease. The main attraction was the bulbous glazed-tile counterfront, as good as new except for crazing, as hearty and vulgar and sanguine as the Victorian age which produced it.

This pub, however, could not compare with the excessive extravagances of another in down-town Belfast opposite the Great Northern Railway station. This had a name to match the splendour of its interior—the Crown Liquor Saloon. Miraculously the Crown had escaped 'improvement', possibly because the original workmanship of 1890 was still in mint condition and looked set to last yet another seventy years.

A pub was first recorded on the site in 1826, an interesting sidelight on the fact that the railway from Belfast to Lisburn opened only a few years afterwards. The Crown was transformed into its present orgy of art works under the hand of a young architect, son of a former owner of the place. The young man travelled in Spain and Italy, falling under the spell of romantic bodegas and cafés. Belfast seems to have struck him as drab and in need of livening up, for on returning he unloaded all the violent emotion roused by his Latin tour into his father's bar.

Up from Dublin came Italian craftsmen who set to work with gusto on the youthful architect's zestful ideas. Glazed tiles of every colour and shape, carved wood panels and posts and bar-tops and table-tops, stained and engraved glass and painted decorated panels, and when the workmen's hubbub subsided there was the Crown Liquor Saloon, transfigured into a glory never before seen in Belfast, or, I suspect, anywhere else either.

As with most late Victorian building the taste was open to question but the craftsmen's skill was undeniable. Almost every conceivable motif of Classical decoration was there and yet, curiously, the place remained quite distinctly a Belfast bar. There was the long counter, with an elaborate theatre-box-like front done in highly moulded glazed tiles. There was the elaborate carved wood shelving behind, housing the barrels and their beautiful brass fittings. There were the Corinthian columns picked out in green and gold, and, most important of all, the box-pews arranged round the walls for small groups to retire in comparative privacy. The most loving work was lavished on the carving of these 'snugs' whose screens were filled with carved panels and engraved glass and whose corner posts were topped like newels with lions and griffins bearing armorial shields with Latin mottoes like *Audaces Fortuna Juvat.*

The local midwife assisted at my entry into the world of Bally-macarrett thirty-five years ago. However, she could not linger for she wanted to join the crowd going the same afternoon to see the wedding of the rector at Laganbank. Three years later, the scholarly Archdeacon of Connor published a book about the state of the Church of Ireland in Belfast. He recommended that the in-cumbent of Laganbank, 'a man of marked ability', should be released from the small riverside congregation 'to use his great gifts' in the large industrial parishes. The good rector was duly sent to St. Simon's in the Meadows. And this man was the one who came to know me in my childhood and early youth better than any other, for I was one of his parish orphans. The Rev. Charles Maguire became more than my father in God when my own window-cleaner father had a fatal fall at the age of 27.

Mine was not the only mouth to be filled in his parish in those grim days of the 1930s. Nor were mine the only wild ways to be kept, within reasonable limits, on the right side of the law. But Charles Maguire sweated and slaved for the less fortunate of his parishioners. He did not desert them even though early in his career the Archdeacon of Connor wanted him for the beautiful and historic parish of Carrickfergus a few miles north on the Antrim coast. We needed him and he would not leave us.

Twenty years after last seeing 'C.W.' when he tried to get me placed as a drummer-boy in the Irish Guards, I went to meet him again, wondering if the years had changed him as they had done me. But they had not. Except for the patina of years and a slight but nevertheless surprising reduction of boom in his voice, the rector had not altered. He was still in the same parish, still a shepherd of

his flock, still now, as then, without thoughts of ambitious prefer-
ment. I wondered what 'C.W.' would say to me after all those years,
for his visits to our home had not infrequently occurred after some
misdemeanour of mine.

'Well,' he began, 'we are all pleased you have done so well.' And
then we delved into the past.

We talked about the rector's friend and admirer of those for-
tunately-over days, John Frederick MacNeice, the Archdeacon of
Connor who became the distinguished Bishop of Down, Connor
and Dromore. We talked of the bishop's son whom Charles
Maguire remembered in his pram. That child was one day to
write:

> *I was born in Belfast between the mountain and the gantries*
> *To the hooting of lost sirens and the clang of trams.*

Louis MacNeice became the *enfant terrible* of Ulster poetry,
a first name in modern literature. Yet I met people in Belfast
who had never heard of the poet but certainly remembered
his father as a great man. Bishop MacNeice died more than twenty
years ago, but memorials are still being made to him, that last
bishop of the united dioceses of Down, Connor and Dromore.
Unlike a famous predecessor Jeremy Taylor—high priest of seventeenth-century prose—MacNeice's life-work still touches everyday
Belfast, for he was the leader of ecumenical thought in Northern
Ireland.

Many people asked me why no biography had yet been written
of this great divine. The present Bishop of Clogher, Dr. Buchanan,
was one of them. MacNeice's influence was felt beyond the
ecclesiastical borders of his diocese, and beyond the political border
of Ulster too. He belonged to the same school as Pope John XXIII
and Archbishop William Temple. When MacNeice's son Louis went
on a tour of Iceland with W. H. Auden in 1936, they wrote a last
will at the end of their amusing travel book. They left a Leander
tie and Pugin's ghost to John Betjeman, a bottle of invalid port to
Lady Astor, and a sprig of heather to Compton Mackenzie. But
the Ulster poet's legacy to his father contained neither levity nor
frivolity:

FORD OF THE SANDBANKS

I leave my father half my pride of blood

And also my admiration who has fixed
His pulpit out of the reach of party slogans
And all the sordid challenges and the mixed

Motives of those who bring their drums and dragons
To silence moderation and free speech
Bawling with armoured cars and carnival wagons.

When the poet was a boy, living with his archdeacon father at Carrickfergus, letters were being written in the rectory which proved to be quite as important to Ulster history as *Letters from Iceland* were to literature twenty years later. From July 1920 to September 1924 letters from Carrickfergus appeared both in Belfast and Dublin newspapers. Between these two seats of religious influence a third influence now intruded—John Frederick MacNeice and his 'League of Prayer for Ireland' in which both Catholics and Protestants, bishops and laymen, Orangemen and Sinn Fein joined to bring peace.

MacNeice's pen was seldom dry. 'In the recent rioting some twenty lives were lost. For what?' he wrote while appeals were posted to every part of the community. 'An Official Report tells you morning after morning that Roman Catholics did this, and Protestants did likewise. By your timely intervention make such reports and reproaches impossible. You could save the city: in God's name try.'

Fifteen years after these appeals were spread across Ulster, Louis MacNeice went off to Iceland with Auden to write their book. By this time, the poet's father had become a bishop and was still fighting bigotry. In 1935 he stood in the middle of the bloodshed in Belfast, bloodshed which sent families fleeing in terror from districts where their own religion was in the minority, bloodshed which terrified me as a boy of 8 so that I feared to cross the Bog Meadows.

To be courageous in those days was to be courageous indeed. But Bishop MacNeice persisted. The Twelfth of July celebrations in 1936 threatened unprecedented violence. But dockers going along Dee Street were bombarded with leaflets and the Bishop personally toured trouble spots. On Sunday 28th June 1936 a pastoral letter was read in every church of his vast diocese, 'It would be a gross misuse of language to describe as Roman Catholics or Protestants those who, in passion or in cold blood, burn houses, destroy property, attack defenceless people, stain their hands in human blood. Much more accurately they might be thought of as anarchists.'

Slowly, perhaps more slowly than even the grinding of the mills of God, John Frederick MacNeice's efforts began to show results. He won peace eventually, and hard on peace's heels the goodwill and toleration of today followed. Not only did the Union Jack fly at half-mast on the City Hall at Pope John XXIII's death, but the two redoubts of entrenched opinion, the Orange Order and the Hibernians, have met to discuss their differences.

When Bishop MacNeice stood on St. Anne's cathedral steps to take the Church Lads' Brigade salute in the 1930s and I shuffled by so hopelessly out of step, looking with awe at the figure with lawn sleeves and crozier, I did not know that the notes for the sermon he had just given us were headed by three Greek words, three words which appeared on every sermon he preached—*God Help Me*.

Bishop MacNeice used to live along the Malone Road, and also in this grand suburb I found St. John's church. Voysey's house was nearby and this architect was reputed to have designed a church in the city though this cannot be substantiated. St. John's had a window filled with the bold design in glowing stained glass of St. Columba by Evie Hone—one of the few coloured windows in the city worth looking at. Surprisingly, Belfast, or indeed the whole of Ireland, had little work by Wilhelmina Geddes, Ulster's only artist who in any way approached the achievements of the Dublin studios.

In 1941, bombs destroyed her *Moses*, reputedly one of her finest works. A black and white reproduction I saw of *Moses*, however, filled me with irreverent thoughts, for the Law-giver looked like Somerset Maugham with a beard and nightcap and the tablets of stone like hot water-bottles being carried up to bed. In the highly stylized manner there was more than a dash of *Art Nouveau*, which perhaps Miss Geddes got via the Glasgow School. Happily her great window at Ypres escaped the fate of the Belfast *Moses*.

Wilhelmina Geddes's first important commission came from the Duke of Connaught in 1919 for Ottawa's war memorial. She died in

1956 recognized as a great artist in this medium and I would have much preferred to see the inferior nineteenth-century German glass of Ulster replaced by her own work.

The art of stained-glass designing is a curious one, for although it must necessarily derive its motifs and genre from painting, long after a particular movement or style in painting has gone the glass remains. The window artist shares with the architect and sculptor the privilege of having the work on permanent exhibition. It is inevitable, therefore, that many stained glass windows have a depressingly dated appearance. Among all the graphic arts of their period, they alone remain on view.

With architecture the situation is aggravated even more. In Belfast, for instance, the stylistic enthusiasms of the nineteenth century have an undue preponderance. It is monstrous that the heavy and ornate Technical College stands obesely across half the façade of the Academical Institution—or 'Inst' as the famous school is called. But then Georgian Belfast was gobbled up whole in this way.

The 'Inst' building had a lucky escape from the greedy boa-constrictor jaws of commerce. A lawn, emerald and bowling-green smooth, still stretches before the long plain façade of brick which bears the date 1810 and has the distinction of being in some degree designed by Sir John Soane. That great architect's intentions were not completely executed but at least his taste and restraint have left its mark on the flatness of the façade and in the almost abstract use of such Classical motifs as pilaster and entablature. 'Inst' must have been dignified indeed in its original context of the Georgian town.

Fortune never favoured my boyhood enough for me to be a pupil of 'Inst' though I did sometimes go to the cinema opposite which, in 1829, had been Lord Kelvin's birthplace. A blue neon sign KELVIN hung outside which no doubt would have amused the electrical inventor. Also near 'Inst', miraculously preserved, is the old museum building, a grave Georgian work with an ingenious portico, and also not too far away, the Belfast Savings Bank which has a broad, serene façade graced by a beautiful doorway with coupled Ionic columns.

When the sun does shine, or is only partly obscured by fleecy clouds fleeing across the lough, Belfast enjoys a sparkling light. It is a light which casts the brilliant highlights and sharp shadows which makes, for instance, Copenhagen assume that unique crispness of cities by water. Although in some ways Belfast resembles industrial towns in the Midlands and North of England none of these enjoys the pellucid atmosphere which, in spring and summer at least, Belfast does.

On such days it is pleasant to wander about the docks and lean over Queen's Bridge looking at the lines of ships tied up and listen to the sea sounds of winches and chains and sirens. The open square leading to the docks has a leaning tower, not at such a dangerous angle as Pisa's companile it is true, but leaning nevertheless. The Albert, a clock tower erected in memory of that prince, is a notable Belfast landmark, but when I saw it on my last visit it had developed a noticeable seawards lunge. I only hoped that the city engineer had his eye on this alarming declination from the perpendicular.

Near the Albert is the Customs House whose fine sweep of steps has always been an ideal place for loungers and loiterers and therefore for preachers. I wondered if hot-gospellers, who still use the steps today, were dispensing fire and brimstone on all and sundry in the days when Anthony Trollope worked in the Customs House. This presumably was Trollope's means of support, reluctantly pursued between writing *The Warden* and his chief delight of going about the Ulster countryside on horseback.

The scene on the Customs House steps would probably look much the same to the Barsetshire author if he returned to his old haunt. Lord Kelvin, however, would completely fail to recognize the stevedores making love in the back stalls of what was his home, just as Sir Samuel Ferguson would hardly recognize the women buying hats in his mother's ex-front parlour.

Samuel Ferguson was, so to speak, the Louis MacNeice of his day. He was born in Belfast in 1810, just in time to participate in the fashion for epics and lengthy poems. The taste for such things, however, has gone and works like *Congal* or his metrical versions of Irish legends do not appeal to me so much as his shorter poems. But this liking may simply be because the short and more manageable verses were all that our teachers could drum into us at school. Thousands of Irish schoolchildren learnt his verse parrot fashion. Having got the words myself when young, the peculiar beauty of them came later.

Can Birmingham or Bolton boast, as Belfast can, that it produced a dreamer who could write *Deirdre's Lament for the Sons of Usnach*?

> *The lions of the hill are gone.*
> *And I am left alone—alone . . .*
> *Stag exult on glen and mountain—*
> *Salmon leap from loch to fountain—*
> *Heron in the free air warm ye—*
> *Usnach's sons no more will harm ye!*

2

Down by the Sea

Like many other children who had to learn Sir Samuel Ferguson's poetry, there was only one word for me which represented the sea—Bangor. Paddling and swimming, sand-castling and jumping on bladder-wrack to make the gas vesicles go pop were only a few glories of the great dream a mere twelve miles away along the coast of County Down.

Even in the cold winds of March we street boys stole rides on the backs of lorries going along the coast so that we could snatch a glimpse of the rolling open sea and turn in the waves breaking on the sands of Ballyholme. History, however, would confirm that our Spartan behaviour was nothing new. As far back as the sixth century the young men of Bangor were moonlight bathers. The difference was that they were monks, who, under St. Comgall, first Abbot of Bangor, were obliged to sit in the cold water in order to subdue the passions of the flesh, reciting the while the whole of the Psalter. It was small wonder that so many died. The survivors of this rigorous brand of holiness spread the knowledge of salvation abroad, earning for Ireland the title 'The Isle of Saints and Scholars' from other European nations.

Ulster people do love to be beside the seaside and particularly at Bangor, which is a kind of Irish Southend. It is small, with most of the town near enough to the sea to fill its boarding houses. Behind the purple bloom of veronica hedges the bay windows look across the bay, themselves crammed with crowded high tea tables, where, in the centre of each one stands a kind of monstrance used in this daily five o'clock ritual—the three-tier cake-stand.

Every boarding house window showed itself not to be inferior to its neighbours in possession of the cake-stand. And indeed, the three-tiers were vital for the tables were loaded, as are all tables in Northern Ireland, with such a variety of different kinds of bread and cake and pastry that one tier alone would not have sufficed. Only in Denmark have I ever found a similar versatility on the baker's part.

While eating out in Ulster it is extremely difficult to find bad food. The incautious visitor, unaware that he is in a land of farmers, finds his waistline increasing in no time at all. And as though the Ulsterman himself cannot bear to prolong the awful emptiness between his midday meal and his evening one, high tea is the order of the day. Despite its misleading name and the fact that high tea can mean huge, juicy steaks and mountains of chips, and wheaten farls and mushroom puffs and home-made cakes, I prefer a later meal.

Looking out at the old harbour, known as Bangor Hole, I could not help wondering if the Scandinavian delight in the bakehouse could be traced to the year 818. There was a momentous day for Bangor in that year. Into the sheltered waters of the Hole slid the long dark forms of Viking ships. The raiders went ashore and reduced the famous university and abbey to ruins. The Norsemen themselves, however, fell into oblivion and their black standards vanished from the Bangor coast, for by the twelfth century an auspicious phoenix appeared in the person of St. Malachy. Once again Bangor became a notable seat of learning and its missionaries sailed out from the Hole to every part of Europe.

The ancient abbeys, like the Norsemen's black eagle standards, disappeared with the passing centuries though the acute sense of religious obligation remained to plague the conscience of the Bangor holidaymakers. Alternate bouts of scorching sun and gentle, wind-driven showers chased each other across the bay and over the sea-front so that at one moment the pavements were wet and the next steaming dry for all the world like streets in a tropical town. When the sun finally conquered and the wind had taken off the clouds like a shepherd departing with an unruly too-woolly flock, I sat on the red stone sea-wall to luxuriate in the penetrating warmth, and to allow the sun to cultivate mildly lascivious thoughts with its sensuous touch. There being no temptation taking me but such as is common to man I did not feel at all guilty, and neither, which immensely cheered me, did the youths and girls pawing and kissing each other on the wall in the sun. The boys could have been boys from anywhere with their tee-shirts and washed out, bulged out jeans. The girls too conformed to pattern with piled up beehive hair lacquered to the same consistency and texture as the candy-floss they were eating.

And just as we had all settled happily to while away an innocent hour along came a fat middle-aged man who looked as if an hour of sun and sin would be of untold therapeutic value to him. We might have guessed his line.

'Ladies and gentlemen,' he began in a stentorian voice, 'I am going to talk about the Lord.'

Inwardly we groaned, but were too transfixed by the sun to bother moving.

'I'm going to talk about the Lord,' he went on. 'I'm not going to talk about Protestants. Have you got that?'

We got it.

'I'm not going to talk about Catholics. Have you got that?'

We got that also.

'I'm not going to talk about religion . . .'

Silent cheers from his audience.

'. . . because there's too much religion in this country of ours.'

We couldn't agree more.

'I'm going to tell the truth.'

We didn't care, just then, about the truth. Fortunately for us, however, both edges of the fat man's spiritual sword were not a little blunted by the arrival of rival groups. The newcomers' secret weapon was a harmonium at which a woman sat pedalling with demoniac fury as though it were a treadmill or a mechanical Tibetan prayer-wheel. They tried to shout our man down, who by now bellowed like a bull. As our man shouted louder and gesticulated more wildly, and as his heavy serge trousers slid lower to reveal an increasingly wide, white strip of underdrawers, the gambling fever came on the beehive girls and their blue jean mates. Which of the preachers would win the race to win a soul.

We never knew because another squall sent us scurrying across the road for shelter in an amusement arcade. The purple lipsticked girls were much more concerned to stamp their names out on a name-plate slot machine than have them entered in the Book of Life. Groups of leather-jacketed boys swarmed round one-armed bandits trying to win 'Fifth Avenue Ten Commandment Bracelets' with instructions to 'wear it and win the Blessing of Thy Lord'.

A stranger might well be struck by the way Bangor seafront was besieged by itinerant soul-savers. But I knew the town of old and could see that the flowing tide of get-saved-or-be-burnt-in-hell was on the ebb. Since my own days of adolescent zeal, when Bangor was a favourite haunt of my evangelical companions, the intensity of the Puritan onslaught had noticeably declined.

A former stronghold of the straight and narrow-minded, the Strand Hotel, had been abandoned and taken over by hedonistic holidaymakers. The hotel had once been the scene for the annual meeting of the Faith Mission whose Pilgrims are still such a feature of the Irish landscape, the girls in their bonnets looking even more Victorian than their sisters in the Salvation Army. Gone, however, from the Strand Hotel were the sounds of Moody and Sankey and instead, for breakfast, I had Elvis Presley and Frank Sinatra. And upstairs, in a pleasant room overlooking the bay, once the scene of our prayer meetings, was the Anglers' Rest where Scotsmen now sat with pints of bitter and whiskies talking over the day's trout fishing at Conlig. Sea anglers were comparing past records of cod, lythe, whiting, wrasse, gurnard, plaice, dab, skate, blockan, conger and spur dogfish.

I saw the influence of these Scottish fishermen when I gave a five pound note for a drink and had change given in a colourful clutch of Scottish banknotes besides a handful of nearly all Irish coins with bulls and horses in place of Britannia. Later on I saw what a hold sea fishing had on residents and visitors alike. When the tide went out, people were down on the sands digging lugworm and ragworm for bait. Every small jetty and sea-wall projection or knob or rock was taken up by a fisherman. Most of them crowded along the har-bour pier, ignoring the fence across its landward end and the notice, 'Warning. The pier beyond this point is unsafe. Many of the support

timbers are missing or decayed. Trespass over the railing is dangerous.' It was certainly unsafe for fishes. The people I saw were using
mussels to take blockan though the more professional had silver
spinners or herring strips for mackerel. One youth was cheating
with an articulated eelet which nothing in the sea seemed able to
resist.

Ulster waters are a perfect place for those who love to go fishing
as I once did. A freckled boy summed up the possibilities nicely
when he told me solemnly, 'We hold the British record for haddock
and the Irish record for hake.' And as though to prove these sacred
truths he cast his home-made line once again into the returning
tide.

Going back to Bangor after so many years was to see it with new
eyes. The town was bound to look different for I had visited or lived
in some of the world's most magnificent seaside cities, from the wild
and exotic beauty of Rio de Janeiro to the copper-spired canals of
Copenhagen. Bangor had no such thrills to offer. Yet, conversely, it
had entirely escaped the crude vulgarities which have long been the
affliction of every coastal resort in England. Bangor's skyline was
still dominated by a slender church tower and a fringe of trees
running across the hills behind. No great concrete hotels, brassy and
blasé, crowded the seafront. It was possible to saunter along the
simple promenade without being either gassed by carbon monoxide
or maimed by impatient car drivers. Unlike Brighton or Bourne-
mouth the streets had not been turned into car parks, and, if the
mood so dictated, it was possible to get away out to the County
Down countryside in a few minutes.

Subject to the same quicksilver changes of light as Belfast,
Bangor's sailing was one of its chief attractions. The waterfront
gave on to the wide lough mouth, and there, sailing was ideal and
sheltered from the running seas and currents of the Channel. When
the sun peered down over pinnacles of high cloud, the cathedral-like
shafts of light fell sometimes on the strings of brilliantly coloured
sailing boats. The scarlet and saffron and sapphire sails picked up
colour and glowed as petals do when soaked in the radiance of the
sun. Bangor had long been famous as a sailing and yaching centre.
In the grand old days grand old men like English kings and German

kaisers sent their craft to the local competitions. The man best remembered in this connection was Sir Thomas Lipton, the tea king, who in all his years of competing for the America Cup sailed under the Bangor club flag.

Apart from its expanse of lough, Bangor's most beautiful sight was its town hall. The building itself, an 1852 Jacobeanesque castle, was of little interest. But the sweep of lawns on which it stood, lawns and cloud-like clumps of trees green as only Irish grass and trees could be, this, and the great park stretching in glades and pine-woods beside the river made the town hall one of the most beautifully situated in Europe.

Having made an oblation of myself at the altar of the high tea table, and also having made a correct astronomical forecast that a young yellow moon would again be riding over the lough, I returned to the park by way of several pints of porter and the company of a young and eager holidaymaker who was anxious to show me that the beech-lined paths made perfect lovers' lanes.

Hand in hand we left Bangor's fairy lights for the moonlit woods and had not progressed far when I spied a weird-looking man concealed in the undergrowth. A peeping-tom with walrus moustache and bowler hat! Not exactly. In fact he reminded me of Bangor's sixth-century monks jumping into the icy waters in order to submerge their unruly flesh, for our intruder was a kind of modern St. Comgall. The bowler hat had supplanted the mitre though he was doing a very conscientious bit of groping for Jesus. Instead of our having to read the whole of the Psalms, however, our man in Bangor presented us with the latest in Gospel tracts—*What God says about Kissing*.

Next morning I resisted my lover's charms and entreaties to go and see Helen's Tower at the nearby Clandeboye estate. Instead I took the bus and went along the superbly beautiful stretch of coast to Donaghadee. Since Helen's Tower is so near Bangor, however, it is a visitor's 'must', though having seen the tower many times I thought I would avoid the detour. As a boy I used to love reading the tributes of various poets to the woman who built it for her famous son, the first Marquess of Dufferin who was a diplomat and statesman. Tennyson and Browning, Lord Houghton and Kipling all wrote her praises. Browning's lines, inserted into the inside walls, begin:

> *Who hears of Helen's Tower may dream perchance*
> *How the Greek beauty from Scoean gate*
> *Gazed on old friends unanimous in hate,*
> *Death-doom'd because of her fair countenance.*
> *Hearts would leap otherwise at thy advance,*
> *Lady to whom this tower is consecrate!*
> *Like hers, the face once made all eyes elate,*
> *Yet, unlike hers, was blessed by every glance . . .*

As far as I was concerned, the most interesting association of literature with the tower was due, fittingly enough, to Helen's son himself. His *Letters from High Latitudes* written a century ago contain passages about Iceland which are some of the finest writing in English about that country bordering the Arctic Circle. This book, more than anything else, prolonged his fame beyond his distinguished career as ambassador and viceroy, and also showed that the ink in the family blood had not dried out with his great-grandfather, Richard Brinsley Sheridan.

I had met many people in Iceland who claimed Celtic ancestry, derived from the Irish slaves of the Vikings. But centuries before the Norsemen settled there, Irish monks had built their cells in the lonely valleys of the Drangajokull glacier. It is not at all improbable that those early and hardy hermits trained for the strenuous Icelandic winters by their recitation of the Psalms sitting in the cold waters of Bangor.

It was easy to imagine the early fathers moving about this coast, for nothing more modern than a few scattered houses stood along the road to Donaghadee. And all the way, the peaks of Scottish hills protruded above the horizon, a soft, melting blue, lighter than the blue-green of the sea and darker than the radiant blue of the sky. The Channel was only twenty miles or so wide at places. On clear days the Scottish coast could look close enough to touch. The road swung gently, sometimes high and sometimes low, and extraordinarily like the road north from Copenhagen which faces the narrow Sound between Denmark and Sweden.

Almost as if the place appealed to them as a home from home, the early Danes had built the original quay at the little village of Groomsport, my first stop. The morning was bright, the air unbelievably clear and sweet and scented with the tang of seaweed. The sun fell dazzlingly on the blinding white walls. It might almost have been a white sea village in Spain or Portugal. The Iberian sun exhausts and drains the colour away leaving an arid monochrome of light. But here the sun illuminated sharply and enriched the myriad colours of the shore rocks and pools.

From the Scottish coast, the distant view of Ireland must have been similar. It was beautiful enough to tempt John Keats to cross from Scotland and to spend his one and only night on Irish soil at Donaghadee. But other Englishmen had come before the poet and their presence in County Down is still seen in the number of episcopal churches.

Bangor was full of Scottish holidaymakers forgetting Glasgow's dourness for a fortnight and wearing kiss-me-quick hats as a badge of temporary freedom. County Down is the most populated of the Six Counties and owes much of its quarter-million people to Scottish settlers. The Scots, with their stern Presbyterian ways, had not always been the contented happy farmers living in Down today. In 1631 many of them built a ship called *The Eagle's Wing* and set sail in the wake of the Pilgrim Fathers. But unlike the *Mayflower*, *The Eagle's Wing* was forced back by storms. They got halfway across the Atlantic and there fought the waves and winds for two months. In the end they returned to Ireland believing this to be the will of God. Some of these would-be escapists from persecuting religious laws lived to see ten thousand men of William III's army land in their tiny village of Groomsport in 1689.

Donaghadee was smaller than Bangor and more beautiful, its moving bay the climax of the little bays of rocks and shale by the road from Bangor. None of the houses was more than three stories and most were brightly painted, the Café de Luxe sharing the same façade of tiny Victorian houses with the Technical School. Donaghadee's bay extended to form a breakwater at one end, where fishing boats knocked each other on the rising and falling water. The Copeland Islands enclosed the bay's other end almost making a lagoon of the gull-dotted waters. By a local tradition Peter the Great of Russia is said to have spent a night in Donaghadee when he came to watch boatbuilding in Belfast Lough.

Although I had no wish to emulate John Keats in his thirty-mile walk to Belfast and back from Donaghadee, I thought I could at least go on foot to Millisle and then inland to Newtownards. The sun was striking hot now and mattresses hung for an airing from the police barracks' windows.

And now the road I trod was as familiar as the lines in my hand for in childhood I came this way many times from Childhaven, a house in Millisle where my boyhood summers were spent, and where I went in and out of the sea like an amphibian or lay on the sands, chin in hand, looking in wonder across the sea to the Scottish hills.

There had been magic in the air then. What would I find now? Surely enough, the sea was still there, quietly edging in and out in a lazy summer way and so, on a rise and set about by trees, was Childhaven itself. But my own boyhood's friends were . . . well, I did not know where.

I walked to the house up the winding path I remembered so well, to see if my old friends the Youngs were still there. But instead I saw 'This tablet commemorates the faithful, devoted service over a long period of years of Mr. and Mrs. John Young for needy children both in the Orphanage and Holiday Home at Childhaven.'

As one of thousands of the needy children on whom the Youngs spent an unstinting love, the least to be done in thanks was to set down the memory of their name. Their name will always be linked in my mind with the golden sands and rock pools and oystercatchers and swooping sea-swallows. I found the orphanage full still, and with feelings mixed of sadness and happiness I silently hoped that the boys and girls who, in these so-called affluent days, still depended on Childhaven for their fortnight's summer holiday would remember afterwards as gladly as I did.

Millisle itself was a bungalow town with caravans parked among the sand-dunes. But old seaside country ways had not all been ousted. In the driveways of smart and desirable residences people had laid dulse out to dry, the nutritious seaweed which is eaten raw throughout Northern Ireland. I walked up through the fuchsia and veronica hedges and came at last to higher ground where stands the eighteenth-century windmill of Ballycopeland, now kept as an ancient monument, a fine landmark seen from miles around.

My thoughts, however, were in the next townland of Killaghy. I used to see the windmill when I worked for six months on a farm there. This was a real, old-fashioned Presbyterian farm owned by a man called James Davidson. With beard and high come-to-Jesus collar and swags of gold watch chain across a rotund waistcoated stomach old Davidson might have been an Old Testament prophet. And he lived like a prophet fearing nothing but his God.

I was gathering sheep on his hill one day in the war when American Air Force surveyors arrived and said they were commandeering all the land around Killaghy. The farmers met in the tiny oil-lit chapel not with the intention of fighting the American and British authorities but simply of asking God to intervene. In those days of my own fevered beliefs I often conducted services for the farmers and their families and I knew of their rock-hard, invincible faith. The American bulldozers moved in but Farmer Davidson and his neighbours did not move out. They stayed and prayed, unshakably convinced that the earth was the Lord's and that He had appointed them husbandmen of that particular patch of it. And nobody was surprised, except the airbase Americans, when they laid their concrete runway, and returned to find it sinking slowly, for the earth *was* the Lord's, boggy earth though it might be. Defeated, the Americans departed and the proposed airbase at Killaghy was never built.

Farmer Davidson was dead but I did find Hugh Martin the blacksmith who, at 87, still gave his son a hand's turn in the smithy. I called at his cottage and talked of old times. 'Mighty changes' was his comment on the last twenty years. He told me of a little boy who recently looked round the forge door and called back to his mother 'Look! There's a horse in the garage.' Tractors have replaced the great Clydesdale mares I used to ride from Davidson's farm, though the forge keeps busy, and now increasingly so, with hunters and children's ponies.

After a meal of crippling proportions Hugh Martin took me down to the forge and its overshadowing beech tree with a pair of doves in its branches. 'More cattle than sheep,' the aged farrier said as I looked out over the hills of my old shepherding. I was surprised to see in his brother John's house, hard by, the fire still on the ancient kind of open hearth with kettles and pots hanging on chains from the crook. And at the gate, as elsewhere in Ulster, were the fat, round, whitewashed stone gateposts on which the fairies dance at night.

I had already discovered transformations and reformations in Ulster and yet at Killaghy, only twelve miles from Belfast, the old Presbyterian ways kept their roots. As I continued my journey I tried to remember the verses County Down Presbyterians used to sing at their choir practices. Since the metrical Psalms were holy writ, the words could not be profaned at practice by the choir-master's directions and interruptions. Instead secular doggerel was inserted, such as

> *In Ireland doth fair Dublin stand,*
> *The chief city therein;*
> *And, as is said by many men,*
> *The chief city for sin.*

When he had a church living in the north and was having his *affaire* with Miss Jane Waring of Belfast, Jonathan Swift may well have heard this and similar rhymes. Swift did not take kindly to Irish Presbyterianism. He put his hatred of it into print and even when he rose to fame later in Dublin the bitterness remained. His *Polite Conversation* is thought to vent his feelings about the superficiality of Belfast society. But the antipathy may have been on both sides for the Presbyterians would hardly have approved the way in which this literary cleric involved himself with various women, and certainly would not have looked kindly on the cruel way he dropped them when the ladies no longer charmed him.

Swift's antics over his Ulster church must also have irritated the intensely serious Presbyterian brethren. On one occasion, Swift's jealousy at the emptiness of his own church compared to the fullness of the Presbyterian one, led him to indulge in something very much like a modern publicity stunt. One Sunday, Swift began wheeling stones from the beach into his church. And so curious were the good people to see what the eccentric rector was doing on the Sabbath that they crowded into the church to find out, whereupon Swift locked the doors. He then conducted a full service, of the kind which his kidnapped congregation's ancestors had fled from in *The Eagle's Wing*.

Despite Swift's disapproval, the Presbyterians did much good and left behind some fine building in their farmhouses and churches, an example of which I saw later in the day at Killinchy, after leaving my old blacksmith friend Hugh Martin. The Presbyterian Church today is still a large and influential body in Northern Ireland and in a harmonious accord with the Church of Ireland which Swift would certainly have disliked. The biggest embarrassment today is not an entanglement with any Establishment but with a minority group who call themselves the Free Presbyterian Church, led by the Rev. Ian Paisley. These extremists recently picketed a meeting held by the ex-Moderator of the Presbyterian Church, because he had attended the World Council of Churches at New Delhi—which for the 'Frees' looks like another road to Rome!

On my travels, however, I was concerned with the road to Newtownards where, until a few years ago, Farmer Davidson used to come every Saturday morning with his pony and trap loaded with home-churned butter for sale in the town.

Possessing a more sophisticated eye than I had in my adolescence when I knew this part of County Down quite well, I saw now, on coming into Newtownards, that the town conformed to the pleasing and simple pattern of country towns common throughout Ulster. Old, higgledy-piggledy, thatchy and indoor-beamy villages beloved by motor coach tourists in England do not exist. Instead, even the smallest village has an imposed sense of order descended from the grand town planning of Georgian times.

Newtownards's regular, straight streets and its town square in which stands the white turret-topped town hall, looked somehow French. I almost expected to find bistros and pavement cafés and cheap wine. What I did find, however, just outside the town were some factories for newly established light industries. Blacksmith Martin had told me his grandson had come home from sea and had gone 'into the nylon' at Newtownards. The traditional skills of linen and hand embroidery were being absorbed by such modern developments.

An intriguing footnote to the town's history lies in the fact that it was here that an early idea of copyright came into existence. This was through St. Columba who was educated at Movilla Abbey outside Newtownards. The abbey was founded in 540 by St. Finian who came back from Rome, where he paid his tribute to the Pope, bearing a copy of the Vulgate text as revised by St. Jerome himself. Seeing this sacred document young St. Columba set about making a further copy, for his own use. When this was done St. Finian claimed that this copy of the copy was also legally his. He did not get it and so appealed to Diarmid, King of Ireland.

This king then gave his famous judgement—'To every cow belongeth her little offspring cow, so to every book belongeth its little offspring book.' And so was established an early principle of copyright. St. Columba smarted under this decision and the great 'Dove of the Church' went to war to uphold his claim on the copy he had made, and many were the souls which 'were sent to perdition'. It was because so many people went to perdition through this battle that St. Columba set off for Iona to try and bring more men to Christ than he was responsible for killing. The disputed copy, however, survived the battle. And when it passed into the O'Donnell family they cased it in a silver shrine and carried it into all their clan battles. St. Columba's copy survived even this, and then all the centuries that followed it until it was deposited in the Royal Irish Academy.

I wanted to get on to Comber and waited for the bus in company with two boys who had trout rods. Of course, they had no fishing licences but were cautious in talking about their angling exploits in case I might be a detective—despite my hitch-hiking appearance. They were off to the Carrigullion Lakes, they said, where the fishing was free and great pike were easily caught by a Colorado spoon.

However, having thoroughly catechized me as to my business in those parts, for Newtownards was small enough for a stranger to be conspicuous, they relaxed. One of them 'borrowed' tenpence and went off to buy another fly for his collection. He kept it in an old tobacco tin which was full of those trout-tempters with such mellifluous names, purple snipe, gold-ribbed hare's ear, Greenwell's glory, Wickham's fancy, boat-wing sedge.

Scrabo Hill brooded over the landscape, the highest point for miles, a rugged hill from which red sandstone used to be quarried when I lived in County Down. I used to pass the quarries on my way to the heathery top, not always alone and for more romantic pursuits than merely to enjoy the fantastic panorama of Strangford Lough. Scrabo—the Sod of the Cow—did not have the holiness for me that sister hills had for St. Patrick when he herded swine.

A square tower stands on the hilltop as memorial to the third Marquess of Londonderry whose home with its exquisite gardens is nearby. This nineteenth-century soldier and diplomat, despite his elevation, was overshadowed on my bus-ride by the fame of another soldier—'Ould Gillespie' as the boys with the fishing rods described him.

But they said it affectionately for Gillespie is still a kind of school-boy hero. The thirty-foot high stone obelisk on which he stood in the little square at Comber does not diminish his dashing story. He remains a pre-celluloid Errol Flynn in spite of the titles and honours inscribed on his statue 'Lieutenant-General Sir Robert Rollo Gilles-pie'. The most pompous memorial in the world could not dim the fact that he was the bravest man in the British Army.

He was born in Comber in 1766 and joined the army while still in his teens. After killing a fellow officer in a duel, 'across a handker-chief', young Gillespie left Ireland and joined the French in San Domingo. Having had the most swashbuckling of wide-screen adventures by shipwreck and bloody cutlass battles he turned up in India in time to take command of Arcot. And from there he rode out to the Indian mutineers at Vellore. During another epic drama he was hoisted into the besieged fortress by a rope, once more becoming a popular hero. All this was too good to last, and he was only 48 when he was killed in India, shouting his most famous command 'One more shot for the honour of Down.'

'He must have been a terror,' my young friends said before they went off on their own piracy of high season trout and salmon.

General Gillespie appealed to a couple of girls who came to peer in my notebook. 'Och,' they said of the bronze soldier, 'what lovely legs he's got.' He had indeed, meaty thighs rising out of top-boots, though the girls soon lost their interest in Gillespie for the real thighs of a farm youth driving through the square on his tractor.

When he had gone the afternoon quiet flowed back again and I was left alone in the square to reflect that Comber, like most places in the world, would be better without its modern improvements. The petrol pumps and neon signs and concrete lamp-posts had nothing to give the simple Georgian buildings which they did not possess before.

Comber was so rurally peaceful that not even a bus threatened its seclusion so I started walking again, in the direction of Killyleagh where I wanted to spend the night. The countryside now seemed to be heavily wooded, though this was an illusion created by fine ash and sycamore and beech left in the hedges by the farmers. The gardens beyond Comber were loaded like flower shows, and wild sweet-pea vied with honeysuckle for supremacy of the hedges where for miles herb Robert was truly jack-of-the-hedgerows. Herds of Herefords seemed also to be competing with red Devons for the heavy-weight contest as they went from one lush meadow to the next.

A grocer stopped his van and gave me a lift as far as Killinchy where I stayed long enough to admire the Non-Subscribing Presbyterian Church of 1845, a plain but dignified, pedimented building. Some of Northern Ireland's most interesting architecture of the Presbyterians belongs to the Non-Subscribing Church. Many of these simple, graceful buildings appear unexpectedly all over Ulster's countryside. They show how the Presbyterians hated the shams of the romantic revivals of bygone styles—an architectural activity associated strongly in their minds with the Church of Ireland. The qualities of these fine Georgian churches also clearly demonstrate the social differences, as well as ecclesiastical ones, between the two denominations at that time.

Swift was not the only member of the Established Church to attack the Presbyterians, who, along with all Nonconformists were made to suffer. Because of the 1704 Test Act many Presbyterians were obliged to resign from official positions, even though they represented the major Protestant denomination in the province. After this Act Presbyterians could no longer sit on the Town Council if they adhered strictly to the views of their fleeing fathers of *The Eagle's Wing*.

Matters reached a climax when a Belfast rector, William Tisdall, tried to have a substantial house tax imposed on everybody to keep his own church coffers full. Fortunately, people were so outraged that they brought Dr. Tisdall to law. The result, however, did not mean that Presbyterians could hold public office—though George I had revived William III's *regium donum* grant of money to Irish Presbyterian ministers.

Faced with Rome on one hand and the Established Church on the other, Ulster Presbyterians soon had a revolution in their own ranks. The battle was over the question of assent to the Westminster Confession of Faith, an accepted procedure to orthodox Presbyterianism. This was no minor teacup affair but a major storm which went on for years and eventually led to a split and the founding of the Non-Subscribing Presbyterian Church of Ireland, whose distinctive early architecture is still such an adornment to the Ulster scene today.

While trying to get from Killinchy I was joined by a 17-year-old Sikh pedlar in a sugar-icing-pink turban. 'I've got something nice for you,' he said mysteriously as he opened his case and spread his wares by the road which was full of traffic going to and from Killinchy Dinghy Championship.

The water here was in fact another arm of the sea, though longer and more lonely than Belfast Lough. Norse invaders originally gave this long stretch of water its name, Strang Fiord or the Violent Fjord. Through the lough's extremely narrow neck, opening to the sea, hundreds of millions of tons of ocean rush up and down with every tide.

Earlier when I had reached the upper end of Strangford Lough the tide was out. And long before I could see, I could hear the cries of the wildfowl delighting in the sloblands and rocks of the shallows. The lough is said to have three-hundred-and-sixty-five islands, great and small. Few of the islands were farmed and most were given over as haunts for Arctic tern and ringed plover, red-breasted merganser, shelduck and oystercatcher. Currents round the neck flow up to eight knots but this only adds to the sport of seals and porpoises.

It pleased me to know that at least one place in Northern Ireland had retained its original Norse name, for not many were left bearing traces of the Scandinavian invaders. To find Strangford Lough with its ancient associations pleased me because the place reminded me very much of Roskilde Fjord in Denmark, a place where I had spent many hours among similar rafts of wildfowl and pagan and early monastic ruins and stories of buried treasure like Strangford's. And a further similarity was shown me by a family called Lyness who gave me a lift to Killyleagh on their way home from the dinghy racing. They took me out to their loughside house which stood looking out over the water and the islands exactly as the house of Bridget Swinton, an Irish painter, at Roskilde. The Lyness's house was called Fool's Penny. An amusing story from the last century tells of the woman who sold stout to fishermen and sailors from the coal-boats, making a penny profit on each bottle. When sufficient pennies had been made from the fools she retired and built the house by the lough. I stood on the lawn of that penny-wise woman while my host talked about the grampus which came into the lough after seals. But my attention was taken by the stately flight of a heron as it disappeared into the gathering twilight on slow, powerful wing-beats. I remembered a line from James Hanley's *The Ocean*—'From this silence he made walls.'

And it was from a rectory also built along the loughside at Killyleagh that the silence of the ancient walls of Egypt and Assyria again woke into speech after thousands of years, for in the rectory lived Edward Hincks, the greatest orientalist of nineteenth-century Europe. As Moses spent forty years in the wilderness so Hincks spent forty years in the obscurity of the loughside forging the keys which would open the hitherto unknown secrets of the East.

Casts of the ancient stones were sent all the way to Killyleagh for his use in deciphering. The principles Hincks laid down then still enable scholars today to translate the hieroglyphic and cuneiform scripts of the Nile civilization. I hope that Hincks's bust in Cairo has received more thoughtful treatment in recent years than did that of de Lesseps, the canal builder who was dishonoured in the first rush of Egyptian national pride.

As though the tiny town of Killyleagh had not given enough material to the Bloomsbury experts another local lad achieved fame by being the founder of the British Museum. Sir Hans Sloane, traveller and physician, was born in a small house in 1660 in Frederick Street, a house still standing and lived in today. There were people who believed that Hans may have been a 'wee love bird', born on the wrong side of the blanket to the Rowan-Hamilton family, overlords of the local estate. Hans Sloane might well have been illegitimate for the founder of the Killyleagh Hamiltons, the Reverend Hans Hamilton, was himself born on the wrong side of the ducal blanket. Sloane at any rate had his education in the magnificent library of Killyleagh Castle.

The town sprawled about the castle foot which rose, towered and turreted over its roofs and above its screen of trees for all the world like a castle in a German fairy story. From behind its high curtain wall the castle looked grim and forbidding, as though dark and bloody secrets lay buried behind its battlements.

I could hardly resist the desire to invest the castle with arms like a knight bent on rescuing a captive damsel. With imaginary accoutrement jingling in my ears I went up to this Rhine Valley fortress, having arranged a knightly hospice in the form of a bed at Killyleagh's ex-manse. But this poor knight, armed in reality with nothing more than his insatiable curiosity, found no breaches in the walls. There was no chance of a half-crown tour for the castle was still the private residence of its owner Mrs. Rowan-Hamilton.

A strawberry ice-cream, bought from the man whose celeste music sent rooks squabbling about the chimneys and lodges and cottages built into the walls, did nothing to help. He could not tell me how to gain admittance. I looked up to the remote inner towers where the rooks settled again by a television aerial. The gate lodges were empty and locked. No bells connected the gates to the castle and I saw notices 'Strictly Private. Trespassers Prosecuted.' I began to think the only way in would be General Gillespie's—to be hauled up by a rope.

The postmistress in the little post office nestling under the walls saved the day. Only for one day in the year, she said, were the gates opened to the public and then in aid of a charity. But nevertheless a telephone call was put through and as a result Mrs. Rowan-Hamilton, from somewhere in the depths of her castle, invited me to call the following morning.

With the rest of that evening to kill I went into the Dufferin Arms to be welcomed with friendly chaffing and inquisitiveness and forceful generosity by the local farmers who would hardly hear of me buying my own drink. A large whisky and a Guinness 'chaser' appeared and I tried to concentrate on at least one of the many threads of talk, for in their enthusiasm the farmers tended to talk and tell stories all at once.

I did disentangle the tale of Captain Blood and the ghosts of Moore Hall, a house which the owner's brother-in-law wanted me to visit. But I had to resist the invitation to 'Come over and see the wee grey lady' abjuring the supernatural for the supernormal in the form of more whisky and Guinness presented by another farmer. He was just getting over a bad dose of 'rat's disease', contracted through taking a horse to the Dublin Show, and rubbing an open cut against rat-infected straw.

The crescendo of talk and laughter increased, and I tried to discover who the 'blonde bastard' in the town was. This character intrigued me, for some avowed and some denied that the 'blonde bastard' appeared recently in a court of law. I asked somebody and discovered that the 'bastard', due no doubt as much to whiskies as to the richness of the Killyleagh dialect, was not a bastard but a barrister. It seemed high time to leave the proceedings though I almost had to use physical force to dissuade my new friends from walling me into my seat with fresh bottles and glasses. The publican's wife asked if I would like to go through the yard, not as a way of escape, but in order to see Sir Hans Sloane's house which was just outside the Dufferin Arms back gate. I was still capable of reading the date over Hans's house—1637, and 1880 as the date of rebuilding.

Sitting on the window-sill of the house next door was Gordon, a youngster who had just come back from shooting hoodie crows.

'Have you seen the stile?' he asked.

I had not, but I knew what he meant, the one I knew of from childhood, the stile in Lady Dufferin's song *The Irish Emigrant's Lament*. She wrote it sitting in a window of Killyleagh Castle, looking out towards the meadows spreading below the castle walls.

Gordon, who offered to take me, reminded me of another song by Lady Dufferin. With his tanned face and thick black curly hair, his talk of wildfowling and fishing he might have been the boy in

Terence's Farewell to Kathleen. I wondered if Lady Dufferin also wrote it looking from the high window towards the ruined churchyard where Gordon was leading me amongst a wilderness of mare's-tail and hemlock and seven-foot-high nettles.

When we got to the stile, Gordon asked about England and about work and wages in the big cities and about the girls who had gone away. Here was Terence of the Farewell, leaving the girl whom circumstances were taking away. If it happened once, it happened a million times in Ireland, and the songs, taken so lightly as sentimental molly-coddle, are in reality poignant comments on the tragic experience of human parting. Desmond Shawe-Taylor speaking of John McCormack's recording of Lady Dufferin's song found it as moving as if Schubert had written it.

> *And when you come back to me, Kathleen,*
> *None the better shall I be off then—*
> *You'll be speaking such beautiful English,*
> *Oh, I won't know my Kathleen again.*

Gordon was not wearing in his coat a small badge of the black Manx cat as were many of the youths in the Castle View Café where I went for my supper. These mementoes of holidays spent over in the Isle of Man had a connection, no doubt unknown to the local boys, with the earliest days of Killyleagh Castle, for one of the first châtelaines, Affreca wife of John de Courcy, was daughter of the King of Man. The Castle View Café was full of talk about shooting, the unlikely shooting of mullet which the boys took at high tide in the lough with shotguns. When I left the café's juke box and Pepsi-Cola bibbers it was night and I wandered slowly back to the old manse which was lost among trees at the top of a rise approached over a bridge lying below a short, steep street of deserted houses.

Morning came in with sunshine again and the sound of birds. I was out early enough to visit Killyleagh's harbour and lough shore before going up to the castle. The miniature town charmed me more than anywhere so far on my visit for it embraced the countryside round about besides fringing the expanse of lough. Trees encompassed it and stood about the meadows. There was good company too, friends were easily made. It seemed also as if the place had been formed through the centuries by the proximity of the castle, a fortress whose foundations were laid in Norman times.

I walked under the trees along one of the outer castle walls and came to a side gate. Away over a hill I saw Gordon, a black figure in a green landscape, going off for a day among the lough islands. The scene must have looked the same for hundreds of years, unchanged since John de Courcy marched northwards from Dublin to make himself lord of Ulster in the late twelfth century. Boys and men had probably wandered off across the hill to fish and shoot ever since the Hamilton family lived in the castle from James I's reign. The Hamiltons believed that part of the castle was built in 1099 and that John de Courcy may only have taken it over for his Manx bride, as he took so many places in Ulster.

Once inside the gate, I saw the main castle building standing on a mound, its stones rising sheer like cliffs. It reminded me of Glamis Castle in Scotland and I said so to Mrs. Rowan-Hamilton, when she admitted me, straining at the leash of a splendid Rhodesian saddleback whose eagerness to inspect the stranger matched my own.

And as we went up through the castle's suites of rooms I had cause to admire Mrs. Rowan-Hamilton's tremendous energy in maintaining the great old house with such consistent taste, for once beyond the thick walls the Grimm fairy story castle, the Glamis of Ulster magically became a charming country house. The secrets of Killyleagh Castle were revealed, not as a series of Bluebeard dungeons, but a succession of surprisingly light rooms.

Mrs. Rowan-Hamilton lived alone in the castle with no company except that of her servants and she devoted most of her time to keeping up the fabric and converting the interior to her own taste with a vigour and success which would have done credit to a professional architect. With her mason, she kept a constant eye on the main walls and battlements and roofs, keeping decay and rot at bay, enemies her predecessors did not have so much reason to fear. Impatient of Victorian varnish and wallpaper and gloomy paint, Mrs. Rowan-Hamilton had stripped much of the beautiful wood panelling clean, as well as the splendid eighteenth-century doors and the strapwork balustrade to the main stair. Here, she had banished the horrors of Victorian varnish to lay bare the Jacobean bones of the fine stair hall complete with surprisingly correct Doric columns and entablatures.

Elsewhere in the castle there were strapwork ceilings, some fine old fireplaces, and to all the rooms, deeply embrasured windows. In one of the corridors I saw a water-colour drawing showing the castle in the eighteenth century when a Georgian house stood between the two outer gatehouses, an anachronism rectified by a central gatehouse put up in the medieval style in the nineteenth century.

In one room was a silver plaque of Charles I which I liked and which my hostess said had also intrigued the head of the Silver Department at the British Museum when he had been at Killyleagh for the recent Hans Sloane celebrations. The plaque was made in a period when it was forbidden for silver to be beaten. Mrs. Rowan-Hamilton had brought the plaque from Glamis. When I looked at the fireplace in the same room Mrs. Rowan-Hamilton said, 'That's the one Harold Nicolson wrote about in his book.' But the upraised hands of the fat Jacobean cherubs had got dry rot and were now removed to quarantine outside the back door. But my hostess's remark reminded me that Harold Nicolson was yet another relation of this literary family and the book, *The Desire to Please*, was about a most extraordinary member of the Killyleagh branch of the family.

Archibald Hamilton Rowan was born in 1751 and became an Irish Nationalist who caused much alarm in high places when he styled himself Citizen Rowan. He played a prominent part in the Volunteer movement and agitation for parliamentary reform. When he actually joined the corps of United Irishmen in 1791, Citizen Rowan was condemned as a spy and sentenced to be hung. But with the resourcefulness of the family he bribed a warder and escaped to France where he became a friend of Robespierre. When the Reign of Terror ended the Citizen had again to escape, this time to America having ferried himself down the Seine. But by 1807 all was forgiven and forgotten and he was allowed to return to his estate at Killyleagh, where he contented himself with being a fierce supporter of Catholic emancipation.

I saw a dungeon in Killyleagh and then, at the other extreme, the battlements reached by climbing an endless flight of spiral stairs. At last we came out on the leads, among the rooks and television aerials. There had been a fire at Killyleagh recently said Mrs. Rowan-Hamilton pointing to her aerial. ('Where *is* the castle?' the fireman asked when telephoned from one of Ireland's biggest, oldest and most unforgettable landmarks.) After some delay the firemen arrived and so did the man who had sold Mrs. Rowan-Hamilton the television set not long before. As soon as he saw the castle was afire he rushed guiltily to the scene with a piece of insulating tape for the set.

From the battlements, despite the aerials and a tall chimney stack in Killyleagh and some council houses just outside the town, the centuries melted away again. I could picture Viking longboats on the lough and the armies of Norman and medieval times making their way across country. Below us, between the castle and gatehouses was a great grassed court and this I populated with archers and jousting knights, and speculated about the people through the ages who must have looked sadly into the court as the gates opened and the men rode out, perhaps to the precarious life at court in London or the more certainly lethal tournaments in France.

The long years could hardly have produced a more colourful warrior than a roadmender called Hugh the Giant. He sailed from Warrenpoint in the mid-nineteenth century armed with nothing but a new shillelagh. His mission was to take revenge on the literary world of London, for Hugh's family name was Brunty, or Prunty, known today as Brontë.

In the late eighteenth century Ulster's athletics was dominated by the five sons of Hugh and Alice Brunty, in the same way that English literature was later to be dominated by their three Brontë granddaughters. Hugh Brunty senior kept a corn-kiln in his tiny cottage at Emdale, County Down, and his eldest son Patrick was born there in 1777.

Hugh Brunty was poor in terms of possessions but rich in terms of story-telling and verse-making. Suitably primed with a local brew made from vitriol, blue stone, copperas and herbs, the neighbours crowded into the cottage, forgetting their prejudice against Mrs. Brunty who had once been a Catholic, to sit spellbound by Hugh's tales. Two of the most intent faces, lit by the kiln furnace, the cottage's only light, were Patrick's and his younger brother Hugh's.

Five big, masculine girls were also born to the Bruntys. Only one of them got married because, as a contemporary put it, 'They were not ordinary women, and I think men were a little afraid of them.' How much more the men needed to fear the five Brunty brothers, whose cock-pit was the county's best and who were also celebrated shots, and still better known as fighters with their fists. Welsh Brunty's bout with Sam Clarke of Ballynaskeagh became Ulster history. Generations of births, marriages and deaths were dated by it. That famous fight was the 'Hejira in the current calendar' according to Dr. William Wright commenting on it in 1893.

It all started because Welsh Brunty had a girl friend, Peggy Campbell, whose little crippled brother went to the village school on crutches, to the amusement of some boys called Clarke. The bullies took the boy's crutches away and threw him into a pond. But Welsh Brunty arrived in the nick of time and made the Clarke boys go into the pond to rescue the cripple. Family honour was at stake and the bullies' big brother Sam Clarke decided to take up the cause against Welsh Brunty.

This was no small village affair. A crowd of 10,000 came from all over Ulster—some estimated that it numbered 50,000—including the sporting clergy and gentry. The fight of the century was held in the hollow of a field so that all could see over the heads of four hundred 'special order preservers' who kept the angry crowd away from the fighters and their seconds.

As Sam Clarke entered the ring his mother gave him something to eat, and infuriated the crowd by shouting, 'Sam, my son, may you never get bit nor sup from me more if you do not lick the mongrel,'— which was a barbed reference to Mrs. Brunty's childhood Catholicism.

And so the two men began their monumental fight. Sam Clarke was an older man than Welsh Brunty, and rather better built. But he soon lost his advantage of size and weight during the fight. Welsh was wiry and quick on his feet and did not tire so quickly as the hours dragged on. Above the silent thousands who stood watching Peggy Campbell's voice rang out, 'Welsh my boy, go in and avenge my brother and the mongrel.' Peggy did not know her words were to be compared in County Down's history with the Duke of Wellington's famous 'Up guards, and at them.' Peggy undoubtedly spurred

Welsh Brunty on and he won the day, though he refused to acknowledge the wild congratulation of the crowd until he had taken Sam Clarke home to bed.

Patrick, the eldest brother, grew up like Welsh and all the rest, having no shoes until he was 14 and even then carrying them to the church door on the odd occasion when he and his family went to the local meeting house. Patrick, also in common with the others, suffered because of his mother's childhood religion and was called Mongrel Pat or Pat the Papish.

He was apprenticed to a weaver for two years at 14, and he proved to be a quick learner whose shuttle flew with as much skill as he showed in the cock-pit on Sunday afternoon. Once he had to take his web to Belfast and returned laden with second-hand books, Milton's *Paradise Lost* among them, which filled the young weaver with delight. He read it aloud as he clecked his sleys and lay on the grassy slope of Emdale fort reciting what he had learnt. And once, on a summer's day, the Rev. Andrew Harshaw happened to pass by Emdale fort and to his astonishment heard Milton's sonorous phrases coming from the weaver's lad who lay looking at clouds drifting towards the Mourne mountains.

The Presbyterian minister spoke to Patrick, inviting him to lessons in the manse. With Virgil and Herodotus in his mind now, Patrick rose daily two hours before dawn and went to his new tutor who coached him by the light of a rosin-slut in his bedroom before the boy left for his weaver's reed. With the burnt end of an ash rod Patrick worked out Euclidean problems on the kitchen hearth to the amazement of his family.

When the weaving firm closed, Andrew Harshaw helped his young student to obtain the post of master at Glascar Hill Presbyterian Church School despite opposition to this son of a former Catholic woman, a young man who in any case came from a family which 'lived like the heathen' because they went so rarely to church.

Master Brunty was soon writing poetry himself and its influence can be seen in his daughters' novels. His *Vision of Hell* written at Glascar in 1796 already had something of *Wuthering Heights* about it, as well as being a starkly real picture of contemporary Ireland.

DOWN BY THE SEA

The clergy aloft on a burning floor
Sat slaking their thirst with bastards' gore,
And gnawing the bones of the murdered poor,
The evicted who died on the silent moor.

This was a reference to the taxes raised by the clergy for the transportation of illegitimate children to the Dublin foundling hospital. Greater scoundrels than these 'bastard-bearers' never existed. Few of their charges ever reached Dublin. They were dropped into the nearest bog-hole while the bearers lived off the taxes.

In spite of such abuses the Rev. Andrew Harshaw persuaded Patrick to study for the Episcopal Church rather than his own ministry for which eight years' training were required. The minister's move was made following Patrick's disgrace when the authorities closed his school. He had kissed one of his senior pupils. This was bad enough, but worse was his wish to court her seriously—him a Brunty, one of the 'Mongrels'. The girl's parents were important farmers and it was they who caused the school to close. The pleasure of learning, the lessons with Harshaw, the reading of Ovid by the turf fire at night, had always been spoilt for Patrick by his being called Mongrel Pat or Pat the Papish. In the end this continual slur against his mother's childhood religion made him leave for England. Before going to Cambridge in 1802, Patrick was known as Brontë, a spelling which by this time his brothers used on their horse carts— a grander spelling no doubt noted by the family when the King of Naples made Nelson the Duke of Brontë in 1800.

He was ordained and given the incumbency of Haworth in Yorkshire, but Patrick Brontë never forgot Emdale and the corn-kiln's red eye glowing in the tiny cottage. He crossed to Ireland and practised pistol-shooting with his brothers. And it was to his brother Hugh that Patrick sent a copy of *Jane Eyre* with the message 'This is the first work published by my daughter, under the fictitious name of Currer Bell, which is the usual way at first by authors.'

Hugh the Giant had been head of the family in Ireland since the death of his father and namesake. He gingerly turned the pages of *Jane Eyre*, thinking how unlike those of *Pilgrim's Progress* they were, the book on which the family had been brought up. Indeed,

Jane Eyre appeared to be 'a parcel of lies, the fruit of living among foreigners'.

The perplexed Hugh took the book up to the Rev. David McKee at Ballynaskeagh manse. The minister read it and pronounced, 'Hughey, the book bears the Brunty stamp on every sentence and idea, and is the grandest novel that has been published in my time. The child Jane Eyre is your father in petticoats and Mrs. Reed is the wicked uncle by the Boyne.' The fact that the minister had said the book was so grand set the Irish brothers and sisters rejoicing. And then they recognized many of their old father's stories in the book and were overjoyed when the Newry newspaper quoted all the English reviews of the novel.

The days of rejoicing, however, were short for the brothers read an unsigned review in the *Quarterly*. After speculation as to Currer Bell's sex, it said, 'Whoever it be, it is a person who, with great mental power, combines a total ignorance of the habits of society, a great coarseness of taste, and a heathenish doctrine of religion.'

If few understood what the book was about or had ever heard of the *Quarterly Review*, they all certainly knew that Currer Bell must have a 'heathenish religion' to be Mongrel Pat's daughter. The slur of Alice Brunty's childhood religion was not forgotten and her granddaughter was, quite clearly, a bad woman.

The family forgathered. They were united in their fury and demanded vengeance on the *Quarterly* reviewer. As Sam Clarke had been dealt with by Welsh Brunty, so the unknown critic must be put in his place. Hugh the Giant was the natural choice of the family champion. He called the village schoolmaster in and made a will leaving all to his maligned niece Charlotte Brontë. A new shillelagh was cut from the hedge and Hugh's oath pledged to the family.

He sailed for Liverpool from Warrenpoint. From Liverpool he walked the seventy miles to Haworth where he arrived on a Sunday morning when everybody except Martha the servant was at church. The old Yorkshirewoman was horrified by the tramp on the door-step who admitted to being a Sabbath-breaker by journeying on a Sunday. Martha was certainly not going to let him into the parsonage. However, when she saw him turn to go into the full church in his dirty clothes she changed her mind and let him into the house.

Patrick's novelist daughters were thrilled when they came back from the church and found their Uncle Hugh. They bombarded him with questions about places in County Down, which they referred to as home. When Uncle Hugh explained his mission, Charlotte was horrified, but Anne was full of sympathy and encouragement. Their father, remembering his cloth, tried to dissuade Hugh from his revenge and took him off to see a prize fight.

In this way, Patrick hoped to 'take the conceit out of him'. But the Rector of Haworth had forgotten his brother's Ulster passion and the fight merely served to whet Hugh's appetite for the *Quarterly* reviewer's blood. He said of the prize-fighters that he 'could have licked them both' and taking his leave of the family and the fighters set off to London. With his shillelagh in his hand he called at John Murray's, publisher of the *Quarterly*, and demanded to see the reviewer.

Fleet Street, however, was not so easily licked as Hugh's neighbours in County Down. Day after day Hugh the Giant called at Murray's until he was banned from their offices as being dangerous. He went next to the publishers of *Jane Eyre* who treated him kindly and arranged for him to be admitted to the Reading Room of the British Museum.

Accustomed though they were in the Reading Room to eccentrics and down-at-heel scholars, none in that august establishment had ever seen anything quite like Hugh the Giant complete with big shillelagh. Some of the people there had a grudge themselves against reviewers and gave a dinner in honour of the man from County Down. His shillelagh was much admired and he made a fiery speech worthy of his still unaccomplished mission. Help was offered him and the reviewer's possible identity was suggested variously as Thackeray or Dickens, George Henry Lewes, Harriet Martineau or Bulwer Lytton. But the real identity of *Jane Eyre's* detractor was not revealed for many years.

Hugh returned broken-hearted to Yorkshire. He had failed in his family duty. Only Anne Brontë was sympathetic to her 'noble uncle' and wanted to take him home to County Down. Perhaps she had presentiments of her own death, which followed shortly after, and wanted to see 'home' before she died. But Hugh the Giant went alone and no gathering of the clan welcomed him when he returned to Ireland. He remained embittered for years, and died without knowing that he lost his giant's stature to the pen of Lady Eastlake.

Nevertheless, Hugh Brunty knew more about *Jane Eyre* than Lady Eastlake did. He had heard his own father recite a poem to lovely Alice McClory, the Catholic he married and whose smile 'would have tamed a mad bull', the woman who became Catherine Linton to her granddaughter. Later, Patrick polished this poem, and his daughters used lines from it in their novels.

In *Jane Eyre* Rochester says, 'Jane suits me: do I suit her.' And Jane goes back to Ulster for the answer, 'To the finest fibre of my nature, sir.' But this was from the poem *Alice and Hugh* composed so many years before in the corn-kiln kitchen of Emdale cottage—

> *The finest fibres of my soul*
> *Entwine with thine in love's strong fold,*
> *Our tin cup is a golden bowl,*
> *Love fills our cot with wealth untold.*

3

The Kingdom of Mourne

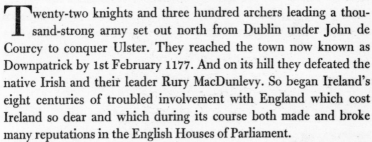

Twenty-two knights and three hundred archers leading a thousand-strong army set out north from Dublin under John de Courcy to conquer Ulster. They reached the town now known as Downpatrick by 1st February 1177. And on its hill they defeated the native Irish and their leader Rury MacDunlevy. So began Ireland's eight centuries of troubled involvement with England which cost Ireland so dear and which during its course both made and broke many reputations in the English Houses of Parliament.

But de Courcy, the knight from Cheshire, probably did not think so far ahead. And now, his battles long done, de Courcy lies, almost certainly, beside his Manx bride in the north transept of Greyabbey, whose roofless ruin stands peacefully subject to decay on the other side of Strangford Lough from Downpatrick.

A grave whose contents were less certain was the one at Downpatrick itself. Under a slab of stone, the mortal remains of St. Columba and St. Brigid were supposed to be with those of no less a person than St. Patrick himself. There are records which say John de Courcy brought St. Columba's and St. Brigid's remains to Downpatrick with much pomp and ceremony and in the presence of Cardinal Vivian who was specially imported for the occasion.

Today, this is disputed by knowledgeable people who maintain that this interment was nothing more than propaganda designed by the Anglo-Norman adventurer de Courcy to win over the religious-minded natives, an astute move in the Cheshire knight's political game of chess. Although the actual site of the three important saints' grave may be open to question, the truth seems to be fairly well established that they were, in fact, buried *in uno sepulchro*. John de Courcy burnt and plundered so many churches during his career that it seems not at all unlikely that he collared the sacred remains. In 1185 Giraldus Cambrensis quotes the famous couplet:

> *In burgo Duno tumulo tumulantur in uno*
> *Brigida Patricius atque Columba pius.*

In spite of rival claims from other places to be the saints' real burial ground, Downpatrick has been a pilgrims' centre of attraction for centuries. Not a little erosion was caused by their taking small amounts of the holy soil away as mementoes. To check this the huge slab of unhewn granite was brought from the Mourne mountains and laid over the Downpatrick grave. But even this has not stopped the pious coming from the world over to collect soil from around the stone.

When I got there a Californian nun was scraping up soil with a nail-file into a paper napkin.

Her family seized on me. 'Can you take us?' They thrust a camera at me, and posed round the granite slab, straining to read the single name Patrick in Irish letters.

'Wish they would put up a better marker,' they remarked as they used cine cameras on the quite unremarkable block of granite. I had no heart to disillusion them about the stone. They obviously thought it was as ancient as the grave itself. It would have been too cruel to have pointed out that, for example, another simple gravestone nearby to 'Patt Smith of Church Wall, July the 18th 1808' had been in the churchyard almost a century longer than the stone on Saints Patrick, Columba and Brigid.

The granite slab only arrived in Downpatrick in 1900, brought there by that most extraordinary of Irishmen, Francis Joseph Bigger. He was born in Belfast and became a fervent Gaelic Leaguer—when he could spare the time from travelling about the country restoring graveyards and castles. A caricature of the time neatly summed him up, the drawing showed him dressed in a kilt and holding a Gaelic banner, and underneath the caption ran 'Occupation: Fellow of the Royal Society of Antiquaries. Recreation: Law.

Favourite pastime: fishing in Lough Neagh, accompanied on the war pipes. Pet aversion: Board of Works and brass instruments.'

I thought it better to let the Americans go on their way rejoicing for if, being disillusioned about the granite stone, they were also to realize that it was odds on whether the saintly trio's bones were there either, their depression might have been unduly disproportionate. In fact, I was beginning to be depressed myself for a gentle, soaking rain had set in which looked as if it had come to stay.

Leaving the Americans to drive away spiritually enriched and happy in their convertible, I went into Downpatrick cathedral which also was a comparatively modern restoration. By 1512 the original building, reputedly the largest and most magnificent church in all Ireland, was in a ruinous state. At the Dissolution it was pillaged and burnt by Lord Leonard Grey, an extravagance he later paid for with his head at Tower Hill in London. After various vicissitudes the cathedral assumed the form of the present building which is less than half the size of the medieval abbey, and of a dullness relieved only by some splendid, richly-coloured and modelled coats-of-arms ranged round its walls.

By contrast, Downpatrick itself appealed to me perhaps because its streets were not flat and the town was arranged about a crossroads, an unusual feature of town layouts in Northern Ireland. The cathedral approach was by a gentle slope, planted with trees and bordered by buildings any one of which would grace any town. The Blue Coat School was easily the best of these, a small-scale, stone-dressed building rather in the manner of William Kent, finished with a neat, central cupola. Immediately opposite the school was a pair of elegantly urban houses with Ionic pilasters about their doors and a view beside them, straight through to the meadows beyond.

As with human beings it is difficult for buildings to be at their best in the rain. I tried to find shelter in a range of decayed Georgian buildings next door. They were hiding in a courtyard shut off from the street by a high blank wall. At one time, these buildings must have been rather grand. As I sat huddled on the steps an old farmer, who looked like a resurrected John de Courcy, drove an ancient car through the archway. I asked if, by any chance, he might be driving down to the coast towards Newcastle. He replied in a dialect which one of de Courcy's soldiers might have used:

'I shan't be stirring till the heel of the evenin'.'

He disappeared for a time, though he peered twice round the archway to see if I had stolen his crock of ages. An hour later, however, his horn croaked beside me in the town. He leaned out of the window, from which all trace of glass had long vanished.

'Are ya holdin' yerself for a ride?' quoted Methuselah.

Terrified that the contraption would disintegrate beneath me, I got in beside him and with a noise like a one-man percussion band we set off on the Newcastle road. He was not going the whole way but, presumably deciding I was not a foot-pad, or rather a motor-pad, Methuselah agreed to take me there nevertheless, the reason being that he wanted to talk—about his marriage. He was, at a conservative estimate, not a day under 70, though he looked 90. When I plucked up enough courage to ask him if, after all, he was married, he replied, 'Not yet'. Then he inquired with as much enthusiasm as young Gordon in Killyleagh, 'What are the wimen like over the Water?'

I explained that, basically, they were the same as women anywhere else.

'Och well,' he said narrowly missing a bus as he pulled up on Newcastle promenade, 'I'll keep a loose leg for another few years.'

My arrival in Newcastle was inauspicious. It was still raining and I was still wet, more wet than needs have been because of exposure in Methuselah's cullender on wheels. Newcastle, like Bangor, was full of holidaymakers, and it took me half-an-hour to find a room in a seafront boarding-house. As far as possible I dried myself but felt disinclined to stay in with nothing more provided by the house in the way of entertainment than the one solitary book *Handbook for Mental Nurses*.

I shared the shelter of some shop awnings with visitors wrapped in plastic macs and got my bearings. Even the rain could not disguise the wonder of Newcastle's setting, though I had already seen enough to tell me that architecturally the little resort had nothing commendable. But its wide sands stretched for miles in a bay whose sea edge was lost in the distance by the salt spray hanging over the waves.

The scene was like the shore landscapes beloved by Bonington and Boudin. It was a most ideal place for children.

As if this were not enough, beyond the town the giant forms of the Mourne mountains, smooth and vast, reared into the sky, sweeping, in the manner made famous in the song, down to the sea with huge headlands. And as I looked in wonder at these mountains, a rift appeared in the clouds. The high profile of hills, obscured a moment before by trails of rain, suddenly became bold and clear and rich with greens and purples and rusty browns in the late afternoon sunshine. The lower slopes were planted with fir, but the upper reaches, culminating in Slieve Donard's peak almost three thousand feet above the sea, were bare except for heather.

The clouds continued to be driven out of sight inland and soon the sun was striking warm again. My own joy at the sun was nothing compared with the children's. I thought I had never been in a place with so many children. They swarmed everywhere, looking Scandinavian with their spun gold hair and blue eyes and butter-golden skin. Newcastle was a place for the young, mooning lovelorn teenagers and young married couples, some of whom were still teenagers themselves. So far as all these people were concerned the rain had not drowned their happiness and something of their enjoyment infected the air. The myriad children were part of this for they were not excluded from any family activity. Wide-eyed without a hint of sleep about them, they sat up to ten o'clock or more with the grownups in the cafés drinking fizzy drinks and eating enormous platefuls of fish and chips.

Partly because of the afternoon's rain and partly because it was the inviolable high tea time the sands were not fully occupied. I walked along them feeling that soft-hard, mysterious quality of sea-sand underfoot which fascinates me now as much as it did in childhood. The tide was right out, so that the sea had withdrawn to the distance. The few figures of bathers looked remote and might easily have been merboys and mergirls sporting at the water's edge.

Near the town's extremity some adventurous mums were exposing grey thighs hoping possibly to get that same tan as a group of Danish Boy Scouts who seemed to have absorbed a hundred summers in their long mahogany legs. On a spit of land some youngsters had turned the scrub-camouflage of a wartime machine-gun post into a love nest, lying prone and immobile in embraces which were still going on, position unchanged, when I returned from the sands an hour or so later.

Wagtails gleaned the last tide's seaweed and toddlers lost themselves in new worlds of rock pools. Some older children were putting finishing touches to sandcastles even though the sandcastle competition was not due until the following day when prizes were to be had from the Milk Marketing Board. I walked on and soon the sands were quite deserted except for an old clergyman I spied behind a breakwater. He wore a black hat and held up a volumi-nous towel so that his tiny granddaughter could change out of her bathing costume behind it, safe from the gaze of gulls and stranded jelly-fish and sinners' footprints in the sand. The retiring sea had left loughs and lagoons of itself behind in the sands' undulations, and away round the bay these caught the light, lying silver against the duns and ochres of the sand. It would have taken hours to reach the bay's extremity so I turned back to Newcastle, and, when I came into the town, afternoon had slipped imperceptibly into early evening. Another seaside day was almost done. The last thermos flasks had been packed up, and the empty strawberry punnets thrown to the gulls.

Soon after high tea a crowd collected on the front to watch the start of the annual, free-for-all cross-country run up to Slieve Donard and back. Twenty-seven young men had volunteered for this tough course up and down the mountain. In shorts and vests and others stripped to the waist they sped off along the front and in a remarkably short time appeared on the lower slopes, white specks scattered across the mountain. People followed the specks with binoculars. An hour passed before they returned, scratched and muddy and sweating. To show they had really covered the course and had passed Bloody Bridge the RECEIVED stamp from the mayor's parlour had been stamped on their arms by helpers stationed at the half-way mark. The winner, in the amazing time of one hour, was a 17-year-old boy with ginger hair who received the prize, again given by the Milk Marketing Board and presented by the Milk Queen herself. He got ten pounds and a shield. The runners loped in one after the other in various stages of fatigue. I talked with one, a student-priest who wanted to go as a missionary to Brazil.

This excitement over, there was time to explore the esplanade which was small and simple boasting nothing much more than lawns and a bandstand and at its farther end a fountain built in honour of William Percy French, composer of 'Where the Mountains of Mourne sweep down to the sea'. On the whole, I decided that the song was a better memorial than the fountain though children liked the fountain well enough for paddling in and courting couples for being photographed by self-consciously.

During the afternoon the bandstand put on a concert for the children and mostly by the children. Without any of the shyness and terror which afflicted my generation, those youngsters, some no more than 5 or 6, stood in front of the microphone and gave a fair rendering of the latest pop songs. And later, it seemed as if Newcastle's entire population had turned out for another concert, of Twist n' Shake, given by four lads with guitars and drums.

The crowd (including me) went wild with enthusiasm, for the rhythm was infectious. Everybody was dancing. Something flamed in the blood. Along the sea-wall stood those who could find no room on the pavement. Locked arm in arm in a long chain they rocked dangerously to and fro just above the sea which had crept in again and now slapped against the wall. The four boys played number after number. The audience, hypnotized by the rhythm as if they were an African tribe, refused to let them go. The twistin' n' shakin' grew wilder, though with Irish decorum girls danced with girls and boys with boys. But the last encore had to be the last, for the not-quite-dark undying night sky had taken over, leaving a glimmer on the horizon as it did in Scandinavia. The crowd, flushed and sea-tanned and more than happy, dispersed until the waves' slumping against the sea-wall was the loudest thing to be heard.

Gulls woke me next morning. The *Handbook for Mental Nurses* lay where it had fallen when I dropped to sleep. The gulls' cries sounded as if a whaling station was in the process of throwing offal into the sea. The mewing and barking, laughing and grating, yelling and wailing followed me down to an early breakfast. It was a typical Ulster boarding-house breakfast of fruit juice, bacon and eggs and three kinds of fresh bread and wheaten farls, all washed down by strong tea supplied in quantities which even a camel about to cross the desert could hardly take.

The landlady, the radio and my own optimism told me that the sun was going to shine uninterrupted all day. As there was no bus to Bryansford until the afternoon I began to walk, taking leave of Newcastle by way of a pleasant road overhung with trees which presently gave on to the Shimna River winding its way over boulders and through pools, where, I suspected, brown trout lurked, a river twinkling in the sun, and flowing amber beneath the boughs of trees along its banks. Schubert could have written *The Trout* here. I jumped down beside the bridge, went upstream a short distance and found a pool and a waterfall to bathe in.

Trusting myself to be out of eyeshot and out of earshot, I sat in that cold crystal water which had the reverse effect on me from that of Bangor's cold water monks. Instead of the Psalms I tried to sing *Die Forelle* and thought, not incongruously, of Austria. It *was* like Austria, with the pines and firs on the Mourne mountains, and that intoxicating, sweetly rarefied mountain air.

Farther up was the lovely stretch of old Tollymore Park in which stood some of the most noble oak boles I have ever seen, rising above the green mist of bracken. And where these cavernous woods ended, the first gentle slopes of the mountains began, curving steeper and steeper, and here ancient oak was replaced by the darker, bluer green of the young pine and fir plantations.

Had I discovered that the cider-coloured river and its pools were paradise I should have been more than content to spend my eternity there, alternately bathing and lying on the bank to be dried and warmed through. But the morning was flying too soon. Already, in the way that stomachs have of interrupting idylls, my gargantuan breakfast had left me with nothing but an even bigger appetite for lunch. So I dried out for the last time, dressed, and made my way back to the road where a travelling grocer stopped to give me a lift.

The road began to rise, bringing the whole seaward range of the

Mourne mountains into view and, flat against the horizon, the sea itself. I saw now that this was not the Otz Valley in Austria but Ireland greener and gentler and more friendly than the remote inhuman nobility of the snow-peaked mountains of the Tyrol. Nestling snug on the Mourne slopes were farms, their white houses and outbuildings protected from winter gales by groups of windbreak trees, while between them the patterned fields of glossy corn spread out.

These were not mountains for daring displays of ski-ing or heroic deeds of climbing but the setting of a quiet pastoral upland life. The white buildings, mostly low and sprawling, seemed to belong to the mountains as though they were boulders protruding from the rock beneath the carpet of rich, dark soil. Everything fashioned by generations of farmers belonged sweetly to the landscape. In Austria, as in most mountainous regions, a feeling pervades that the farms and villages along the narrow valley floors are somehow menaced by the mountains, a prey to avalanches. Perhaps that was one of the reasons why Baroque architecture flourished with a peculiar genius on the Alps' northern side—the highly sophisticated decoration being an expression of men's defiance of the inhospitable mountains.

We rose higher, the view extending on every side and came into the heart of the Kingdom of Mourne. We stopped several times for flocks of black-faced sheep filling the narrow roads which were stone-walled and earth-banked with whins and foxgloves. The young driver stopped at farms and cottages by the road, mostly to sell ice-cream. He sounded the horn and children came streaming out, followed by their mothers and grandmothers.

'Two pokes and a slider,' they asked, meaning two ice cornets and a wafer. At one such halt we stayed longer than the selling of ice-cream demanded to laugh and to tease a girl with copper beech hair and bright emerald eyes who might have been a colleen for any tourist poster.

The grocer had to turn off the road eventually to carry his packets and tins and ices to the remoter parts of the mountains. With a cheerful grin and a wave of the hand he rattled down a stony track and was soon out of sight and sound. I was left alone feeling as strange and blissful as Gerontius did when he woke after death, and thinking that if the holy angels bright flying through the realms of light ever stopped for a breather then this place, high up in the Mourne mountains, must surely be a favourite alighting point.

As it was, the only things flying about were bumbling bumble-bees whose drone filled a silence otherwise unbroken except for the cor anglais call of sheep scattered among the hills. I began walking again, to cover the last two miles into Hilltown, passing through that lovely land of standing cattle and trees, white farms and sweep-ing valley floors patchworked with a thousand tones of green, squared with hedges and dry-stone walls, the hills radiant in the noon light.

These were delectable mountains indeed. And as though the language of its people were poetry the places were called by such lilting names as Hare's Gap, Silent Valley, Eagle Rock, Trassey Burn, Deer's Meadow, Spelga Pass. Was it the fuchsia growing in the hedges which moved W. R. Rodgers to write

> *Of the Mournes I remember most the mist,*
> *The grey granite goose-fleshed, the minute*
> *And blazing parachutes of fuchsia, and us*
> *Listening to the tiny clustered clinks*
> *Of little chisels tinkling tirelessly*
> > *On stone . . . ?*

Although later I went along the coast road on the other side of the mountains and fell hook, line and sinker for its own sea beauties, that day along the inland, upland road stayed in my mind as the more splendid experience. I went later along the coastal road to see the Prawn King receive the ancient Kingdom of Mourne—a cele-bration doing just a small honour to the Down fishermen who specialize in prawns that compare favourably with the *élite* of Dublin Bay.

Nearer Hilltown a farmer joined me. He was taking a cow to bull and slowed his pace to mine.

'A brave day,' he said to passers-by as we got nearer the town.

'A powerful day,' they answered.

And a powerful brave day it was too. I was hot now and went straight to the Downshire Arms for a quencher in company with an equally thirsty drove of cyclists who with their jersey shorts and caps came straight off William Roberts's canvas *Les Routiers*. Their bright colours and the shiny bright efficiency of their machines were not out of place in Hilltown, which sported bright colours itself. The single wide Georgian street wore an air of gaiety with the houses painted yellow with blue window-frames and white doors, or grey with white woodwork, or blue painted quoins. The shop windows were dressed smartly enough but in the style of the 1920s with drapers' dummies looking forlornly from the bedroom windows. Clustered around shop doorways was all the accoutrement of country life, scythes, spades, chicken-feeders, pig troughs, sheep dip, cross-saws, and to add more to the colour, plastic buckets and bowls and brooms.

Several ponies and traps clattered down the street full of tinkers who seemed too sad to notice the glory of the day. Sprawled in the sun on top of a lorry loaded high with farm meal sacks were two young labourers who said there was no bus but I could climb up and have a place in the sun beside them for they were just going to drive off to Newry.

Those who have never tried to hold on to a bag of pig food fifteen feet off the ground tearing along at thirty miles an hour will have no idea of the difficulty of that ride from Hilltown to Newry. The young men laughed as I rolled about but made a grab at me once or twice as we took corners on what felt like two wheels. I nearly shot off the top altogether when we pulled up sharp at a junction of seven crooked lanes, called Seven Sisters, to let a dead horse lorry pull in front of us. But the pig food grandstand could not have been better for seeing the country and overlooking the hedges thickly golden with drifts of honeysuckle and the quick flight of yellow-hammers, who fled from our lorry which interrupted their familiar song *a-little-bit-of-bread-and-no-cheese*.

So we rode along, rocking and swaying, my two young companions laughing and trying to push each other off the top. And my mind went to two other young men who had travelled the Mourne roads together, long ago. Just before going over to Northern Ireland I spent a week-end in Cambridge. While talking to E. M. Forster in his rooms at Kings the Mourne mountains drifted into the conversation like a recollected dream. In 1911 Forster went to Northern

Ireland, the year *The Bracknels* was published. Intensely moved by the book's delicate beauty Forster wrote to its author Forrest Reid. By coincidence Reid was living very near Forster's lodging in Belfast and the authors became friends. They went rowing up the River Lagan, explored the Mournes, and spent winter evenings round the fire with Reid's latest menagerie of cats and dogs.

And when the Ulsterman died thirty-six years later E. M. Forster wrote in his book *Two Cheers for Democracy*: 'He was the most important man in Belfast, and, though it would be too much to say that Belfast knew him not, I have sometimes smiled to think how little that great city, engaged in its own ponderous purposes, dreamed of him or indeed of anything. He who dreamed and was partly a dream. A dream not only compounded of visions, Mediterranean and Celtic, but of the "moral fragrance" which he prized and pursued and diffused.'

After the growth of his friendship with E. M. Forster, Forrest Reid wrote his trilogy of boyhood *Young Tom, The Retreat*, and *Uncle Stephen*. Although the setting is Ulster, the boys could easily have been young Greeks. I can approach the dreams of Forrest the dreamer more through his *Apostate*, one of the most beautiful and disturbing stories ever written about growing up. Somebody commented once that E. M. Forster's own characters were simply Forrest Reid's boys grown up.

The Ulsterman was already old when I spent some of my own boyhood in the Lagan Valley, but he was a familiar sight. I remember him looking rather as James Sleator painted him years before—intense eyed, pince-nezed with more than a glint of mischief in the expression—though it was not 'remarkable' as Reid himself described Oscar Wilde whom he saw in his own youth, reading in Belfast's Linen Hall Library. And so, as I sat on top of the pig meal lorry with the two happy young labourers I could not but think of the two authors, as young as my companions, as carefree and as happy, riding along the same road, looking at the same hills and valleys to the same song of yellow-hammers.

I knew I was hungry but did not think I was famished to the point of seeing illusions. When I climbed off the lorry at Newry the first thing I saw was an elephant. It was walking down the street quite casually as though it did so every day of its life. I hurried quickly into a restaurant wondering what they had put in their cellars at Hilltown's pub. The waitress did not seem at all put out by my carefully worded statement that I was under the distinct impression I had just seen an elephant wandering on its own in the street.

'And well you may have indeed, sir,' she said, 'the circus is in town.'

A glass of milk, followed by a thumping great farmer's midday dinner soon dispelled any traumatic tendencies. Sober as St. Patrick I went into the busy Saturday streets of this biggish market town, which my guide book called an 'industrial town' and which St. Patrick, or somebody thereabouts in time called Newry or Place of the Yews after the trees which St. Patrick planted there.

I saw neither the yews nor the industry. There *were* some factories on the outskirts and some warehouses in the town, but not enough to ruin the place as industry inevitably does. Newry, in fact, had escaped comparatively unscathed from the nineteenth century, and looked very much as it must have done from the seventeenth century onwards. In character, the town shared much of the regularity and the idea of straight streets common to most Ulster towns. But Newry also had an alien and pleasing quality, approximating to the Dutch flavour found in Fenland towns in England. Newry had a canal lined by merchants' warehouses and this alone was sufficient to suggest an element of the Netherlands, an influence not altogether out of place since King William III himself came from the Lowlands and there are a few Dutch gable houses in the town dating from his reign.

Newry grew up at the important point at the head of Carlingford Lough, a thin finger of sea inserted deeply into County Down's southern coastline. The town was also a halt on the road to Armagh, and was the scene of many battles, standing as it does in the 'Gap of the North' where expeditions from Dublin met and fought the Northmen. The road from Tara brought fiercer men than pilgrims up to Armagh. Lady Gregory's version of the Irish saga, *Cuchulain of Muirthemne*, sums up the situation, 'There is neither in Alban nor in Ireland an army that can put down the men of Ulster when once their weakness is gone and their anger is kindled.'

In the last few years so much of what used to be regarded as the essentials of life have been closed down. Local newspapers have met their fate, theatres have been pulled down to make way for office buildings. And now, not only in Ireland but in England too, much of the railway is disappearing. It is surprising to realize that Newry had its own newspaper as long ago as 1817 and that the paper made literary history on at least one occasion. A fill-up poem appeared which Byron declared to be 'the most perfect ode'. Many people immediately claimed the poem as theirs, until at last *The Newry Telegraph* was obliged to reveal that the true author of *The Burial of Sir John Moore* was a shy curate, Charles Wolfe of County Tyrone.

Certainly not a drum was heard in Newry that Saturday afternoon as I walked through the town on my way for a week-end in the cathedral city of Armagh. The Newry canal was green with algae, the Dutch looking warehouses were all shut up, and not a typewriter tapped in the town hall under whose arches the canal ran charmingly. Several farmers waiting at the bus stop looked awkward in their Sunday-best suits going off with their dogs to the Sheep Dog Trials.

At Newry, County Down becomes the County of Armagh and going out of the town by way of Sugar Island Quay I had no difficulty in getting a lift. By now I was taking this particular kindness of the Ulster people for granted. I had only to step off a kerb, raise my hand thumbs-up like a Roman emperor, and a car would draw up. On this occasion a chemist going with his violin from Newry to a musical *fleadh* at Sligo took me on board.

We set off and he noticed then that his speedometer was registering nil. He pressed the accelerator, notwithstanding this technical inconvenience, and rounding a corner at sixty miles an hour he pointed to a disused railway station. 'Two hundred children were killed on a Sunday School outing here, before they closed the old Armagh–Newry line,' he said.

Taking wrong turnings at crossroads because he was going too fast to read signposts, my new friend discoursed with more wit than earnestness about music and politics and religion, he being a Roman Catholic. 'Of course,' he said, 'I'm sorry to see the Twelfth of July dying out. There's a lot of colour gone out of life. Mind you,' he went on cheerfully, 'I think the bottom of the Twelfth got knocked out when they discovered that King Billy's charger was not white at all but *brown*.'

I could not display as much amusement as I felt over this ironic revelation for the driver's own amusement about the Crossing of the Boyne caused him to turn laughing towards me, rather than concentrate on the roads. Fortunately the Irish Saturday traffic was almost non-existent so that our danger lay more in the possibility of hitting trees and stray animals rather than other cars. 'Lots of my friends got so fed up this year with the dismal Twelfth,' said the chemist going back to his earlier theme, 'that they went down for a day's spree in the Free State.'

'Anything but a dull life,' I agreed, seeing this as about the one drawback of the new tolerance abroad in Ireland. Or, to be more correct, *not* the new tolerance, for understanding between Catholics and Protestants had its champions in many great churchmen, even in last century's troubled times. Armagh, the seat of both Primates, had its brighter episodes. When Archbishop Alexander, husband of Mrs. All Things Bright and Beautiful Alexander, was the Church of Ireland's head he sent a carriage to meet his Roman Catholic opposite number returning from Rome. This was Cardinal Logue whose portrait by Lavery I had so much admired in the Ulster Art Gallery.

Besides the troubles, the Irish situation had, and still has, its comic incidents and one of my own favourites concerns Armagh's two famous archbishops. The Viceroy of Ireland, Lord Dudley, decided to visit Armagh and while there lunched with Archbishop Alexander. The Primate and his wife and daughter quite understood when the Viceroy, almost immediately after the meal, excused himself saying that important business called him to Dublin and that he must go at once to catch the afternoon train. Meanwhile, His Excellency's aide had slipped round to Cardinal Logue's palace to fix up a clandestine afternoon tea for Lord Dudley. The Viceroy wanted, tactfully and diplomatically, to please everybody and offend nobody amongst the rebellious Irish he was supposed to rule. And so on taking his leave of Archbishop Alexander and family, the Viceroy went not to the station but to the Roman Catholic Archbishop for tea. And as the Cardinal took him into the drawing-room, Lord Dudley was confronted by a young woman sitting behind the silver teapot. 'Does Your Excellency know my neighbour's daughter, Miss Alexander?' asked the Cardinal. 'She often comes here to act as hostess.'

A more recent visitor to Armagh was Julian Huxley, who suffered no such embarrassment as Lord Dudley when a friend of mine, then aide to the Governor of Northern Ireland, showed him round the city. The distinguished biologist was amused, however, to see a shop sign—*The Primatial Hatcheries*.

It is unlucky that amongst ancient Icelandic sagas now no longer extant was one written on Brian Boru which described what Ireland was like at the time of the Battle of Clontarf. About the nearest in time is the gory chapter in *Burnt Njal* on the 1014 battle. It would be interesting to know whether Wolf the Quarrelsome or Erling of Straumey were among the hundreds who gathered in Armagh cathedral for the twelve days lying-in-state of the great king Brian Boru.

Although the Icelandic writings of the twelfth century are not as informative about Ireland as one would wish, there remain, nevertheless, a whole series of Irish tales dating from centuries before the Vikings ever reached Iceland. They tell of events happening in Ulster long before Christianity came to its shores. These tales have been likened in character to the Homeric tales. One of these cycles of stories goes back to the days when Ulster was the biggest and most powerful of the five Irish kingdoms. Conor MacNessa was King of Ulster then and he had his capital beside the site of the present city of Armagh.

It was he who founded an order called the Red Branch Knights. The greatest warrior amongst the knights was Cuchulainn, whose birth had resulted from the union of the Danaan god, Lugh, and a Red Branch girl called Dectera. Cuchulainn was handed over at birth to the Ulster knights and later received his education at the court of King Conor. The great things prophesied for Cuchulainn were justified by his first act of valour—the killing of a huge hound with his own bare hands. He fought and destroyed the fierce dog which was guarding the palace by smashing it against the doorpost.

Cuchulainn's death, like his birth, was surrounded by portents which seemed to be messianic and precursive of Jesus Christ.

Cuchulainn was a saviour of his people. By his heroic deeds he kept Ulster independent and released the people from an old curse so that they threw off invaders in one of Ireland's greatest-ever battles. Cuchulainn was wounded in this, his last fight, but refusing to give in, he asked to be tied in an upright position so that he could still face the enemy with his sword in his hand. Otters came from the river and drank his blood and ravens came to eat his flesh and only then did Cuchulainn drop his sword and die. The hero's death, as prophesied, lifted the curse and the Leinster armies were driven back over the border.

Such deeds and exploits of the Red Branch Knights were sung by court harpers for centuries. Legends perpetuated their greatness until the Red Branch was driven into what today is Down and Antrim. Less than two miles outside Armagh a great entrenchment can still be seen encircling the hill where, for seven hundred years, the Red Branch Knights had their headquarters. Queen Macha is said to have traced the palace outline on the ground with a brooch, three centuries before the coming of Christ.

Armagh of the sagas and of medieval times must have been rather different from its present aspect. The city must have been barbarous to judge by some Latin lines which have survived:

> *Carnes crudae,*
> *Mulieres nudae,*

No raw meat was given to me in Armagh nor were any naked women roving the streets when the Newry chemist set me down in The Mall and went off to his *fleadh* at Sligo. The wonder of that golden, Attic morning had changed now into a sumptuous afternoon. Armagh looked like a Ford Madox Brown painting with every leaf, every blade of grass, every stone in every house, looking more real than real, the detail picked out by the strong light and bathed in the golden atmosphere beloved of the Pre-Raphaelites in their more cheerful moments.

The butchering Red Branch Knights and their swords had been replaced by innocuous young men in white flannels with cricket bats on the wide greensward of The Mall. I took a nap, a pleasant dreamy doze filled with the voices of children playing under the beeches and oaks surrounding the green. As so often in Ireland, I had a sense of calm and serenity and of a way of life still persisting long after it had vanished in a neurotic England.

Nor was this entirely an illusion, though as I saw from a statue standing at one end of the green, the rural calm had been threatened by the same storm clouds that broke over late Victorian England, ending in the deluge which swept the old order away in 1914. The most eloquent sculpture I saw anywhere in Ulster was Kathleen Shaw's bronze figure of a young Irish bugler about to sound the Last Post, Armagh's memorial to its men killed in the South African War of 1899.

This sculptress was undoubtedly skilled at her art and perhaps was intensely moved by the occasion of this work. Yet she avoided the false sentimentality so typical of academic art at that period. Her bronze has transcended its immediate purpose, and like great sculpture does, has expressed universal human experience. Armagh should be proud of this figure. The 1914 memorial cannot be compared, nor indeed have I seen any memorial so fine—not even the first of all 'Unknown Soldier' monuments, Bissen's *Valiant Peasant Soldier* at Fredericia in Denmark.

Armagh is, however, justly self-conscious of its architectural beauty as a city, not only in its individual buildings but in the town as a whole. Armagh is a most striking city on several points. Firstly, it rejoices in several hills, not steep as Basel's hills are steep, but nevertheless steep enough to allow that variation of level, that changing viewpoint which makes, for instance, Bath a more interesting city than Cheltenham though both consist of fine Georgian buildings. And then, curiously, Armagh retained a medieval kind of street pattern, so that surprises occur at every corner, surprises which include some exquisite Georgian houses.

Francis Johnston was born here in 1760, a man of unusual sensibility who became one of Ireland's great architects in a period when much fine work appeared. Although Johnston spent most of his life in Dublin designing some of its finest public buildings, he left his native city with examples too. The most notable perhaps was the row of silver-stone houses in Charlemont Place which overlooks the green and its trees. He also designed the court house whose pedimented Doric portico looks sedately down the long stretch of grass. The court house was built with the same kind of pearly, light-catching stone as his houses, a stone which is peculiar to Armagh. Another house, now used by the Bank of Ireland, of extremely graceful proportions, also by Johnston, hides away in one of the narrow streets.

But apart from its Georgian ware, Armagh possesses one of Ireland's most splendid Victorian buildings. On a hill, twin towers and spires needle the sky in a paean of . . . well, those who cannot stomach Victorian Gothic would call the Roman Catholic cathedral a pain in the neck. Certainly a pain in the neck was what I got from standing at the top of the long imposing steps which lead up to the west front, in order to gaze at those skyscraper spires of the beautiful light grey stone radiant in the sun.

Well I remember those towers being described to me in childhood as the Devil's horns! The Devil, I am sure, would be pleased to sport a pair of horns as fine as those, in the same way as the archbishop must be pleased to have such splendour in which to exercise his office. The cathedral, in fact, is a completely untouched gem of Victoriana, and it was a tribute to the kindly air of Armagh and the diligence of church workers that the building looked quite new. To step inside was to step straight into the 1870s. The interior was astounding. It had clarity and precision and a quite extraordinary aerial effect. It was also all very odd, for this was no mere eclectic collection but a positive jubilee jamboree of Gothic and Italianate motifs, an exciting rag-bag of architectural sources.

It ought, by all the dictates of fashion and taste, to have been terrible. It had that agglomeration of mutually antipathetic materials which was one of the seventy deadly sins of Victorian architects. Polished white marble writhed and wreathed about the sanctuary like thick undergrowth in a tropical rain-forest. Crawling patterns and pictures executed upon the walls in ceramic mosaic gave off the colour, and almost the smell too, of Ovaltine. The tall, narrow nave, of French proportions, was closed by a queer vault—a sort of cross between a barrel-vault and a hammer-beam roof. Yet all this added up to a most magnificent sight.

The building stone, the beautiful white limestone which graced Armagh, was taken from a quarry close by the Navan Fort where

Queen Macha scratched the palace outline on the ground with her brooch and where the young Cuchulainn slew the watch hound. An unusual sense of exaltation derived from this cathedral perched high on its fine site. Curiously, the immediate surroundings have an atmosphere more reminiscent of Victorian secular gardens rather than ecclesiastical precincts. I almost expected to hear the knock of croquet mallets on wooden balls. At the top of the great flight of steps, which went up between pleasantly sloping banks of grass, two statuesque prelates stand on pedestals. In the background, copper beeches made a sombre and sumptuously-coloured background to the gleaming limestone.

Colour must be the keynote inside also, when the nave is full and the sanctuary is ablaze with candles, with canons in their stalls and the priests in the beautiful vestments given by the Empress of Austria, with the Cardinal Archbishop in the scarlet mantle of a Prince of the Church, and the cathedral's high vaults ringing with a Palestrina Mass.

However, it was none of this, nor the cathedral's unfortunate copies of Thorvaldsen's swan-winged angels which took my mind to Rome—but the Romans themselves. A whole coach-load of them arrived, twittering and chattering like a cageful of exotic birds, all, it seemed, bent on behaving, when in Armagh, as Romans do. Excitedly they pointed out the wondrous detail, the women's heads clad in black lace-like mantillas shrunken in the rain, the men taking off their sun-glasses as a mark of reverence. I left them to their tour hoping that they would be able to resist the temptation to which a certain vandal called P. Duffy succumbed, a visitor who I saw had cut his name crudely and deeply on the particularly fine white marble balustrade of the altar.

What a different situation in Armagh from penal times, when the city was made famous by the Bard of Armagh. Of all the bishops and priests who risked their lives to celebrate Mass in secret during penal times none was better known than Bishop Patrick Donnelly. Ballads have recorded his exploits and given him the title of the Bard of Armagh. Patrick Donnelly was Bishop of Dromore and travelled the countryside disguised as a harper. He would find a quiet wood and begin to sing and people gathered around him.

When Bishop Donnelly was certain no informers were present, he set his harp aside and the aged, withered fingers would celebrate their priestly duties.

I walked back to the city's centre to find a reasonably priced roof for my head that night, for Armagh was no place to be 'done' in an hour. Every aspect of the city fascinated me. Even the shop names set up a kind of *Under Milk Wood* resonance in my head—Quinn, Kells, Wishart, Vallecy, Rolston, Ballantine, McArdle, Hillock, Whitsitt, Toner, McKeever, McAleavey, McShane, McGovern.

In this noble company stood Black's Hotel in a tall narrow house, whose roof-high bedroom suited my mood which was largely regulated by my pocket. Black's must be one of the few hotels in the world with an organ in the bathroom ante-room. The bedroom window afforded another view of this lovely, small city. The sun was still high, turning the whitewashed walls and shining slate roofs into dazzling Greek villages islanded in a Reckitts-blue Mediterranean.

I swilled the pig-meal collected on my lorry-ride off in the bath, and then went masochistically to suffer the slings and arrows of another banquet-sized Ulster high tea and then sallied out again for Armagh's Saturday night.

'How ya doin', are ya rightly?' asked the first man I stood beside as I downed my first drink. He eyed me up and down as though he were a tailor estimating. Then he said that because of my height I must be a powerful singer. He called for silence.

'Give us a bar,' he demanded.

'I can't sing,' I said, whereupon he himself started to give us an old country ballad. The barman behind the counter had other ideas.

'You're disturbing the people,' he said, turning the television set on louder.

As in many other pubs in Ulster, the fun and the fiery talk and the tipsy, gipsy singing is dying from televisionitis, that creeping paralysis which, to mix metaphors, may be one man's private meat but is certainly everybody's public poison. Singing, once inseparable from drinking in Ireland, is now outlawed in many pubs. With the thunder of Wild Western guns, the telling of *real* stories, as distinct from true ones, has gone too. Nevertheless, Armagh has so much violence and bloodshed of so many centuries in its history, that it can probably stand the interruption of such modern upstarts as television.

Armagh's hey-day, so to speak, was already waning when the Red Branch Knights were ultimately defeated. Armagh ceased then to be the centre of government for Ulster. But already as early as A.D. 444 Armagh was so holy a place, so pregnant with the tradition of kings, that when St. Patrick came he asked the local chief, Daire, if he might have the hilltop for building a church. At first, Daire would only let St. Patrick have the site where the Bank of Ireland stands now. Later the chief consented and St. Patrick began to build a church on the hill.

It was a stone church and its story is told in the *Book of Armagh* which may be inspected in Dublin's Trinity College Library, a book built on slightly more substantial lines than a paper-back for it was compiled by one Ferdomnach, a scribe, at the beginning of the ninth century.

By 447 St. Patrick declared that Armagh should be the mother church of all religious buildings in Ireland, which position it still holds today. Due reverence, however, was not always forthcoming for the hilltop church. Danes plundered Armagh in 832 and for a century and a half afterwards the pyromaniacal Norsemen ravaged and pillaged the church. St. Paul would hardly have had cause to complain that Armagh was lukewarm! The Danish burnings of this already four centuries old church were carried out long before Christianity was accepted in Denmark itself as a smart political move by King Poppo.

And then came to Armagh in 1004 that great King of Ireland, Brian Boru. He visited the cathedral and presented gold upon the altar, before which, ten years later, he was to lie in state prior to his burial on that hill of kings. Although Brian Boru sent the Danes packing, he could not alas, once dead, prevent the continual burnings of Armagh's church. By 1125 the cathedral was completely restored, but then the English kings' Lord Deputies started a series of raids on the city.

John de Courcy set fire to the city and cathedral in 1199 and again in 1206, setting a pattern of destruction and reconstruction which went on through the centuries until 1642 when the cathedral was again burnt, this time by Sir Phelim O'Neill. But nothing, it seemed, could daunt or discourage the men of Armagh. After each sacking, they patched the ruins. The cathedral walls, in spite of all, still consists largely of the restoration of 1268.

And so, at last, came I. For fifteen centuries people had done precisely that—gone up to the hill to worship or to destroy the church on its top. My own approach to the cathedral was already coloured by childhood years of association with this mother of all Irish churches. However, I tried to be as open-minded as might be, not even allowing Swift's words to prejudice me, 'High Church, low steeple, dirty streets and proud people.'

Armagh's now-Protestant cathedral certainly had a low steeple, a steeple which, right up until the 1939 War, rang out the nine o'clock curfew. But its churchmanship could hardly be described as of the 'high' variety. The people of Armagh had cause to be proud of their city whose streets are paved with marble and were by no means dirty. But Swift may have been unduly influenced by his own cathedral in Dublin to spare much charity of thought to Armagh.

I climbed the hill which had become the site of houses and trees and gardens. On reaching the top I found the cathedral standing on a little plateau, which allowed sweeping views over the city and the countryside beyond. Possibly invaders had destroyed the succession of churches because its position made a good observation point.

I pictured the flames and smoke of centuries ago. Where I stood, Brian Boru had stood, sword in hand. Hereabouts also the great warrior was buried. I looked at his monument which was a mere stone plaque announcing Brian Boru's presence. Was this north side of the church *really* the thrilling place I had heard of so often in childhood—the 'Side of the Slain Men', of the High King Brian and his son and nephew, of Malachy MacDomnald another eleventh-century High King, and of warriors from sixteen centuries of Irish history? And had it been of this Side of the Slain Men the Icelanders sang at the open-air parliament of Thingvellir?

> *I have been where warriors wrestled,*
> *High in Erin sang the sword,*

THE KINGDOM OF MOURNE

Boss to boss met many bucklers,
Steel rung sharp on rattling helm;
I can tell of all their struggle,
Sigurd fell in flight of spears,
Brian fell, but kept his kingdom
Ere he lost one drop of blood.

Veneration for age in a building often blinds the eye to its true merit as architecture. Anything old is presumed to be interesting, as if by virtue of simply being present at sieges and murders, the stones took on qualities they would not otherwise have possessed. Armagh's cathedral stones certainly took on qualities they did not formerly possess, though literally and physically by virtue of attention from a bad English architect-cum-restorer called Cottingham. This man's good intention did almost as much harm as the raiders. He arrived from England in 1834 and spent the following six years in covering up every trace of the original buildings with his own inferior work. His work was, in fact, so outrageous that even as shortly afterwards as 1888 the authorities were pulling Cottingham's restoration down. When I went inside the brown sandstone building I thought that the authorities had not pulled nearly enough of the restorer's excesses down.

Cottingham must have covered up a good deal of interesting detail, but nevertheless the feeling of generous spaciousness remained, an illusion partially induced perhaps by the dimness, for, as might be expected in a building so long used to marauders, the windows were not large. Military banners, in various stages of decay, hung about the walls with their memories of bygone glory. The brightest part of the cathedral was the modern chapel of the Royal Irish Fusiliers. Not seen to best advantage in the low light were the cathedral's wall tombs and monuments. They created something of a Westminster Abbey atmosphere, inevitable perhaps because many of Armagh's tombs were executed by the Westminster sculptors—Rysbrack, Roubiliac, Marochetti, and a bust by Joseph Nollekens of Archbishop Robinson. For all their fame, none of these things, in my opinion, could compare with Kathleen Shaw's beautiful bronze figure of the bugler down on The Mall. The best in the cathedral was the bust of Archbishop Alexander, who only needed an irreverent and fat cigar in his mouth to look like Sir Winston Churchill.

I wondered what Mrs. Alexander looked like. She too ought to have had a sculptured head for her hymns. So should another of Armagh's most distinguished sons, whose contribution to church music made him one of the principal figures in modern British music. Not only has the cathedral no bust of him, but (and here I had a singularly large bone to pick with the city of Armagh) his name and fame were nowhere mentioned in the city's official handbook. This most notable native was Charles Wood, born in Armagh in 1866.

The city handbook listed generals and admirals from the Royal School, including Wellington—though the booklet omitted to say that Wellington was only sent to the school because, as the Duke's mother put it, 'My ugly son, Arthur, is only fit for powder.' And in view of such modern phenomena as Common Markets and N.A.T.O.s and Councils of Europe, one may reasonably wonder if the Duke of Wellington's efforts to keep Britain British were really worth the trouble. But beyond dispute is the long-lasting and civilizing effect of Charles Wood's life. The noise of guns is soon, fortunately, forgotten. But as Shelley knew and as Charles Wood emphasized by setting to music,

> *Music, when soft voices die,*
> *Vibrates in the memory.*

Voices were the principal medium by which Wood expressed his genius. He succeeded Stanford as Professor of Music at Cambridge and poured out a stream of anthems and cantatas which moulded the whole conception of modern English church music. It was the period when the Church of England could boast splendid choirs not only in its cathedrals but in every great parish church also. And whereas the contrapuntal ingenuity of Tallis and Byrd and other Elizabethan composers would have been beyond the resources of lesser choirs, Wood's music was designed especially for such performers. He continued where Stanford left off, extending and building on the tradition of simple melodic line whose tunefulness and emotion might well have derived from the same potent characteristics in Irish folk-songs.

Folk-song setting was an art highly developed by Wood's contemporaries Vaughan Williams and Cecil Sharp, but Wood himself joined in this work of rescuing many beautiful songs from obscurity. These are less well known today than his own songs. The Shelley setting, Herrick's *Cowslips for her covering*, and *Ethiopia saluting the Colours* from lines of Whitman show Charles Wood's feeling and knowledge of poetry.

The Ethiopia song, at first hearing, does not sound characteristic of Wood. But the secret is in the piano accompaniment—a marching rhythm with broadly expanding chords, whose boldness perhaps inspired Vaughan Williams in his magnificent hymn tune *Down Ampney*. Wood was prolific. Whenever tuning forks are struck in Welsh valleys, whenever grammar schools compete, whenever music-sheets are set out in Oxford chapels and whenever cathedrals open their organ manuals, there, somewhere will be the music of Charles Wood. When lofty anthems like *O Thou the Central Orb* echo round the fan vaulting of St. George's Chapel, Windsor, there can be no doubt as to his supremacy in the English choral tradition. But, though he loved and worked in England, he did not forget Ireland. He called one of the finest hymn tunes simply—*Armagh*.

4

Scherzo

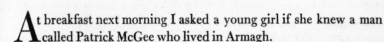

At breakfast next morning I asked a young girl if she knew a man called Patrick McGee who lived in Armagh.

'Ya wouldn't be meanin' Master McGeee—the father of the fella on the telly?' she said.

'The very one,' I replied, whereupon she told me how I must go to get to Lower English Street.

Her directions were reliable and soon Pat McGee himself had me sitting beside his fireplace with a bottle of whisky within reach. Patrick had retired from schoolmastering and spent most of his energy on fishing, in one way or another. I was not surprised Patrick had an actor son in films in England for the father was a first class raconteur with a flow of stories as fascinating as the trout streams he talked about. He filled my glass again and told me about Wynne's hare crossing the goose-green.

'It was October,' said Pat, 'when the dollaghan came up the Black-water to spawn.' He went on to sing anglers' praises for dollaghan— dollaghan being a confusing general name to cover the several and wonderful kinds of trout indigenous to Lough Neagh.

Pat went on: 'When Edward VII came on a visit to Ireland he was presented with a dollaghan of forty pounds.'

I hoped His Majesty did not receive the great trout at the hands of Patrick McGee for he might have insisted on the King eating the whole thing there and then as he was insisting that we finish the whisky bottle—not that much insistence was really necessary. How-ever, these king-size dollaghan are exceptional and rare, and the lough trout usually vary between four and eighteen pounds.

Patrick talked most about the black boddagh species, the best fighter among the three kinds of dollaghan. The extremely dark colour and large fins make the black boddagh unmistakable. Also, the black boddagh is the last of the three trout to run the rivers in autumn from Lough Neagh. When hooked, the great trout will almost certainly dash downstream, giving the big-game fisherman a thrill which can only be compared with the taking of a fresh-run salmon.

'Mind,' Pat went on, eyes gleaming under bushy eyebrows, 'there's good salmon too in Ulster. We had a fantastic run in 1962. A wonderful year, with more salmon in the one season than we usually get in ten.'

The rivers, however, were not enough and the local club had just replenished a lake with 30,000 trout fingerlings obtained from the Inland Fishery Trust across the border in the Republic. Since some of my happiest memories of boyhood in Ulster were of fishing and evading water-bailiffs I was content to listen to Pat McGee all morning, not forgetting the story about Jimmy Wynne's hare which, of course, was magic. Hunting the hare with hounds on foot was a great sport among County Armagh farmers and they looked down their noses at their neighbours in County Tyrone who degraded the sport by bringing in city greyhounds.

It was an ancient pastime and the hare, being possessed of supernatural powers, always got away back home to its owner, like Jimmy Wynne. The hare would, in any case, always go free even if the hounds could catch up with its swift changes of direction because the farmer-hunters allowed it an escape route, for it was sport and not blood they were after.

In the Archbishop of Armagh's register there was an entry, made in the fourteenth century; 'The Archbishop by authority of the present Council inhibits all the faithful under pain of greater excommunication from hunting any wild beast, and especially the hare, on the Holy Day of preparation before Easter.' But long before this, Arrian of Nicomedia was writing nearly two thousand years ago, 'There would never have been a hare coursed in Greece had not the hound first been brought from Ireland.'

SCHERZO

We have some jolly sportsmen down here from Pomeroy
Cookstown and Dungannon and likewise the Moy,
With their pedigree greyhounds they come from afar
And they travelled to Creggan in their fine motor car.

This verse came from *The White Hare of Creggan* collected by
Sean O'Boyle one of Ulster's chief authorities on folklore and now a
master at St. Patrick's College, Armagh. Pat McGee wanted me to see
the county round and about and asked Sean O'Boyle to go with us.
But though people turned up their noses at 'fine motor cars' for
hunting we decided that one was necessary to get us round the hare-
hunting countryside in one day. So Pat and I went on a car-hunt first,
and soon found a victim, a fishing companion of Pat's who with the
usual Ulsterman's generosity put not only his car but himself at our
disposal. I appreciated this even more in discovering that Jerry
Lennon was not only a busy lawyer but a senator in the upper house
of the Northern Ireland Parliament and also the leader of the Ancient
Order of Hibernians.

Politics and religion, always so inseparably entwined in Ulster,
did not occupy our talk that afternoon except for an inquiry from
Sean O'Boyle who asked how the meetings were going between the
Hibernian and Orange leaders. Senator Lennon had held several
discussions with Sir George Clarke trying to define their differences
and find ways to ease much of the bigotry which has plagued Northern Ireland for so long.

Although fishing was Jerry's main pastime he also grew roses.
While he got ready to go off with us for the day we sat on his lawn
eating strawberries and cream, listening to the birds singing in the
trees crowding round the garden, and drinking in the cloying scent
of his fantastically rich rosebeds. An English friend joined us and
remarked that roses seemed to be much more of an Irish emblem than
the shamrock. Certainly rose trees flourished and produced extraordinary blooms on Ulster soil.

When Jerry brought the car round we set off for Loughgall. Just
outside Armagh we had to stop for a group of young men playing a
game of bullet-throwing in the road. The youngsters had taken off
their jackets and were throwing the iron bullet, smaller than the

wood used in bowls, along the road, the winner being the one who could cover the set distance with the least number of throws.

I had not seen this game since it had puzzled me as a boy on the Belfast Hills as to why it was strictly forbidden by law. I used to wonder if it was because the iron ball damaged the road surface, or whether there might be some political significance to bullet-throwing. The police kept a hawk-eyed watch for the game, no less vigilant than their look-out for smoke rising from poteen stills hidden in the heather. Nowadays, the game has all but disappeared. Only the districts round Loughgall and County Cork in the south seem to have preserved bullet-throwing as a sport.

Shortly afterwards we stopped again to watch a hare which was poised, insolently, at the roadside. We talked then about the writer and poet who had been the Presbyterian minister here for twelve years—W. R. Rodgers. Some months before returning to Ulster I had listened to a B.B.C. Sunday afternoon concert and during the interval heard a soft voice begin the interval talk *The Full Circle*, 'For the hare I was told runs always in a circle. Any lad who wanted to hunt had only to go to a hilltop and blow the horn and instantly, from every valley-farm within earshot, a hound would emerge and hurry to the spot.'

It was only in 1946 that W. R. Rodgers left his manse in Loughgall to join the B.B.C. in London. It seemed odd for a man immersed in some of Ireland's most beautiful countryside, out of contact with the smart world of contemporary writing, to emerge suddenly as a significant poet. Rodgers's poems intelligently controlled violence of imagery, and their underlying sensuality was a surprise. Accusations that his verse is Hopkinsesque or that traces of MacNeice can be discerned in his use of epigrams do nothing to alter the fact that Rodgers found a new way to sing, even if the songs were old. Armagh hare-hunting and the streets of London do not have much in common—though perhaps through Rodgers they have, for he has taken many hayseeds in the turn-up of his pants into the city streets.

W. R. Rodgers brought country Ulster to London, and his late wife's aunt, Helen Waddell, brought the Middle Ages in a similarly real way into literature. Her novel *Peter Abelard* is recognized as a classical historical work, and with *The Wandering Scholars* contributed to a modern understanding of the Middle Ages.

It is curious to see how Ulster scholars have been caught by the romance of far away times and places. Oriental studies occupied many people from Northern Ireland. There are little villages where such scholars worked at translating Korean classics, or, like Edward Hincks of Killyleagh, spent forty years interpreting Egyptian hieroglyphics. In Armagh cathedral I had seen the memorial to one Turner Macan, who was 'unsurpassed in his knowledge of the language and literature of Persia and to him is owing the first perfect edition of her great poet Ferdousee'. Helen Waddell besides being an authority on medieval matters, also worked as a translator; apart from French prose she also rendered Chinese poems into English.

As Jerry Lennon took us along the Armagh roads and lanes we all talked more or less at once, not always on such serious topics as writing. I heard someone mention local 'gas chambers' and had visions of genocide, which was not a ridiculous conclusion for me to make since between Loughgall and Portadown was fought the Battle of the Diamond which resulted in the founding of the Orange Order. But the gas chambers turned out to be not for people but for apples —the pride of County Armagh, Ulster's Kent.

Loughgall was in the centre of this fruit-growing country and its apples were stored in great chambers until after Christmas when prices rose. The small town looked innocent enough of any such twentieth-century ideas, especially about the gates of the local mansion, in the grounds of which sits the little lough. But since we were aiming for a large lough, the largest in Great Britain, we did not disembark at Loughgall. Our way took us near Ardress and we stopped there to look at this unusual country house.

Travelling about Ireland yields surprise after surprise. There seems to be no part of the country which does not hide away secretly a beautiful park and a gracious house. Ardress was not large. The winding drive, which led under a tunnel of trees gave suddenly on to the pink-walled house and to glimpses of the landscape, neat and parti-coloured reaching uninterrupted to the horizon, a horizon made infinitely far by the blue silhouette of hills of Tyrone. The house, though Georgian, looked almost like a Dutch colonial building. And we might indeed have been in the Java hills that afternoon what with the warmth and the sight of an occasional palm tree which had survived Ulster's mild winters. As we left Ardress I saw a farmhouse protected by a magnolia in full bloom and this again made me think of the south. It was almost like Madeira, except that the sub-tropical Atlantic island has no peat factories—another surprise in the garden-like County Armagh, where peat is processed for use in gardens and stables.

Out through the open car windows blew the cigarette smoke of Gallagher's 'Blues' or 'Greens' and in blew the intoxicating scents of the hayfields, some already gathered with golden stubble, others still newly cut. And so we came to Lough Neagh, a stretch of inland water so big that it could easily be mistaken for an inlet from the sea. Five of Northern Ireland's six counties have shores on Lough Neagh and so its bland surface is seldom out of sight.

Legends inevitably surround the lough. The giant, Finn MacCoul, is said to have dug the lough out with a single stroke of his spade, flinging the earth far out into the Irish Sea, so forming the Isle of Man. The Norsemen who sailed up the River Bann to make Lough Neagh their headquarters had a similar legend in their own homeland. They believed that Gefion, a goddess, had turned her sons into oxen and set them to plough up Lake Vänern in Sweden, so forming the Danish island of Zealand on which Copenhagen stands.

Mysterious monsters were supposed to lurk in Lough Neagh's depths about the spires of a long-submerged city. But the only monsters which interested my companions were the monster dollaghan which they had seen coming out of the nut-brown waters. Though the simple-minded modern man may scoff at legends, not to be derided was Lough Neagh's ability to fossilize sticks although these were not from trees growing there before Noah's flood as some supposed. Tinkers used to sell these stone-sticks in the streets when I was a boy, and they were commonly used as hones for razors. One of the first jingles I ever learnt was:

> *Lough Neagh hones! Lough Neagh hones!*
> *You put them in sticks and you take them out stones.*

We pulled up and parked the car at Maghery, a tiny village on the lough shore, where a group of men were playing pitch and toss behind the church. Most activity seemed to be along the Blackwater riverbank, where it entered the lough. The others strolled along to see what the fishermen were after and I talked with a farmer, who was also called Pat McGee, the main difference being their age. He was 94 and was both proud and amused by this and looking forward with excitement to his hundredth birthday. Twenty-five years of his life had been spent in the Scottish pits, but he came back to his family farm on the shores of Lough Neagh. He had a perky air and an independence which even extended to doing his own dentistry since he had not approved of the way 'a black fella' had pulled the first tooth out.

Offshore from Maghery lay Coney Island and while we waited for a boat to take us out I sat with the others watching the fishermen trying for perch and bream. The ripples from their casting lines gave the water-lilies that movement and sinuous line which so fascinated sculptors in the thirteenth century. The curves of water-lilies were often carved into roof bosses. They appear in Westminster Abbey and in Lincoln's famous Angel Choir. Lilies were also an object of fascination with the Pre-Raphaelite painters, possibly because their waxed flowers had a nice way of suggesting the pale consumptive condition which they so admired in women. Paleness was occasionally permissible for men too as with Keats's poor knight.

> *Oh what can ail thee, knight-at-arms,*
> *Alone and palely loitering;*
> *The sedge is withered from the lake,*
> *And no birds sing.*

There was, however, nothing pale about the fisherman and his son who picked us up in their boat and chugged away through the yellow lilies to Coney Island. Neither were the lake's sedges withered, although a sudden squall had come up and I sheltered under a canvas sheet. Strictly speaking, the birds were *not* singing, though as we approached the tiny tree-covered island we could hear the cries of wildfowl.

It was emigrants from Maghery village who gave New York's Coney Island its name, though a bigger contrast between two places would be impossible to imagine. The first Coney Island, now owned by the National Trust, has no trippers, indeed no inhabitants at all except the ubiquitous hooded crow and countless water birds nesting in its reefs and reeds, and the whitethroat and wren competing for the underwood spiders. There were some sunbathers hoping for the rain to clear—shaggy donkeys who took not the slightest notice of our exploration.

Apart from its trees and somewhat dank air, the island's principal item of interest was the ruin of a circular church, a monument announcing that St. Patrick often 'resorted to this island'. There was also a mound of no known purpose and a house built in the last century which was not nearly so interesting as a branch of a tree by the back door which had ingrown on itself, in the shape of a perfect horse-collar. St. Patrick would probably find Coney Island little changed if he were to return.

Although the lough water was now choppy, the rain kept away and the two fishermen took us off the island and over towards some rocks which barely emerged from the clear amber depths. They slowed the boat down and, standing up, clapped their hands loudly to make the huge rafts of mallard take wing. A great panic ran among the birds. All around us flocks of ducklings, who could not yet fly, dived for safety under the water while their parents put on the limping and fluttering of their wounded bird act trying to draw us away from their defenceless chicks. Clouds of angry gulls and terns screamed abuse at us. But the two fishermen were delighted when they spotted eighteen swans together far out in the lough, a sign, they said, of good weather.

Then one of the fishermen also spotted, amazingly among that medley of birds, a kind of duck which had not been seen on the lough for years. From their immense, almost goose-size and the characteristic flight, I guessed them to be sheld-duck. There were stones heaped up on the flats and wildfowlers used them as sconces for shooting duck. Perched upright on these rocks were the cormorants standing erect with wings outspread like the brass eagle-cocks of church lecterns.

We turned towards the mainland again and seeing the spires of Dungannon in the distance somebody suggested we should go there for our high tea. The afternoon on the lough had sharpened my own appetite. We climbed ashore at Maghery once more and drove off to Dungannon variously anticipating our tea. What a pleasure it was, I said, to eat in the simple Irish restaurants, off real linen and out of china instead of plastic cups and saucers. 'Plastic spoons nothing,' somebody said, 'you ought to go down to Dublin. A pub there has just been fitted with a *plastic thatch*!'

The thought that such terrors could even exist, let alone in Ireland, sobered us and we crossed the border into County Tyrone serious as a funeral. But at least Tyrone was not yet reduced to plastic thatch and as we bowled along towards whatever high tea could be found in Dungannon I saw that the county was as green and lush as ever. I could also see why Tyrone people throughout the world say 'among the bushes' when their county is referred to. The phrase, descriptive of Tyrone's landscape, comes from a poem by William Collins:

> *Oh, God be with the good old times when I was twenty-one*
> *In Tyrone among the bushes. . . .*

One young man who never even reached twenty-one has left his mark deeply in Irish hearts. As though he had not died so young his name is kept alive in Irish Republican songs. When we were going into McAleer's Hotel, Jerry Lennon pointed to a window-sill. The name 'K. Barry' was carved into it with a penknife. The Gaelic-speaking landlady explained that the young Kevin Barry had cut it himself, saying, 'It will be here when I am not.' When he was barely 18 he joined the Republican Army, and having shot a British soldier was hanged in Dublin on 1st November 1920.

In view of the meteoric flight to independence from Britain of some modern African and Asian states, Ireland's patience was phenomenal. At Dungannon, for instance, in the Presbyterian Church of Scotch Street, as long ago as 1782 a body known as the Irish Volunteers met to demand the independence of the Irish Parliament and the relaxation of the penal laws against Roman Catholics.

Inside McAleer's Hotel I saw a fine St. Briget's cross which a farm boy had recently made the landlady for protection against fire and other dangers. These traditional crosses were made from rushes pulled, not cut, on St Briget's Eve and formed by winding the rushes round in the same direction as the sun's course. In origin the crosses were pre-Christian. Curiously, South American Indians use similar devices and at a wedding in the Himalayas I had seen the newly-weds riding off on a horse decorated with a whole fringe of these good-luck swastikas and lozenges.

Dungannon, like Armagh, featured early in Irish history. The O'Neills, Ulster's ruling dynasty, centred on the town, and it was from their family that Ulster took its emblem of the Red Hand. To the O'Neills, this hand in the act of blessing was that of God Himself—from whom the O'Neills, like other pre-Christian royalty in Ireland, claimed direct descent!

In its correct form, the Red Hand of Ulster is a right hand without drops of blood. In present day heraldry, however, baronets' coats-of-arms show a left hand with three bloody drops. Such titles with such arms originated in Ulster and were given to the English who were awarded the Plantation after the O'Neills and other indigenous Irish families were deported or driven from their homes and farms. The sale of these baronetcies also helped to swell the coffers of the impoverished House of Stuart.

The use of this left-handed and bloody coat-of-arms derived from the legend about two warriors who swore an oath that the first one to cross the Channel and touch the soil of Ulster would be its possessor. As they approached the Ulster shore the one who was lagging behind cut off his hand and threw it on to the beach in front of his rival.

Because I was not always a well-behaved child, I was often termed 'a dirty wee Tory', particularly after some incident such as the theft of a barmbrack from the baker's van or my 'interference' with the girls. Those who called me a dirty wee Tory, however, were all staunch Protestant Unionists whose representative members at Westminster all voted Conservative. 'Tories' meant for us any bad characters in history such as the O'Neills and others who had been thrown out by the English settlers and forced to live wild on the mountains and moors.

In the days of these outlaws, or Tories, Tory-hunting became a great sport of the new English landowners. Indeed one such gentleman of the seventeenth century found that Tory-hunting was his 'chief delyghte and recreation'. There were many famous outlaws such as Redmond O'Hanlon, and on the other hand there were also many famous Tory-hunters such as the Johnston family who lived like royalty in the Fews. The Fews was the old name for the south-west upland district of Armagh, once part of the O'Neills' kingdom. Johnston's old house and model village have disappeared, but his name lives on in the famous couplet:

> *Jesus of Nazareth, King of the Jews,*
> *Protect us from Johnston, the King of the Fews.*

Little did the English Whig party realize how the name would stick when they called their political opponents 'Tories' to associate them with the Irish outlaws.

The Tories we have with us always, to paraphrase Scripture, but the O'Neills, or at least their castle in Dungannon, has long since gone, leaving only the scrappiest of remains. The O'Neills proudly refused to bow the knee to the English sceptre and, almost as though it were a punitive measure, Dungannon today bears no trace of its ancient character. Not that in terms of architecture this was any loss, for Dungannon, subsequently laid out as a typical Plantation city, had the broad streets and squares, the simple stucco and paint houses and the absence of ugly modern accretions which make Ulster country towns so delightful. Dungannon's speciality was the main square which tilted steeply. The English kings, having deposed the Irish ones, set about establishing the English way of life among the Irish, and to ensure that the Planters' sons would have a public school education, buildings for these were put up. James I founded the Royal School at Dungannon, so continuing the town's royal connections.

When Jerry Lennon drove us back towards that part of the Black-water River which separates Armagh and Tyrone it was after nine o'clock. We came to the charming little village of Moy—or rather *The* Moy as it is always called. Lord Charlemont originally laid out The Moy in 1754 after he had been to Italy and seen Marengo there grouped around a piazza. The Moy certainly had an Italianate feeling. Its trees stood in circular, walled beds whose stones were whitewashed, a piece of grooming unusual for Ireland's free and shaggy trees. Until recently these trees and the piazza had been the scene of The Moy's celebrated horse fair. People came from all over Europe to buy horses and the little town made its fortune by supplying chargers to the armies of a score of nations.

Besides an Italian square and a name for horse-dealing, The Moy also had a band marching that evening to perform at the football field beside the Catholic church, even though it was late. But it was summer, and in that Scandinavian way, the light lingered in the western sky for hours after sunset. The Rev. P. Moore came out of his presbytery and asked the accordion band to play for us before it went into the football field. And so there was music in the air, the wistful, nostalgic wail of accordions which is one of the most melancholy sounds in the world.

Father Moore would not hear of me trying to find an hotel so late in the evening and kindly telephoned Benburb Priory, just a few miles away, to see if they would give me a bed for the night. They would, so taking leave of The Moy and Father Moore we all clambered into Jerry's car again and set off along the twilight lanes for Benburb. I was particularly pleased with this idea, for in the grounds of the priory stood one of the most historic castles in Ireland. By a strange coincidence the Order now occupying the large red brick house at Benburb were Servites from Chicago whose journal was called *Sancta Maria*—the battle cry of an Irish army who defeated the Scottish invaders of Benburb. Under the command of General Robert Monro the large Scottish forces marched to this castle of Benburb standing on a high cliff above the Blackwater River. There they were met by the Irish forces, badly armed and far outnumbered, under Owen Roe O'Neill. But their blood and their courage were up and they went out 'in the name of the Trinity' and routed the Scots in the famous Battle of Benburb on 5th June 1646.

Silence enveloped the place when a young novice opened the priory door and then went off to find the Reverend Prior. Darkness descended imperceptibly while we stood in the shadowed forecourt and when Jerry Lennon, Pat McGee and Sean O'Boyle finally drove off at the end of our good day together, the night was complete.

It was ironical that the domain of the warrior chief O'Neill should now be given over to a school for spiritual training, and ruled by an American priest. Father O'Malley, the Prior, showed me as much of the buildings and gardens as could be seen by star-light. Several of the other brothers and lecturers were American also and they had a staunch friend in the Protestant rector whose church stood by the priory gates. Both in its architecture and its atmosphere the priory reminded me very much of the Anglican community at Kelham in Nottinghamshire. Inevitably, of course, American occupation of the building had left its mark.

The students' centrally-heated rooms would have done credit to any university hostel, and the interior decoration generally was much more Scandinavian than Irish, with the modern furniture and some simple modern carvings and paintings done by members of the community. I was shown to my room, which could hardly be called 'a cell'. The window was wide open, and the night air blew in, heavily scented with the smell of new-cut grass which, like honeysuckle, yields its sweetest, strongest smell at night when the dew has fallen. I fell asleep with the musical murmur of the Blackwater River tumbling over the weirs below the cliff.

And morning revealed the range of hills and distant mountains, and in nearer landscape, the quiet pattern of farms, innocent of the battles and bloodshed of more troubled times. In the kitchen gardens young novices were picking strawberries. The world seemed far away to me. How remote the vitality and clamour of Chicago must have seemed to them. But their years in the priory were only a storing up of spiritual energy.

The Servites, or Servants of Mary was begun by seven young men, as was the Egypt General Mission. But unlike the seven Belfast men the Servites were thirteenth-century noblemen. The Order they founded in Florence was dedicated to the alleviation of the suffering caused by poverty and ignorance and vice. Soon Benburb's novices would become priests. Some would then go home to America, toughened spiritually to combat the tough materialism of their own country. Others would go elsewhere in the world, perhaps to one of the Order's missions in Africa where they would teach in the schools.

Although Benburb Priory was seated in such an isolated, rural place and seemed to be beyond the reach of the world's cares, nobody, having visited it, could accuse its priests and novices of running away from the world. They were training, not for escapism, but for involvement.

I spent the morning exploring the rest of the priory, enjoying particularly its fine library, and also in wandering about the O'Neills' castle. There had never been a keep in the Norman fashion, nor a stone building of any sort within the bawn enclosed by the outer defensive walls, though there had been stout house-like towers at the corners. To one side, where the wall followed the contours, was a drop of two hundred feet to the Blackwater River flowing fast and foaming over the weirs. A little white footbridge crossed it, disappearing at each end into the woods thickly crowding the banks.

After O'Neill's victory against Monro, Cromwell's soldiers bombarded the castle. But the walls still stand, as impervious to time as to their former attackers. Small cottages have since been built on the grassed bawn, occupied now by lay brothers. But going into the house-towers or peering through the perfectly preserved musket-loopholes, I had the feeling that Owen Roe O'Neill had never gone away, and that if I went quietly enough up the spiral stone stair, I might surprise him and his soldiers at their recitation of the rosary.

Prior O'Malley had a simple lunch with me and afterwards we drove into Portadown. He dropped me at the station with an injunction to be sure and visit them again. The change of mood between Benburb and Portadown was abrupt. The train I wanted to catch had gone, and two hours or so needed killing before the next one. I used the station's Asiatic lavatory and then sat on a platform bench.

To regale waiting passengers there was a poster, TO GIRLS TRAVELLING, put up by the Girls' Friendly Society. I got up and wandered along the platform, picking my way between baskets of racing pigeons and stacked commuters' bicycles, and found an even more startling notice put up by the Belfast Girls' Help Society—'WARNING, Girls travelling to Belfast are warned by the above Society against leaving any station with a STRANGER—man or woman —or taking advice as to changing trains, etc., from anyone but a Railway official.'

SCHERZO

The dramatic effect was, if anything, heightened rather than diminished, by the poster immediately beside it. A sexy girl in a bikini lay stranded on a lonely beach in Galway Bay with a muscle-bound youth in short shorts. The sexy girl was obviously beyond reach of the dread WARNING for whatever had just happened to her, or was about to happen, caused her cheeks to bloom with exaggerated poster good health and her lips to part in an ivory smile.

And as though the WARNING had only been pasted up in the nick of time I found the town itself plastered with pictures of other near-nude muscle men—professional wrestlers whose forthcoming bouts in the local cinema appeared to be Portadown's big entertainment event in the near future. One of the Tarzan types was Bobo Matu, 'friendly guy from the Friendly Isles', who was naked except for a necklace and skirt. There were photographs also of the Black Prince, 'Heir to the Chieftainship of the famous Natashi Tribe'.

A wrestling match of a different kind, but none the less amusing, was the commercial one between two stores, glaring at each other across the street, with almost identical shop-fronts and name signs and the same red and gold colours. This was a struggle of titanic odds for one was called F. A. Wellworth & Co. Ltd. and the other F. W. Woolworth & Co. Ltd.

Portadown, strung out largely along its main street which crossed the River Bann at one end, was a busy town. For better or for worse it harboured industry which used quays by the river as well as the railway. Loaded lorries thundered through the town, almost touching the sides of the decorative arches still left standing from the Twelfth of July celebrations.

In common with most other towns, Portadown was reluctant to dismantle its highly decorated, temporary arches spanning the streets. Just as singing in country pubs is giving way to television so the ingenuity lavished at one time on these arches and gable paintings is dying out in the face of growing tolerance and understanding between the rival political-cum-religious parties. But, although the gradual decline of bitterness and hatred is good, a form of folk-art is disappearing as a result.

SCHERZO

When I was a boy, I was always on the look-out for paint which could be used in touching up the gable wall paintings of King Billy on his white charger. And the men in our streets spent months making the Orange Order symbols for the street arches. As best as they knew how they made miniature castles, Arks of the Covenant, plywood crowns and wooden Bibles, the Coffins of Death, and the weird, all-seeing Eye of God. Not the least important inspiration of this art was the desire of one street to outdo the next in the splendour of its arch, a competitive spirit almost as fierce as the anti-Catholic spirit on which the whole affair of the Twelfth was then based.

Besides the crude wall paintings and the gaily painted street arches, and the hundreds and hundreds of fluttering Union Jacks, there were the huge banners carried in the processions. The be-tasselled banners were an art form in themselves, done now entirely by commercial artists with larger-than-life portraits of British Royalty and fathers of the Orange Institution on one side. The reverse side was reserved for historical scenes. There William III could be seen landing at Carrickfergus. Ridley could be seen burning with Latimer at his stake. Luther would be nailing his famous theses to the Wittenburg door, and Wycliffe translating the Bible. Two battles were popular too, the Boyne of 1690 and the Somme of 1916. And it went without saying that almost every procession had, and still does have, a banner called 'The Secret of England's Greatness' —whereon a turbaned and kneeling Indian proffered the Holy Bible to a young (and upstanding) Queen Victoria.

But the variety of banner subject is endless—an exotic variety like the names of the lodges and bands. These come from all over the world to display their Protestant allegiance on the Twelfth of July 'walk'. One follows another in a fabulous succession—Sir William Young's Chosen Few, Israel's Truth Defenders, Pride of Mother-well, Purple Star Ladies, Hearts of Oak, The Silent Valley Flute Band, The Saintfield Amateur Silver, Bailliesmills Accordion, Britannia Temperance Reed, and, of course, the Girls' Pipe Bands. Trades are also represented by such bodies as the Transport True Blues complete with banner pictures of big lorries similar to those which I saw grinding their way carefully beneath Portadown's Twelfth arches.

SCHERZO

Industry was not so highly developed as to turn Portadown into anything even approaching the grimy horrors of England's Black Country. The sky was bright, the air clear, and the River Bann innocent of effluence. In fact, Portadown is renowned on account of its roses, grown commercially but spectacularly. With a nice roseate touch the mayor's chain of office is composed of gold medals won for rose-growing by Sam McGredy—Ulster's equivalent of England's Harry Wheatcroft.

Though no roses had yet escaped to grow wild along the banks of the Bann there were at least islands of water-lilies and rank margins of Himalayan balsam. A century ago, jealous gardeners nursed this rare *Impatiens* from the Western Himalayas as tenderly as Sam McGredy nurses his experimental green roses today. But in the end, like Catherine in *Wuthering Heights*, the Himalayan balsam escaped from the prim elegance of Victorian conservatories and ran wild and free. It flourished on every canal, along every industrial stretch of river where its moisture-loving, thick red stems could find room.

Himalayan balsam was such a familiar sight that not only were Victorian conservatories put out of mind but the plant's origins in the East too. Also easy to forget in connection with the East was the life of a man born at Lurgan, near Portadown, in 1867. Like his friend Gurdjieff he turned to the East to find a philosophy for the 'Harmonious Development of Man'. This was Æ—George Russell, poet, painter, economist. Æ drew his personal brand of mysticism from a mixture of Bhuddist scripture and a potpourri of Gurdjieff and Ouspensky. His high altar, however, was not Fontainebleau or Virginia Water but Dublin's literary circles where he could tune his mood to 'Keltic Twilight'. And perhaps there was no better exponent of the mind's twilight than the Ulster mystic who wrote:

> *Twilight, a timid fawn, went glimmering by,*
> *And Night, the dark-blue hunter, followed past,*
> *Ceaseless pursuit and flight were in the sky,*
> *But the long chase had ceased for us at last.*

Even the real world outside Æ's metaphysical one was peopled with fairies. He often painted the 'wee folk' whom he claimed to have seen throughout his life.

SCHERZO

I was to discover Æ only later in life. Certainly I knew nothing of him when, as a boy of 10, I marched through Lurgan in an Easter juvenile Orange parade. But I did know of Marjorie MacCall from the same town. I am sure that none of Æ's dabblings in the supernatural would have given me such nightmares as did the story, the only too true and dreadful story of Marjorie MacCall. It was a story literally from the tomb.

Marjorie died and was buried in Lurgan's old cemetery. On the night after the funeral, a knock was heard at the door of her house. The servant girl, no doubt in a nervous state over the funeral, was too terrified to open the door for the knock sounded exactly like her dead mistress's. Marjorie's son, however, was not a prey to nerves and nonsense, and opened the door himself. A corpse stood there, its hair disarrayed, the damp of the grave still on it, wrapped still in its shroud. It was his mother. She had walked home from the graveyard. Her death had not been death at all but only a deep coma. Marjorie had been brought out of her coma when thieves opened the coffin to steal her rings.

Her son's horror on opening the door is difficult to imagine, but Marjorie herself lived on for years afterwards, though it is not recorded whether she was given to a morbid turn of mind. In my childhood I knew several old women who feared to die, not because of death itself, but because they feared grave-robbers who once dug up bodies for sale to Glasgow medical students.

To make sure that I had missed nothing of significance in the flax spinning town of Lurgan (flax, incidentally, which is nowadays imported from the Continent) I consulted the official guide: 'When Queen Anne was on the throne William Waring, M.P., introduced diaper manufacture, and from that time Lurgan never looked back'.

The importing of flax into Ulster sounded rather like taking coals to Newcastle, but perhaps this connection with the Continent was not so strange since a French Huguenot had been responsible for organizing the Irish linen industry in the first instance. William III appointed Louis Crommelin, a man whose name was always afterwards linked with the town of Lisburn. Even more famous was Lisburn's own son John Nicholson of the Indian Mutiny. Although

118

the General has been dead a century, he still tended to dominate the scene.

Lisburn's main street contained a frightening statue of Nicholson, holding a pistol in one hand and brandishing a sword with the other. The figure was frightening because he had, in fact, been like that. It was impossible to ignore him, just as it was impossible to go to the ancient cities of Taxila in the Punjab without passing even bigger memorials of him. In the matter of monuments the General did quite well, all things considered, though one of them was incorrect in stating he was born in Lisburn. He only grew up there, being born in Dublin.

Lisburn cathedral had yet another monument to this hero. It was beautifully carved in white marble, a low-relief, wide-screen sort of affair full of rolling smoke and cannons and piles of bodies all in the best Alexander Korda-Cecil B. de Mille tradition. General John Nicholson was shown standing atop the breached walls of Delhi, beneath which walls in actual fact he was afterwards buried when he was killed at the famous Siege of Delhi on 23rd September 1857 aged only 34. No wonder—he could not have stood the pace.

The inscription at Lisburn cathedral said, in that dead-pan Victorian way, he had '. . . an iron frame and mind, a terrible courage, an indomitable will, unselfish, earnest, plain and true . . . the type of the conquering race.' I presumed this to be a euphemistic way of saying he was brutish, pompous, obstinate, unfeeling and ignorant. I felt thankful for being born at a time when the type of the conquering race has all but died out to the general relief and benefit of all and sundry.

Choked by cannon smoke and drenched in blood at Delhi, the General would probably not have been amused to know that his efforts were to achieve far less in India than the influence exerted in London drawing-rooms by a woman. And by yet another strange coincidence she too hailed from the Lisburn district. Her father was the bailiff to the Marquis of Hertford who gave Lisburn cathedral its clock. The cathedral, however, contained no memorial to this most striking woman.

Young Laura Bell left Lisburn and went to work as a shop-girl in Belfast. By the 1850s she had moved to England and had become one of London's most prosperous courtesans. Sir Francis Burnand described her as 'the theme of songs of the period'. At the end of a performance, when she left the Opera House, the whole audience stood to watch her departure.

While young thunder-guts John Nicholson was putting the natives in their place in India, Laura Bell saved thousands of lives simply by lifting a finger, a finger adorned by a ring. The chief of the Nepalese princes, Jung Bahadoor, gave her the ring when he was her lover. There was also a letter, worthy of any fairy-tale prince, saying that if ever she needed his help, she was to return his ring and he would move heaven and hell to oblige her. The India Office in London knew of this ring, and during the Indian Mutiny persuaded Laura Bell to send it to the Prince with the request that the Government of Nepal should side with the British. The Prince kept the promise made to his Irish lover. Nepal never did join the mutineers and its famous Gurkha regiments remained loyal to the British Raj.

Laura Bell's fame might well have rested there but she was caught up in another fashion of the times and became converted. The 'Queen of London whoredom', as Sir William Hardman called her, became the queen of London Bibledom. From her drawing-room in Grosvenor Square she now ruled the smart evangelical society of London, a drawing-room in which no less a person than Mr. Gladstone himself often led prayer meetings. Lady St. Helier left an account of Laura's fiery preaching and of the 'magnificent jewels she wore round her neck, and the flashing rings on the hands with which she gesticulated'. But Lady St. Helier knew, just as Queen Victoria and the Queen's own son knew, the source from which the 'Ambassadress for God' got those jewels.

In view of her career, it was not perhaps surprising after all, that Lisburn had no memorial to this remarkable woman. One more strange coincidence, however, connects her with yet another famous man from Lisburn and he at least has given London a memorial of Laura Bell. The man was Sir Richard Wallace, the connoisseur and art collector who gave London its renowned Wallace Collection. Amongst its treasures is Ernest Girard's portrait of Laura Bell painted at the height of her 'early reign'.

Sir Richard Wallace himself had two windows as memorials in

Lisburn cathedral, but I could not make out if he was represented in the East window. I spent a wet afternoon studying this splendid window and wondering why the flax-expert Louis Crommelin was put between Martin Luther and the Holy Innocents, and why St. Edmund was put next to Jeremy Taylor, whose high church views the clergy and congregations rejected, causing him much unhappiness. The great divine was Bishop of Down and Connor and his *Holy Living* and *Holy Dying* are amongst the finest prose works of the seventeenth century. He died in Lisburn in 1667.

Laura Bell had the Opera House on its feet and the aged Mr. Gladstone to tea-fellowships. But another person from Lisburn, years before, had taken Drury Lane by such storm that the army was called out to turn the crowds away from the theatre. Mr. Pitt adjourned the House of Commons so that members might attend the theatre. The extraordinary actor playing Hamlet, whom all London wanted to see, was only 13 years old, William Betty, the Young Roscius.

In 1801 he went to the theatre for the first time and saw Mrs. Siddons play Elvira in Belfast. Afterwards, young Master Betty declared he would die if he did not become an actor. Two years later, Betty made his début in Belfast at the age of 11, already playing Osman from Voltaire's tragedy *Zaïre*. Much is said nowadays about the fortunes made by pop-singers and film stars, and about the supposed over-enthusiastic behaviour of teenage 'fans'. Yet this is nothing compared to the near-riots caused by William Betty's appearances. Bishops and peers clamoured to be first with gifts at his dressing-room door. And as for payment, in a single season lasting twenty-eight nights Master Betty made what today would be £200,000. No wonder he was able to leave his profession soon after 30, having made box office records and retire, as one contemporary newspaper said, 'in the quiet enjoyment of the large fortune he had so early amassed'.

Perhaps while still in Lisburn the Young Roscius got his love of period costumes from seeing the Guards at the neighbouring town of Hillsborough. In magnificent Elizabethan uniforms these Guards gave Ulster a spectacle comparable with the Tower of London's Beefeaters. It was only recently that this spectacle, seen in

SCHERZO

Hillsborough for three centuries, came to an end. Every Sunday morning, accompanied by their own trumpeter and drummer, the Guards marched to church like the Military Knights of Windsor.

The Guards were originally appointed to the Marquis of Downshire's family as Hereditary Constables of Hillsborough Castle. But noble families, who nowadays can barely afford enough staff to run their houses and estates, could hardly be expected to provide pensions for a score of military warders. The Guards have had no replacement in their ranks during recent years, so that now only one bugler remains to blow the Fall-in by the castle gates and march on a Sunday morning all alone to church.

There were, of course, still guards at Hillsborough, for it was the residence of Northern Ireland's Governor, but these guards were khaki ones on routine sentry duty. The castle they guarded was a modest Georgian stone manor rather less interesting than the forecourt's splendid iron gates. The gates were only brought to Hillsborough in 1936 and had formerly stood at the entrance to Richhill Castle in County Armagh, and were almost certainly the work of the two Thornberry brothers from Falmouth who settled in Armagh early in the eighteenth century.

Like Armagh, Hillsborough stood partly on a hill and the town's main square was at the top of it with the famous gates closing one side of it. From this elevated place there were views out to the surrounding countryside. Elegant Georgian houses surrounded the town and gave it perhaps a stronger English flavour than could be found in other Plantation towns. Islanded in the square was the court house, a small but nevertheless fine building—the best I had seen since leaving Armagh. It was painted in pink and grey and white and besides its turret also had urns against the skyline.

Samuel Brown's pub opposite was an excellent vantage point from which to admire this little architectural opus of 1780. A farmer beside the pub door bolted out to capture a sow which somehow escaped from the trailer behind his car. The beast was caught before any damage was done to the sedate Royalty-planted trees on the lawns of Government House. One frightened sow can make quite a noise, but it was only a tiny squeak compared with the din that filled Hillsborough on its former fair days. The jostling farmers and moaning cattle and bleating sheep, the cries of country women with honey and butter for sale made dissonant music a thousand times over. But it was not dissonant for a Hillsborough boy who years afterwards recalled the joy and excitement in the scherzo of his *Irish Symphotny*.

Walking about Hillsborough breathing the sweet airs of County Down I thought of how often that boy, who afterwards became the great Sir Hamilton Harty, must have longed to return to his native town. The renowned musician did try to visit Hillsborough at least once a year. But music in the form of the Hallé Orchestra kept him prisoner in Manchester, a place he hated. On retiring from his post as the Hallé's permanent conductor he said, 'When well-intentioned people ask me how I left Manchester I reply "With pleasure".'

Harty was known for his wit, which no doubt developed early in repartee with Hillsborough's farmers and perhaps also with the good people of the parish church where his father played John Snetzler's eighteenth-century organ. Hamilton Harty was also playing it eight years after his birth in 1879. By his ninth birthday he was appointed organist in the church of Magheragall five miles from Hillsborough, a walk the boy made every Sunday morning.

Hamilton Harty was bursting with talent. By his twenty-first birthday he had already become a figure in London's musical landscape. He began as an accompanist. Busoni's letters contain a reference to a young pianist, 'Hamilton Harty, who did supremely well'. And doing supremely well everything he did, was the hallmark of Harty's life.

Although the Hallé Society did not invite him to be their Orchestra's permanent conductor until 1920, Harty had made a name by then as a composer. When he was 27 a concert overture of his was given at the Queen's Hall Promenades. *With the Wild Geese*, inspired by a poem by Emily Lawless, put Harty among significant young British composers.

In Manchester, Harty slipped into the shoes of two great predecessors, Charles Hallé and Hans Richter. No Arts Council existed in 1920 to help lame musical dogs over stiles. The Hallé Orchestra was in financial trouble. Hamilton Harty soon drew the crowds. He cared only for music. His music making was magical. His interpretation of the classical repertoire was enriched by his experience as a performer and composer. But he extended the Orchestra's horizon and played works never heard before in Manchester or London. Under his baton all seven of Sibelius's symphonies were introduced from Finland.

The Hallé became the first orchestra in the country, but Hamilton Harty never descended to showmanship and though he was revered by musicians, the public's eye was caught by flashier conductors who assaulted their audiences with shock tactics both musical and verbal. Nevertheless, when Harty gave a performance of Berlioz's *Grande Messe des Morts* critics came specially from Paris to hear it. Mahler's Fourth and Ninth Symphonies received their first performance in Britain under him as well as *Das Lied von der Erde*. Mahler is notoriously difficult but Neville Cardus, then the *Manchester Guardian* music critic, wrote of Harty thirty years later, 'no conductor outside Austria has more eloquently and comprehensively interpreted Mahler than Harty'.

Hamilton Harty, however, never lost his head, or his heart, nor his ear for light, airy tunefulness amongst the turgid, depressed Romantic Germans. His own music was full of Irish lilt. In his piano concerto, Irish tunes lurked like leprechauns behind every lyrical bar. He could be simple as only a master could be, as for instance in the lullaby *O men from the fields*.

Harty could not hide a peculiarly Irish mystical strain. In earlier years, like Charles Wood, he had set music to Whitman's poetry in *The Mystic Trumpeter*. In 1939 his *Children of Lir*, based on a Celtic legend told him as a child by fiddlers and fishermen of Antrim, was performed by the B.B.C. in the still un-bombed Queen's Hall. Harty said of this himself, 'The legend is the least known and perhaps most beautiful of the Three Sorrowful Stories of Erin. King Lir's lovely daughter Finola and his three sons were changed by his evil second wife into swans, doomed to haunt the lakes and seas of Ireland until they heard the sound of a Christian bell. They wandered through storm and sunshine until they heard a church bell off the Antrim shore and became children again. But as they were being baptized they died.'

Bad health took its final toll of Sir Hamilton Harty two years later and while only just over 60 he died at Brighton in 1941, and his ashes were taken later, at his own request, home to Hillsborough in County Down, where he was born. His death must have affected many thousands of people for he endeared himself as man as well as musician.

Would the *nouveau riche* titled Lancashire woman remember how the young Harty went with a quartet to an industrial town and played to a factory audience and how, as hostess, she remarked to him afterwards 'It was lovely, Mr. Harty, but next time you come I wonder if you would mind bringing a bigger band?' Would the American man remember how Harty took no notice when he rushed to the rostrum and struck Sir Hamilton while playing at the Hollywood Bowl, because, as the man said, Harty was drowning his solo 'cellist daughter by a too-loud orchestra? Would the players in Chicago remember the orchestral fanfare they accorded Harty when he conducted there, an honour given previously only to Paderewski and Rachmaninoff?

The great Ulsterman, who never lost his brogue, was remembered at Hillsborough when his ashes were interred to the playing of his own arrangement of Handel's *Water Music*. And this is the memorial which perhaps Harty would most have liked, for the *Water Music* will be played as long as Handel himself is heard. There could be no greater compliment.

Twilight had come again when I left Hillsborough church and walked down a long, darkling avenue of limes. This was the time of day, everywhere in Ulster, when hundreds of swallows and swifts and martins appeared, wheeling and whirling in the glowing sky, dive-bombing in swoops for insects, the shrill *chee-ree-eee* giving away the swifts' presence. When I came to Dunmurry, these birds were still feeding on the wing though it was practically dark.

It was a golden, velvet evening, and masses of dark foliage standing close together to form even darker masses of impenetrable shadow hid Dunmurry's houses. Not all of Northern Ireland's population lived in Georgian buildings or the early nineteenth-century terrace houses of the country towns. Like England, Ulster had its share of modern housing estates, of which Dunmurry was partly one. But with a foresight and feeling unusual in council estate builders, the great trees of the old village had been spared the axe and expanses of grass prevented monotony. I was reminded a little of Steen Eiler Rasmussen's housing group at Tingbjerg which is as far from Copenhagen as Dunmurry is from Belfast.

Life behind Dunmurry's tulip beds and chromium letter-boxes, behind the net curtains stretched like modesty vests across the bay windows was typical of life in modern affluent Ulster. The house at which I was going to stay resembled its neighbours except for the lawn which looked shaggy instead of shaven. The principal furniture consisted of bookshelves and heaps and piles of books, and instead of three plaster ducks in plaster flight on the walls there were original Dan O'Neill paintings, for this was the home of James Boyce.

James was an Ulster edition of his friend Gilbert Harding, with whom he worked for years on B.B.C. programmes. But, unlike Gilbert Harding who remained a bachelor, James was blessed with a wife and family whose home in the housing estate at Dunmurry is the meeting place of politicians and artists, actors and writers, the new rich and the poor aristocrat. During each of my own visits the house swarmed with people—those who had just been interviewed on televison by James, or those acting in a current play by Ralph Spence, James's son-in-law. In one part of the house Charlie Brett, the young lawyer leader of the Labour Party would be arguing with young Paddy Boyce who went to the local Quaker school and to the Aldermaston marches and was keen on National causes. Alfred Arnold, the English Civil Servant who fell in love with Ulster was always there, looking among theatrical people for likely talent for his new musical plays.

People wandered in and out of the Boyces' without either getting or requiring any specific invitation as, during the war, soldiers on leave used to climb in at the windows looking for a bed, to the discomfiture of the local police. The house was always open, like the MacCanns' in Belfast and indeed, their guest Stanley Spencer delighted in James Boyce's cooking—another field in which this actor-personality was expert and about which he wrote a weekly column in the press.

Besides this gamut of people occupied in the arts and politics, the Boyces' neighbours also dropped in, and so the old Irish custom of an evening *ceili* was kept alive in the least likely place—the heart of suburbia.

Before each night's crowd began to disperse, or James's long-suffering wife Dorothy got blankets out to make shakedown beds for whoever decided to stay until morning, a lull interrupted the talk and singing, and as though the tide was ebbing across Newcastle's sands, the hubbub gave way to silence as James read aloud, Swinburne perhaps or one of the Irish poets who had sent their books as mementoes of other evenings of readings after an exotic, Oriental supper.

For me, there will never be another story-teller who in any way could compare with Karen Blixen, the late Danish authoress, who told in her extraordinary, deep rasping yet hypnotic voice the tales of her beloved Africa with the waves of the Sound in sight of her window. Nor will *Eine Kleine Nachtmusik* ever sound so romantic again for me as it did under the open tropical sky of the Venezuelan Concha Acustica in Caracas. Nor will poetry reading ever be the same again as it was to hear James Boyce reading in the improbable environment of Dunmurry's garden suburb.

5

Live Men and Dead

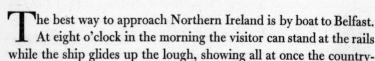

The best way to approach Northern Ireland is by boat to Belfast. At eight o'clock in the morning the visitor can stand at the rails while the ship glides up the lough, showing all at once the country-side and the hills beyond and the city's spires and stately towers of steel gantries in the shipyards. Also to be seen from mid-channel is the striking difference between the lough's opposite shores.

County Down lies on the port bow, a soft, undulating landscape of blues melting into greens, a gentle landscape set with trees and studded with cloud-shadows as soft as wool. White cottages and farms and seaside villages nestle there. Gulls whirl in the brown velvet of newly ploughed uplands among straggling forests of beech and oak.

To starboard the forbidding escarpment of County Antrim rises from the sea, changing its colour and mood with every change of sunshaft and cloud. The Antrim coast alternates between ranges of black basalt cliff, as impregnable as the dark Norman walls of Carrickfergus Castle at its feet, and other stretches of cliff like blue-veined cheese. At nightfall, the Antrim side becomes a vaguely menacing mass of indeterminate indigo.

The lough's two shores have each their own beauty but County Antrim's black and white is more dramatic than County Down's green. The two extreme colours of black and white symbolize Antrim. Even the names of places around its coast echo the curious interplay of black and white, the counterchange between chalk cliff and black basalt. Blackhead stands close by Whitehead.

Whitehouse lies before the Black Mountain which stands sentinel over Belfast. Charles Kingsley was so taken up with this black and white counterchange of the Antrim coast that in *Westward Ho* he described its island of Rathlin as 'looking like a half-drowned magpie'.

Paul Henry, the Ulster painter, caught this mood of huge cumulus poised over the changing Antrim coastline. His paintings of the coast show well the strange alternation of colour and of form too, which on a still bright day reflect from the sea swells. But behind those towering cliffs and buttresses of basalt lies a landscape of immense glens, valleys and sweeping hillsides which filled Moira O'Neill's poems. Moorlands stretch across the high ground, desolate and deserted.

I took a bus to Antrim town itself. No clock was necessary to tell it was late afternoon, for we stopped several times to let women pass who were driving their cows home for the evening milking. When the bus drew in at Antrim I saw at a glance that it followed the pattern of a wide main street, laid out specially for the holding of fairs and markets. The court house stood islanded at one end of the piazza-like street. This building of 1726 reminded me of town halls I had seen in the islands of the Azores, for its main entrance was on the first floor approached by an external stair and the windows of the main front had Baroque-looking lintels. But the carriages and carts of the eighteenth century were replaced by the haulage vehicles of the twentieth. Huge lorries thundered by the old building day and night, carrying cattle and sand, creamery cans, bales of wool and 'Early Riser Bulk Foods'.

Close by was a Tudor gateway leading into Antrim's fine park and castle, which gave the town a unique distinction. The great house, once the home of Lord Massereene, stood by the Sixmilewater River, a fine Plantation house which survived all the vagaries of Ireland's violent history until the troubles of 1922 when it was burnt, leaving a ruined shell which still remains, none the less impressive and romantic. The whole place was heavily impregnated with a ghostly, abandoned atmosphere, that kind of flourishing decay which, in a house, has more appeal than buildings in good order.

The romantic 'Gothick' feeling of the early nineteenth century, with its sham ruins, may have been more than a fashionable whim. Perhaps it struck chords in human nature, chords rooted deep in the contemplation of mortality, playing on mankind's love of surveying time's ravages while being himself, momentarily, beyond time's power. John Piper has translated this love of decay and ruin into a modern idiom. His dramatic drawings of derelict country houses, and especially his famous war-time paintings of bombed buildings in Britain, touch a more fundamental experience than mere interest in the pictorial records of damaged or neglected buildings.

Standing by the river, among the trees around the grassy fore-court, I looked at Antrim's ruined house and saw it as though John Piper had painted it. The walls, textured with lichens, reared up with empty, gaping windows, through which I could see, where magnificent rooms once were, a tangle of elderberry and ivy, brambles and hawthorn, while above, ragwort and clover flourished on the parapets.

It was an impressive ruin, and perhaps because forty years of exposure after the fire had left little mark, it looked like a 'Gothick' sham ruin, for the carvings were well preserved. Of most interest was the centre-piece and doorway with coats-of-arms and Classical detail. Two mermaids floated beside a sea-shell over the door. The door itself, like the windows, had gone, leaving no trace except sockets in the stonework. And crowding out the sky and the nearby town were the park's trees—great cypresses, yews and chestnuts, white spruce and copper beeches, all overfull, suggesting that nature had stepped beyond the bounds within which man had once confined it.

Lawns and grassed terraces at different levels surrounded the ruin, and there were broad walks which gave on to woodland glades, cleverly contrived with an art that almost, but not quite, concealed the art. These wide walks ran in straight lines, meeting and crossing with others, now in a tunnel of planting, now in the open, now affording a view of the river and its fallen bridge, now shut in with only the light falling through a clearing ahead.

Chaos reigned within the ruin, a jungle had sprung up to choke the space once occupied by the rooms. But order prevailed in the landscaped gardens, and, moreover, an order foreign both to accidental waywardness and the deceptive natural grouping of English landscaping as men like Capability Brown and Repton handled it. At Antrim Castle there was a suggestion of Classical gardens whose shady groves were the haunt of fauns and nymphs and even of Pan himself.

I wandered slowly along one grassy walk, sheltered by overarching trees whose boughs swept to meet the ground in long graceful tresses, and came upon a perfectly circular pool. Swans glided mysteriously across the algae-bright surface, causing hardly a ripple and indifferent to my presence. They alone, in all this emerald world, were white. The place was utterly quiet as though bound by a spell.

And, in a sense, it was, for this garden was the work of Le Nôtre. I remembered a broadcast by James Boyce who called it the Versailles of Ireland, and this explained both the garden's orderly, grand layout and its foreign character. Andre Le Nôtre was among that group of brilliant architects, artists and craftsmen whom Colbert inveigled into the service of Louis XIV. Le Nôtre's first great work of garden design in France was at the huge château of Vaux-le-Vicomte, the magnificent country house of Louis XIV's ill-fated finance minister Fouquet. Here, with a glory of fountains and terraces *tapis vert*, Le Nôtre exploited for the first time the megalomaniac handling of natural terrain by giant vistas and avenues which later reached their supreme point of exaggeration in his masterpiece at Versailles. Antrim Castle's garden was a slight work compared with Le Nôtre's vast undertakings for the French king, but nevertheless the hand of master landscape designer is felt by walking through its carefully arranged sequence of lovely scenes.

Fortunately, although the castle is a ruin, the park has been kept up more than tolerably well by the local authorities. Instead of becoming rank and overgrown, the trees and hedges were well kept, the grass was trimmed where it required to be so, and the all-important walks were maintained free from weeds. And to keep the garden alive, the people of Antrim used it. Lovers strolled in the dusk down to the long avenues to lose themselves in the shadows.

Possibly less in tune with Le Nôtre's intention but serving nevertheless to keep the park alive, was an impromptu game of football played by youths in the twilight, their shouts and laughter echoing amongst the wooded groves. Other youngsters were fishing in the river, too absorbed to answer the saucy remarks of girls who prowled about the park entwined in each other's arms like Siamese twins. Occasionally, shots rang out from boys shooting at rats scurrying along the riverbank.

The castle's coach-house and stables escaped being burnt and have since been converted into a charming residence, occupied by Captain Collis, who came out while I was trying to decipher the heads of carved stone on his gable. According to the late Lord Massereene the sculptured heads of the blind man and his ugly wife were portraits of two local worthies. When the blind man was miraculously cured and saw how ugly his wife was he prayed to be made blind again.

Captain Collis invited me into the house for a drink and we wandered from room to room looking at things of interest. In the hallway was a plaster bust of Maurice Collis the distinguished surgeon, the grandfather both of my host and of the author who today bears the same name. Somebody had given the bust's white mouth a generous coating of lipstick. But somebody who was much more desperately in need of make-up was the Countess of Desmond whose portrait hung in one room. The Countess looked bloodless, which perhaps was not altogether unexpected in a lady who lived to be 150 years old.

In common with many young shepherds and shepherdesses, fauns and wood-nymphs, who were bent on the pursuit of love, I was locked in Le Nôtre's classical dreamscape and had to walk miles to get back into the town. In Hall's Hotel a man in a tee-shirt was reading a missal behind one of the three-tier cake-stands. Most of the other guests seemed to be 'commercials' absorbed in making up the day's books. Several times on my travels round Ulster I was mistaken for a 'commercial' myself with a consequent and pleasing reduction in hotel bills!

The 'commercials', however, had their cars, whereas I had to rely next morning on a bus to Ballymena, the 'City of the Seven

Towers'. Ballymena may once have sported seven towers. But it had nothing to compare with Antrim's own round tower, a perfectly preserved example of pre-medieval skyscraper for which Ireland is renowned. Antrim's is almost a hundred feet high, and shares with the tower on Lough Erne's Devenish Island, the honour of being one of Ulster's only complete two such towers, all of which were probably used for a variety of purposes, belfry, look-out, safe deposit for monastic treasures.

Ballymena had little of architectural interest—even some of its houses' front gardens were concreted over without so much as a geranium in a pot to keep company with the park seats, which many people in Ulster have outside their front doors.

The Adair family brought Ballymena into prominence in 1732 with the setting up of linen industry in the town. One of their relatives, a carefree young doctor, fell in love with Admiral Keppel's daughter, gaining a name for himself in Lady Keppel's song *Robin Adair*. To make quite certain that other young ladies do not fall foul of young Ballymena lads, as dashing as Robin Adair on their motorbikes, the station bore the same awful 'Warning to girls travelling' as Portadown had.

I got on a train to Portrush with a Japanese businessman who, with his wife and two beautiful children, was making a twelve-hour tour of Ulster. Like John Keats, they had been drawn across from Scotland by the beauty of the Ulster coast and rather than never see the country they thought it better to have half a day than nothing at all. The Japanese kept their eyes on the green, fertile land rolling past the carriage window but two R.A.F. boys returning to camp were fast asleep after a restless and berthless night on the cross Channel boat from England.

There was also a stage-Irishman in cloth cap and silk scarf knotted at his neck and crossed over his body. He appointed himself guide to the Japanese, indicating places of interest with his blackthorn stick. His highest praise was for Bushmills—'Home of the wee Bush' as he called the famous whisky, though he thought 'cowl rain eight say' equally as good—his dialect version of Coleraine H.C. Whisky, as once supplied to the House of Commons. It did not seem to bother him whether or not the Japanese could follow his fast, slurred Ulster accent and local slang. But they did, and having had whisky breathed over them for an hour they could hardly fail to see where his principal interest lay. When we all got out at Portrush I bid the family a safe journey home to Japan. The wife said of the stage-Irishman now disappearing down a side street, 'I think he wanting a very big wee Bush!'

Portrush was built on a promontory only three hundred yards wide, so that the Atlantic's waves break on sandy beaches on three sides of the town. The sea could be seen from the end of almost every street. Boarding-house advertisements with '3 mins. sea' was no exaggeration in Portrush. The town's boarding-houses were, in fact, advertising two centuries ago. One, dated 1761, reads 'At the house commonly called Bushfoot, where John Dunkins, Esq., usually lived, there will be lodgings kept for bathers or those who have a mind to drink the salt water, by Edward Fayth. Any gentlemen or ladies who will favour him with their company may depend on clean and orderly attendance with a reasonable charge, his wife being an Englishwoman. Also he will keep a cake-house for those who pass by or repass to the Giant's Causeway with cyder and mead, and a fish dinner will be dressed for any that inclines to dine, and those who come to bathe are desired to give a week's warning to your most obedient humble servant, Edward Fayth. N.B.—He intends keeping of goats.'

As at Newcastle, teenagers are among the thousands who abandon themselves to the sun and salt air of Portrush beaches every summer. And the abandonment was not only to the sun but to other sensuous delights, especially at Easter, delights which the older and established residents looked upon with disdain. A friend of mine was asked by the B.B.C. to investigate these exciting rumours about Portrush. He asked a teenager when the supposed orgies began 'Och,' the boy said, 'not until the last train comes in from Belfast on Good Friday night.'

The only orgies I could find in Portrush were those of spending, Barry's Amusement Arcade, the ultimate in Ulster's funfairs, coming in for a fair share of the visitors' purchasing power. Barry's could offer the newest and most novel in sideshows and one-armed bandits. It sported the flashiest of dodgems and flying cyclones and helicopters, the sight of which made me feel seasick with their plungings and swoopings. But to forgo such pleasure was one of the penalties of being the wrong side of 30 though the right side of 40. On the other hand, normally, being a teenager has its disadvantages too, and being under 10 has even more. When I was a boy under 10 years of age, we may have smoked an occasional butt-end in secret, but we would never have dared to do so brazenly in public like a party of children I saw reaching up to the one-armed bandits.

I saw the Japanese family several times, for Portrush is the kind of friendly, intimate place where it is impossible to lose people. The golden bodies on the golden beaches reminded me of chickens turning on the spit in those automatic mass-produced barbecue machines. They were trying to make an orgy of the sun which slid slyly behind the clouds like a tantalizing dancer of the seven veils. And, alas, the dancer's veils did not all come off. Rather they increased, for a wind drove clouds in from the sea so that the golden bodies began to disappear under coloured blouses and tee-shirts as the broken coast of Scotland was disappearing, as distant light drew away from the Paps of Jura above the smudge of Islay, the long leg of Kintyre enfolding the hills of Arran.

Since sunbathing looked as if it was finished for that afternoon, I hopped on to a bus going along the clifftops, for there, I knew, was a dramatic, dark beauty which the patchy showers and wind would do nothing to lessen, a beauty as wild and rugged as the legends which even time's mists could not hide. There were facts as well as legends connected with a castle standing on a frowning, beetling cliff a few miles along the coast road from Portrush.

The road passed the town's famous golf course, now turning into a vivid emerald colour in the rain and tenanted only by gulls standing with yellow beaks all pointing in the same direction. I would have liked some of Edward Fayth's cider and mead inside me as I began the clifftop journey, though I was hoping for more than a fish dinner when I got to the Causeway Hotel where Colin Kane is king of Ulster's kitchen—a mine-host who will don the white hat himself to cook specially for any guest.

Within minutes, the modern world of golf was left behind and high above the long lazy Atlantic breakers the old world extended all around with the rough grandeur which neither the battering sea gales of centuries nor the hand of man had softened or brought to ruin. But both had wreaked a terrible vengeance upon Dunluce, the cliff-edge castle which once dominated the sea approaches to this wild, deserted north Antrim coast.

In keeping with the grim aspect of the castle remains as they stand today is the meaning of Dunluce—Stronghold of the Sea-sprite. The stronghold was taken in 1513, according to the *Annals of the Four Masters*, by one O'Donnell from the sons of Gerald MacQuillan and given to the sons of Walter MacQuillan. By 1558 the MacQuillans seemed to have been routed from Dunluce altogether by Sorley Boy— a MacDonnell. Sorley Boy was still at the castle in 1588, in spite of having been a prisoner of Shane O'Neill meanwhile. When the *Gerona*, one of the Spanish Armada's ships returning home foundered on the Antrim coast, Sorley Boy salvaged three of its guns and mounted them on Dunluce.

The sea-sprite's stronghold saw many festivities when the châtelaine was the Duchess of Buckingham, the same duchess who had run in her nightdress to see her husband assassinated in Portsmouth High Street. She put up a monument in Westminster Abbey to the unfortunate duke and then escaped from high-powered politics to Dunluce as wife to the head of the MacDonnells, who had become Earl of Antrim.

But although the Duchess escaped the assassin's knife in Portsmouth another waited for her at Dunluce, and this was the sea itself, the hungry sea which never ceased to gnaw the rocks on which the castle stood. In 1639, while the Duchess was preparing for a banquet, a domestic part of the building collapsed and fell into the sea hundreds of feet below, carrying all with it, the servants, the pheasants and sucking-pigs. Only a tinker survived who was sharpening knives in an embrasure, still seen today as the Tinker's Window. Miraculously, the Duchess herself escaped. There was presumably no banquet that night. But later on, the Duchess became involved in more drama. She saw her first husband move to his dramatic end through the pomp and intrigue of Europe's courts. Later, she entertained the Scottish General Monro under Dunluce's roof quite unaware of his intentions to take her second husband prisoner.

After his capture, the Earls of Antrim went elsewhere and the castle was left to the Atlantic winds and its contents were scattered. A painting by Rubens of the duke went to Italy, and long after Monro went to his own defeat at Benburb and Cromwell's troops had ravaged Ireland, a portrait of the dashing George Villiers by Janssen found a resting place in London—appropriately enough in Buckingham Palace. Dunluce's ruins rear up still above the cliffs, waiting during who knows how many centuries more for the final dissolution of its drum towers and Scottish turrets, stone ovens and crumbling walls.

The coastline, indented with sandy bays, could have changed little since Dunluce's windows shone with flares and lanterns for the last time. But as though the local council was afraid the tragedy of the seventeenth-century pantry-boys and sucking-pigs would be visited again on tourists, a notice had been put on a beautiful stretch of sandy beach at Portballintrae—'The removal of sand from beach without a permit is strictly prohibited.' A whole mountain of sand would hardly be missed from all those miles of beaches.

To the relief of an American beside me the road swung away from the perilous cliff edge and turned inland towards the village of Bushmills. That double-decker buses ran this route surprised me, for although the winds were only a summer's day they gave more than a hint of what winter gales would be like. And the uplands were spaced with white farms hugging the ground and protected by wind-break trees whose tops were shaped by gales like the fantastically cut hair of some African tribes.

The River Bush runs through these wind-shaped woods, and is frequented by anglers out for salmon, lurking in its twists and bends which snake about the hills, making islands of the wild, open country. My American fellow-traveller in the bus was going to fish in hopes of getting sea-trout below the weirs. Good though the salmon leaps of Bushmills are, the town enjoys its renown from *Uisge Bheatha*, two Irish words meaning 'water of life', which is the origin of the word whisky, and may even have been linked with the stage-Irishman's description in the train from Ballymena of his crying need for a 'wee Bush'.

'Wee' is a word used very much in Ulster. It conveys endearment and has a curious parallel in other languages such as *cafezinho* in Brazil—a wee coffee, or in German such words as *Mädchen*—a wee girl. 'Wee', however, was hardly the term to describe the inhabitants in this part of Antrim, who, by all accounts, were once giants. Apart from legends connected with the Giant's Causeway, there are stories and traditions to do with Dunseverick Castle, another fortress along this coast, though now in a more ruinous state than even the under-mined Dunluce.

Dunseverick, however, was of more ancient foundation. Mention of it occurs in legends circulating long before the neighbouring stronghold of the O'Donnells was built. In the days of the Red Branch Knights, Dunseverick was the home of Conal Cearnac, a famous wrestler and swordsman. Conal went with other Red Branch warriors to Rome and pitted his skill against the soldiers of Tiberius Caesar. He was the Roman army's delight and went off to the East with the soldiers in their occupation of Jerusalem. Conal was present at Christ's crucifixion. And he was so close to the Cross that when the soldier pierced Christ's side, a drop of blood fell on his brow. He joined the soldiers in casting lots for Christ's seamless coat but when he won Conal refused to accept it. His powerful muscles were called upon when Joseph of Arimathaea wanted the stone at the sepulchre rolled aside for the entombment of the Saviour's body. Conal's castle in Ireland, with its vast walls, stood long after the Crucifixion and it was left until Cromwell sent a Captain Venables to end Dun-severick's centuries of invincibility.

Almost in the same decade as Conal was delighting the Roman army with his swordsmanship, a Roman author was writing about an island off the coast, opposite Dunseverick Castle. This was Rathlin, which Pliny mentions as Ricnia, an island which saw two of Ulster's most savage massacres. The Campbells of Argyle committed the first, and English troops carried out the second, against Sorley Boy MacDonnell.

Sorley Boy had evacuated his wife and children for safety to Rathlin, but they were among the six hundred people killed. Those who did not actually die on English swords were dashed to death on the rocks below the four-hundred-foot-high cliffs over whose edge they rushed in panic and terror. The old fighter Sorley Boy watched this massacre, powerless to help in any way, from the mainland. He was 'likely to run mad from sorrow, tearing and tormenting himself and saying that he had then lost all he ever had'.

It would be interesting to know if Queen Elizabeth I was told of the screaming children jumping from the cliffs when she congratulated Essex on these savageries, which were supposed to have broken the power of the Irish chieftains. But Sorley Boy came of granite stock and although he was 80, he married again and had another family.

A less harrowing story of Rathlin is of Robert the Bruce who also took refuge there after one of his defeats. In one of the island caves he saw the spider which encouraged him to try, try again. Unlike the Bruce, I decided not to try the four miles of sea between Ballycastle and the island, for the tides and boats were not to be depended upon, as I knew from a previous crossing when I had to spend three days on Rathlin waiting to get back again.

For the visitor who has never been on the island and who is a nature lover, Rathlin is one of Antrim's 'musts'. Apart from its rugged beauty, the cliffs themselves teem with razorbills and puffins, guillemots and kittiwakes. Until I went as a war-time evacuee to the West and discovered Fermanagh's lake islands, Rathlin had always been my boyhood's dream island.

In spite of the radio weather forecaster's 'occasional rain', the road beyond Bushmills had a reasonable amount of traffic bound for the Giant's Causeway, now available for sightseeing free of charge since its recent designation as a national park. The presence of an attraction, such as the Causeway, tends in most cases to destroy the general amenity of an area as, for instance, at Stonehenge. In the season's height, nobody could pretend that the motor-coaches and litter assist the sense of atavistic mystery of Salisbury Plain's monument.

At the Giant's Causeway, luckily, the worst effects of tourism were kept to a minimum. In spite of hotels and trinket shops, the old ways still clung to this part of the Antrim coast and the last cottage we passed before getting to the hotel had a well-built turf stack in its garden. I often caught a whiff of peat being burnt in these coastal villages. High hedges of escallonia acted as wind-breaks by the house near the track down to the Causeway. Escallonia's cloying smell was one of the first scents I ever associated with holidays for it grew prolifically in the gardens at Childhaven, County Down.

I am brave enough to face any accusations of snobbery and affectation which may be incurred by confessing to a distaste for the vulgarity which attends the sightseeing of places like the Causeway. It is undoubtedly a wonder—the world's eighth it has been called. But on the other hand, the Causeway was no more a wonder than a thousand other, though possibly less spectacular, wonders to be seen in Ireland, wonders which the madding crowd neither see nor wish to see. It is not perhaps, the best imaginable approach to this amazing geological formation, to pass a hideous and obtrusive public lavatory and a car park and one of those unexploded war-time mines used as the collecting box for a charity which may be seen in many coastal parts of the British Isles.

However, it might, I suppose, have been worse, for the Causeway itself lies concealed by a headland from these modern necessities of life, and even the visitors who arrive by Rolls-Royce or Cadillac are obliged to make the final half a mile of their pilgrimage on foot down the rough path which brings to mind the Valley of Rocks in North Devon. This reduction to a common denominator of all visitors even obtains in the lavatory where one turnstile alone gives access to the compartment for both sexes, guarded by a woman behind iron bars who allows ingress upon payment of one penny.

Half-way down the track there is a shack where coloured postcards may be bought—as though the postcard shops in all Ulster were not already full of Causeway pictures. How much better the scene must have been in the days when all this *kitsch* was unheard of and the Causeway was a lonely, deserted place, peopled only by legendary figures like the giant Finn MacCoul and his rival Scottish giant living across the narrow stretch of Channel.

According to the light in which these things are seen, the praise or blame for the Causeway's fame in modern times rests with Frederick Augustus Hervey, who is said to have been the first man to call attention to the extraordinary rock formation.

In 1766 Hervey was in Italy collecting art, which was his principal occupation though he had qualified for Holy Orders. He visited the crater of Vesuvius while in a state of agitation and was badly wounded in the arm by a falling stone. However, Vesuvius fired his imagination and thereafter he made a study of volcanic formations. When his brother was appointed Viceroy of Ireland, Hervey forsook the art centres of Europe and managed to get the first Irish bishopric which fell vacant.

In 1768 he was translated to the very well-endowed see of Derry and began one of the most extraordinary careers in Ulster's history, for the new Bishop of Derry soon succeeded as the Earl of Bristol and built a series of great country houses which became the seven wonders of domestic architecture in the province. He was a father-in-God whose Te Deums were in stone. The Earl Bishop was also a friend and patron of the Italian naturalist Fortis, and was quite overwhelmed upon seeing the Giant's Causeway, and it was his unbounded enthusiasm which began the tourist draw which has never slackened from that day to this.

The regularity of the Causeway's hexagonal basaltic columns is impressive, though more like a giant's honeycomb than anything else. But I had never been able to see that it was more beautiful than the rest of Antrim's northern coast where every mile reveals a drama of frowning cliffs and heaving seas and long stretches of sandy beach, a paradise for bathers and children all but deserted. Places like White Park Bay have also been taken over by the National Trust and for me, this unspoilt beauty is worth more efforts of preservation than the Lady's Fan, the Giant's Loom, Lord Antrim's Parlour, the Giant's Organ and other phenomena of the Causeway.

White Park Bay is one of Ulster's little-known wonders. The prehistoric Ulsterman certainly had Frederick Hervey's eye for beauty when he built his wooden hut on the green turf in the sand dunes under the white limestone cliffs. The mile-long crescent of finest white sand, the sweeping amphitheatre of dunes and grass banks give the bay everything that holidaymakers from 7 to 70 could possibly demand of the seaside.

But Antrim is more than just its fabulous coast whose dunes and beaches rival those of Jutland. Visitors with no particular love of the shore or sand in their cucumber sandwiches on the beach, have unhindered miles of moorland in Antrim's hinterland. Waiting for them, equally as unfettered by crowds and improvements, is the lonely splendour of the steepsided Glens of Antrim lying between the vast stretches of moorland. The Glens alone could devour whole weeks of the summer, for each part of them has, as it were, a secret which only patient exploration would discover. But even on the journey by road from Ballycastle to Cushendun tantalizing, luring glimpses can be caught of the heathy desolation and grandeur of the moors.

I had a delicious swim in White Park Bay and coming up the twisting lane from the beach was fortunate in catching a country bus. The conductor saw me scribbling in a notebook and for the rest of the journey acted as a well-informed guide.

'I heard Woodbine Willie preaching in that church,' he said when we got to Ballintoy.

The conductor had heard more than I ever did of the 'prophet who burnt himself out for the sake of the Christian faith', as the *Sunday Times* called Geoffrey Studdert Kennedy. But Woodbine Willie's wife once wrote to me in thanks for a haunch of venison I sent her son—little knowing I had poached it when I was a shepherd in the Morven Hills across the Channel in Scotland.

The bus stopped again to pick up some people who had been to Carrick-a-Rede, a huge knob of rock separated from the mainland by a narrow, treacherous chasm. Fishermen go out to this rock for the salmon which are lured to the area by the mixture of sea water and fresh water spilling from the gorge in the cliffs a hundred feet above. Unfortunately, the only access to this rock pinnacle is by a long rope bridge which 74-year-old Daniel Wilkinson dismantles in autumn and re-erects in spring. Though the rope bridge is sturdy enough, its use can only be recommended for anglers with a good head for heights, for even in summer the bridge is a plaything of the winds.

The occasional rain was more occasional than ever when I got to the coastal resort of Ballycastle. I was glad to shelter in Holy Trinity Church, where people had presumably been sheltering from climatical or spiritual storms since it was built in 1754, a plain, decent Georgian building with a coved plaster ceiling and an apse with gold stars. Other holidaymakers had dropped in to avoid the rain. Two women were making reparation, not for their sins, but to their disarrayed hair. With no thought of irreverence they used a highly polished brass wall plate as a mirror, not bothering to read its sad words, 'Cecil Sparrow aged 20 and Tom Hay aged 19 who were drowned off Fair Head, May 11th 1895. In death they were not divided.'

Driven away from the body of the kirk by the outraged glances of the *dames de coiffeur* who thought my interest was in their impermanent waves, I went into the small porch and comforted myself with the Visitor's Book Remarks' column. The remarks ranged from 'Born in Ballycastle 1920, Trust Him' to 'Lovely clean church'. A young boy from an English vicarage had written 'Lovely embroidery'. The schoolboy hand in which these two words were written reminded me of a Forrest Reid novel in which a young boy sits down to write in Ballycastle.

At least the church embroidery did not consist of shamrocks, spinning-wheels or colleens in red cloaks which cluttered the linen in the town's shops. Nothing so frivolous was to be seen up on the moors, though I would not have been surprised to find real fairies appearing through the mists which had come down. Here, away from civilization which clung precariously to the cliffs and valleys, there was nothing except a few widely scattered and isolated houses merging into the moors' shapes and hiding behind dry-stone walls and the wind-break trees which seemed to have escaped from the woods folded one upon another in the steepsided glens.

Following Ballypatrick's miles of young fir trees a landscape quite different from anything yet seen, emerged, a harmony sweet and stern but undisturbed by any harsh sounds of modern life. Here on the Antrim uplands the ancient Ulster, an Ulster already old in wild legends and pagan religions when Christ was born, remains boldly indifferent to the passage of time.

Beside one stretch of lonely road lies the Lake of Loughareema whose waters appear and disappear in an uncanny and unpredictable fashion. Tradition says that the lake sometimes drains away overnight. A local poet wrote:

> *Loughareema! Loughareema!*
> *Lies so high among the heather,*
> *A little lough, a dark lough,*

LIVE MEN AND DEAD

The wather's black and deep,
Ould herons go a-fishing there,
And seagulls all together
Float round the one green island
On the fairy lough asleep.

When the bus passed this peculiar lake the water level was low.
But round the turn of this century there had been enough water for
a Colonel MacNeill and his coachman to be drowned in it. The lake
overflowed across the road and the horses shied at the cold water,
and, in their panic, plunged deeper into the lake taking the colonel,
coachman and coach with them. Such scientific minds as have applied
themselves to the mystery of the coming-and-going Loughareema
have concluded that the phenomenon is explained by escape fissures
in the boulders which are hidden until the lake empties itself in dry
periods.

The scientific explanation possibly does not have the same kind
of appeal as the romantic one, personified by Moira O'Neill, poet of
the *Fairy Lough*. Her book *Songs of the Glens of Antrim* is now em-
bodied as part of local tradition. Although Miss O'Neill's sentimentality with its fairies was neither heroic nor hardboiled, at least her
verse had a built-in capacity for being turned easily and naturally
into songs which both Stanford and Harty did. The poem of the
Fairy Lough has been lent a beauty greater than its mere words by
Stanford's most lyrical of settings, now made famous too by Kathleen
Ferrier's recording.

Sir Samuel Ferguson had sung the praises of this part of Antrim
before Miss O'Neill came upon the literary scene. John Masefield
also found inspiration at Cushendun, though which inspired him
more, the village or its people, is difficult to detect, but at any rate
one of Miss O'Neill's neighbours became the poet laureate's wife.

Cushendun struck me as being quite different from any other
village in Northern Ireland, though neither then nor now could I say
exactly why. The village was small and spread along the shore and
along each side of the river which tumbled from the sombre hill of
Glendun behind the village and ran over rocks and under a bridge
and so, through a small, beautiful harbour to the sea. All this, and

heaven too—in the form of yet another marvellously sandy bay, has been taken over by the National Trust. Also included in this take-over is the group of cottages built in 1912 for tenants of the local estate. They are an interesting period piece and though rather twee and coy still have a good deal more charm than most of Ulster's council estates. I found that Cushendun provided its inhabitants with do-it-yourself entertainment such as a 'Whist drive for Apostolic Work' and a performance by the Faulat Girl Pipers.

Hedges bejewelled with fuchsia and gold-plated with honey-suckle lined the road from Cushendun to Cushendall, a town with a red stone Muslim-like tower with projecting windows which, said a woman beside me in the bus, was a curfew tower, the curfew bell, she assured me, being rung at nine every evening. This lady was extremely talkative and informative and she spoke so fast that the bus had whisked by the various objects and places of interest she was pointing out to me before I had time to take them in.

Red Bay, one of the greenest of the glens, spread itself like a pea-cock's tail to meet the blue and jade now radiant in the early evening sky. We passed an arch of rock with a gaping hole, called Madman's Window as the result of a suicide incident some years ago. And it was here, as a youth full of evangelical zeal, that I used to turn inland and go up the valley of Glenariff. It would need a strong heart indeed not to be moved by the sight of that valley's waterfalls and pools lying below the wooded flanks and the flat-topped Lurigedan Mountain which looked like a pagan altar raised up to a pagan sky on black cliffs no less awesome than those frowning over the north coast of Antrim.

Thackeray called the valley 'Switzerland in miniature'. Cows wait to be milked by every farm gate while the air tinkles and hums with the sound of falling waters from such cascades as Fall of the Mares or Fall of the Hoof. The glen spreads out towards the shores of Red Bay so that its own scents of water and moor and of rich farmland mingle with the smell of the sea, as its birds' song mingles with the mewing of gulls.

And now, unlike the north coast road which is an eagle's eyrie of a road, the Antrim shore itself ran alongside the road. I could have put my hand through the bus window and almost have picked up those wonderfully rounded pebbles, or almost, in places have trailed my fingers in the sea, so near did it seem. But I was torn between looking at the near scene of the shore boulders which, perhaps centuries before, had crashed down from the cliffs, and between watching the distant scene of sky and sea and headlands unfolding one behind the other, lying on the horizon like sleeping whales.

The weather changed twice. And the lowering clouds were stopped off in a long line, creating the gradation of rich tones which a water-colour artist makes by holding his colours at the edge of a wash. Beyond this watery and purple-blue edge of cloud, the headlands were bathed in a misty yellow light. Distant fields and trees and hedges rose above the water like a sea-mirage.

Beyond the village of Waterfoot, where women sat knitting on benches outside their cottages, the sea took on a green luminosity like copper roofs in sunshine. Purple appeared again mixed with brown in layers, so that the tints of the wet seaweed strewn about the shore were repeated in the sea itself.

But more beautiful than the colours was the sea sculpture, littered prodigally for miles along the whole shore. Some of the rocks were as rounded and black and shiny as seals. Others were white and sharp edged, and still more were of a yellow ochrous stone wrought into weird shapes by tides of a thousand years. At some places the white and yellow rocks were piled up in suggestion of gigantic castle ruins which, like the ill-fated Dunluce, had fallen from great heights.

In the darkest of the sea's purple-indigo passages the wave crests broke lazily and luxuriously into trails of ermine. The foam gleamed white as though spotlights played on the slow turning breakers. Occasionally, on the landward side of the road, woods reached down to the shore. We passed fishermen in small boats riding the swell, their occupation made starkly dramatic by the curiously theatrical lighting so that they looked like symbols of all fishermen in all boats there had ever been since the beginning of time.

The summer afternoon had declined without haste into evening and as the sun moved with a graceful, parabolic gesture westwards, pure gold was poured over the sea. Then a flush of delicate, rose light suffused the whole sky and as we rounded a bluff Larne came into view. A large ship was leaving harbour, balanced on the glassy water as gently as a swan. Its lights were already turned on, twinkling across the water. This was the ferry to Stranraer, but at that moment the majesty of the ferry's movement and its utter isolation on the sea made me think of all those sea voyages I had taken since I was a boy with envious eyes watching the boats slide out of Belfast Lough bound for the ends of the earth.

It was from Larne, and not from Belfast, that I made my own journey across the water on leaving Ireland for the first time. The lough's mudflats surrounded Larne so that at low tides the town was seen rising out of long horizontal perspectives, a mere smudge between the sky and the mudflats where, with the forlorn serenity of a Millet painting, groups of men dug for lugworm amid the unperturbed curlews probing with their bills for shellfish.

Larne's chief attraction was its setting and the excitement which any harbour lends a place. I did not stay on this occasion to haunt the scenes of my youth, since at Larne they had only been brief ones of departure. The bus drew up in the station forecourt and I went to get a train, so bringing my run along the Antrim coast to a climax at Carrickfergus.

Besides mud, those few miles between Larne and the ancient fortress of Carrickfergus had seen blood. Ireland, irresistible through history to ambitious armies, was particularly vulnerable here to invasion from the sea. Edward Bruce probably sailed in at Larne with his three hundred ships and six thousand men in a disastrous attempt to make himself king of Ireland. Famine resulted from the ruthless plundering and even his own Scots followers were reduced to eating their own dead. Countless tides and the shifting, silting mudflats have since covered this and other horrors enacted here, and the railway line, running just above the high water mark, revealed no scars other than those made by the excavations and dust of a cement factory.

The tide was out and on the shining mud dozens of men were digging for bait, while farther out, low in the channel, the sea swirled sluggishly, secretly gathering its forces for the slow return at high tide across the flats. There were redshanks by the score stalking disdainfully, stabbing their bills fastidiously into the mud.

I was in no mood to be fastidious myself on arrival in Carrickfergus for hunger asserted itself. Yet Dobbins Inn was precisely the place where I could have been as fastidious as I liked, for Dobbins enjoys a well-earned reputation for its table. Feeling in the mood for something on the scale of oxen roasted whole, I went through the inn's old passages to find a dining-room whose simple furnishings, wooden floor and white rough plastered walls, were, though much restored, agreeably expressive of the inn's long history.

With enthusiasm and skill, the hotel people had collected items once used in everyday Irish life and had employed them as points of interest in the public rooms. The collection included some fine examples of the blacksmith's craft, such as weavers' lamps and bread irons, a craft on which people of bygone days depended more than perhaps we realize today.

I did not have whole roast ox, though to turn the spit for such a feast would have been possible in the huge stone inglenook fireplace in one of the bars. The fireplace and walls were only discovered a few years ago and were thought to be part of the castle—Dobbins Castle—which once stood on this site. The hotel itself, however, has been an inn since at least the seventeenth century.

No doubt the inn did a roaring trade in those times also, especially during such occasions as the Spring Assizes. At the Assizes held at Carrickfergus in 1711, I read over a Guinness by the old fireplace, eight women appeared before Judge Upton for 'exercising witchcraft on the body of Mary Dunbar'. They were found guilty and sentenced to a year's imprisonment and were pilloried four times. The pillory was no joke, as may be seen from the fact that one of the witches lost an eye from rotten eggs and cabbage stalks used as missiles by the enthusiastic townsfolk.

A superior kind of witchcraft was performed in Dobbins Inn kitchen, for scrumptious scampi were set before me. I gave myself up to those 'allurements of smells' which did not over-concern St. Augustine before setting off to enjoy those 'delights of the ear' which he would have approved of—*Son et Lumière* at Carrickfergus Castle.

The Château de Chambord on the Loire is a far cry from Carrickfergus on the Lough. But Carrickfergus is brought into the company of the noble houses of the Loire by having its history performed in sound and light, an idea conceived by the French architect

Robert-Houdin after seeing Chambord itself vividly displayed during a thunderstorm.

Darkness was complete when I left Dobbins Inn and walked to the shore where Carrickfergus Castle stands at the water's edge, still looking across the wide lough up and down which sailed so much of Ireland's history. I walked up the wooden ramp and through the barbican and took my seat beneath the keep and let *Son et Lumière* carry me back through hundreds of years.

Fergus, King of Dalriada, set out from here in the sixth century and brought the Caledonian Picts to heel, and from his Highland capital of Dunstaffnage established the Scottish nation. From Ireland he took with him the *Lia Fail*, the Stone of Destiny, which was believed to have been Jacob's Pillow. This stone became known as the Dunstaffnage Stone, until removed to Scone Palace, whence King Edward, the 'Hammer of the Scots' removed it to its present place in Westminster Abbey.

The slab of sandstone was rather a heavy talisman to carry about, and in spite of doing so, King Fergus did not save himself from getting leprosy. He returned to Ireland to wash his white spots at the holy well of Carrickfergus. Unfortunately he was shipwrecked on the rocks, which event gave the town its name. Fergus was not the only leper to be seen at Carrickfergus, for at one time the town had a leper hospital and the disease remained in Ireland until 1500.

John de Courcy was responsible for Carrickfergus Castle as it is today, still largely unaltered after a long existence involving some of Ulster's most significant military and political events. The *Son et Lumière* production was completely beguiling. The voices of Ulster's distinguished actors Joseph Tomelty and Robert Mac-Candless created an extraordinary illusion of reality. Instead of sitting on a wooden seat in a stand specially erected in the courtyard I felt that I was actually walking about with John de Courcy as he inspected the erection of the castle in 1180. And so, right through to King William III's landing at Carrickfergus and the Duke of Schomberg's siege of 1690.

Carrickfergus deserved praise for mounting this wonderful entertainment which carried me completely away. I could not tell the difference between the gulls crying in the drama's sound effects and the real ones flying up from the rocks below the castle walls, angered by the cannon shots and smoke from the ramparts. And as the lighting played about the castle, silhouetting the black darting shapes of bats, appearing now in a window, now in a doorway, I looked out across the lough also and saw the lights strung out marking the towns and villages of the far County Down coast, while Belfast shimmering at the head of the lough looked romantic in its night attire. Mysteriously beautiful in the summer night's darkness were the ships, invisible except for their lights arranged in a geometry of pinpoint portholes. The boats glided noiselessly up and down the lough, like Chinese lanterns floating in a pool.

Son et Lumière of a rather different kind lit up the lough when the American privateer Paul Jones sailed up in the *Ranger* in 1778. The British government had enough on its hands fighting the French and trying to quell the revolt in the American colonies, without having its fleet involved in Belfast Lough. No doubt the good people abed in Dobbins Inn, whither I also went after the castle show, pulled their nightcaps over their ears and dived below the bedclothes.

A pint of milk was standing outside the castle door when I went back again next morning. It was not that I begrudged the castle custodians their cups of tea but it seemed wrong, somehow, for an ordinary bottle of milk to stand on the front doorstep as though Carrickfergus Castle was no more than a suburban semi-detached. On the other hand it did not surprise me so much as did the furniture in my bedroom at Dobbins Inn. When I woke I realized that the white painted wardrobe and dressing-table were in the *Art Nouveau* style of the Glasgow School, fine examples beautifully made. Who, I wondered, had bought and brought these period pieces over from Scotland?

Although the castle looked dramatic by night and *lumière* it was, astonishingly, even more so by broad day. The preservations had been done extremely well, and because even eight centuries had left little mark it had a curious sense of being occupied and used. In the bright morning sun it was possible to see the castle's commanding position and how its cannons must have been a formidable obstacle. The curtain walls rose from the rocks and shallows and the tall, square Norman keep looked impregnable. The whole thing reminded me of Lisbon's Bethlehem Tower which stands on the Tagus in a similarly dominating position.

The *pièce de résistance* at Carrickfergus was undoubtedly the keep's interior, particularly the spacious upper chamber once used for banqueting. Its deeply embrasured windows and great stone arch spanning the whole width of the room had a vigorous architectural character worth going to see for its own sake apart from its historical associations. An interesting but not overpowering collection of bits and pieces connected with the castle was displayed in the keep. Besides such things as cannon balls and locally minted coins recovered from the mud during restorations, there were some ancient boats thirty-feet long, hewn from a single log and once used for war purposes.

Just beyond the harbour was the site of another of de Courcy's buildings, St. Mary's Abbey of the White Canons dedicated to the Holy Cross. A large factory now stands on the site, dedicated to the fortunes of Courtaulds. And a few miles beyond Carrickfergus was Kilroot, and thinking of the salmon steak Dobbins had promised me for my midday meal, I regarded an enormous appetite as only polite and decided to walk out to Kilroot.

I wanted to see a thatched cottage there which was not only an architectural curio by being oval in shape, but had also once been Jonathan Swift's rectory. This was the house from which he went back and forth to Belfast while in hot pursuit of his 'Varina'—Miss Jane Waring. It is still in dispute whether the famous rector of Kilroot actually wrote part of *The Tale of a Tub* in this cottage, but some of his best couplets about the parish's daily life were undoubtedly written there.

My favourite amongst these is the one Swift wrote as a result of finding a tinker and a girl under a tree in the rain. Swift demanded that their act of love should be immediately solemnized into a holier matrimony. His outraged sense of what was proper would no doubt have given Miss Waring in Belfast cause for saucy comment. However, Swift regularized the tinkers' union with the lines:

> *Under this tree in stormy weather*
> *I join this rogue and whore together.*

Swift's cottage has gone. Not a straw or a stick or stone remains and this disappearance had happened since my last visit seven years before. Swift's church was also long gone to ruin, looking little better than the heap of stones he wheeled into the church as a trap for unwary Presbyterians.

Long before salmon-steak time I was back in Carrickfergus and so went down to the beautiful little harbour sparkling in the sun and bright with the colours of pilot boats, sailing dinghies, and a small freighter unloading loose salt. Sitting or sprawled over the sea-wall youths in jeans and leather jackets were fishing, successfully for saithe and flatfish. A light wind ruffled the lough so that the water took on a kind of silken sheen as the breeze grew contrary to the tide. The hills across the lough changed from blue to green, advanced or receded as the light changed, as the luminous clouds passed across the sun, filtering its rays on to the land below.

Dobbins duly did me right royally on a monster steak of salmon, the enjoyment of which practically amounted to gratification of fleshly lusts—hardly the right prelude perhaps for my visit to St. Nicholas' church, another of John de Courcy's buildings. I wondered if this church would still please me as it had done in the days before I travelled and acquired a taste for the brilliance and colour and floods of light and the elegance of gilded gewgaws of the Baroque church. But I need not have feared for St. Nicholas. Although it has that random quality often found in medieval buildings and which is anathema to the Baroque, it had a kind of charm, especially in the magnificence of the huge Chichester memorial of 1614.

This tomb had more than a flavour of Renaissance exuberance and piety—florid carving, including a fine Corinthian order as a frame to kneeling figures in bas-relief, carved shields and spears and breastplates and banners in panels below, and above, hanging on the wall, a knight's real helmet and coat-of-arms. Besides Sir Arthur Chichester and his wife and their only child was a brother, Sir John who was ambushed and killed by the MacDonnells in 1597. A few years after this unfortunate event Sir James MacDonnell is reputed to have gone into Carrickfergus church and saw the splendid marble and alabaster monument with Sir John's effigy. MacDonnell asked 'how the deil he came to get his head again, for he was sure he had anes taen it frae him?' Whereupon MacDonnell, according to popular stories and the church guide book, drew his sword again and beheaded the statue. This story, however, seems to be a tall one. Sir James MacDonnell had been dead several years already when the Chichester memorial was erected. And in any case, the Chichesters command no sympathy. Sir Arthur was a captain with Sir Francis Drake and helped to singe the King of Spain's beard. Afterwards he was sent to Ulster where he distinguished himself when, in his own words, 'I burned all along the Lough, within four miles of Dungannon, and killed one hundred people, sparing none what quality, age, or sex soever, besydes many burned to death; we kill man, woman, and child, horse, beast, whatsoever we find.'

I was thinking of other lines about this church in a poem simply called *Carrickfergus*:

> The Norman walled this town against the country
> To stop his ears to the yelping of his slave
> And built a church in the form of a cross but denoting
> The list of Christ on the cross in the angle of the nave.

When young, the poet had plenty of opportunity to reflect on this inclining of the nave to represent Christ's head, because the boy who was to become the poet Louis MacNeice, was the rector's son.

It was impossible to separate Carrickfergus's fine church from the name of the MacNeice family and their in-laws the Greers. When I went into the church the sexton came over to me and took me to see the various church furnishings, most of which had been gifts from the two families. 'Bishop MacNeice gave more to the parish than he got,' Edmond Love informed me as he pointed to the late bishop's crozier of bog oak carved by his brother-in-law. Edmond Love told me much about the MacNeices—he was an authority, for before becoming sexton he had been gardener to the Greers. He told me some amusing stories of the rector's children and their mischievous ways of years ago. I stored these stories in my mind to tell Louis MacNeice when I next met him in London. But before the poet could be reminded of these episodes from his childhood he was dead.

'It seems almost grotesque to write about Louis MacNeice in the past tense,' said Cyril Connolly in the *Sunday Times*. So it is. It is also grotesque to think that Louis MacNeice will go to watch cricket at Lords no more, nor to see rugby football in Dublin, nor sail up Belfast Lough again, straining for the first glimpse of Carrickfergus where he saw the *Titanic* pass by, and where the curfew rang in the days when his father took him to eat plum cake with the soldiers in the castle on Christmas Day.

Louis MacNeice's ashes lie across the lough on the County Down side. In a moving funeral address delivered in London on his dead friend, W. H. Auden said that Louis MacNeice did not write his own epitaph, but these lines might well be written on his tomb:

> *Live men and dead*
> *Being each unique*
> *(Their pain and glory),*
> *Yet some will have left*
> *By force or freak*
> *To us the bereft*
> *Some richer story;*
> *Their say being said,*
> *They still can speak*
> *Words more unique,*
> *More live, less dead.*

6

Among the Bushes

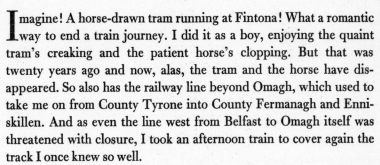

Imagine! A horse-drawn tram running at Fintona! What a romantic way to end a train journey. I did it as a boy, enjoying the quaint tram's creaking and the patient horse's clopping. But that was twenty years ago and now, alas, the tram and the horse have disappeared. So also has the railway line beyond Omagh, which used to take me on from County Tyrone into County Fermanagh and Enniskillen. And as even the line west from Belfast to Omagh itself was threatened with closure, I took an afternoon train to cover again the track I once knew so well.

The uncertain days of fitful weather had changed overnight into a sultry summer heat-wave. Men, women and children moved about in the meadows winning hay. Baling machines crawled slowly across many of the fields depositing their oddly geometric packets of hay in regular lines across the fields, a geometry oddly discordant with the voluptuous curves of Tyrone's landscape. But many of the farmers had no machinery and the haymakers worked in the mown fields stooping and bending and lifting, skilfully building up the small hayricks whose round forms and round shadows on the stubble harmonized with round forms of hills and trees and clouds.

The baling machine has changed the soft forms of the Classical landscape into an angular, Cubist world. Yet dereliction has changed the scene I knew in boyhood even more. The farmer in me felt disturbed, on looking from the train windows, at the sight of so much land which I had known ploughed and reaped during the war, now lying waterlogged and gone to rushes and rough pasture.

For miles, out beyond the railway verges, out to the far mountains, meadowsweet was indeed *regina prati*, queen of the meadow. The milky white bloom of meadowsweet has a pale beauty, but it makes bad hay, and the days when it was used for scouring milk-churns are as legendary as the days of Fintona's horse-drawn tram. Meadowsweet does not seem yet to have found a place in modern life though in bygone centuries people had scores of uses for it. 'Queene Elizabeth of famous memory did more desire it than any other herbe to strew her chambers withall,' wrote John Parkinson in the seventeenth century of meadowsweet, which the Druids once regarded as sacred.

When I was shepherding in the Highlands of Scotland, I heard the meadowsweet called *crios Chu-chulainn*, the Belt of Cuchulainn, Ulster's great hero. But I was not thinking of the Red Branch Knights as the train wound about Tyrone's hills, snaking and shaking on its way to Omagh. I was thinking of El Dorado.

The late afternoon glowed with gold. The harvest fields were gilded. And now, in the greatest heat, before ever suspicions of sweet evening airs blew from the hills, the haymakers went to cool off in rivers and streams, as cattle stampeded across the countryside, seeking cool shade from the biting clegs. And farm boys laughed and waved at the passing train, as they splashed naked in the shallow amber waters, their sun-tanned bodies golden also in the late light, as though each was El Dorado himself gone to wash the gold dust from his body in the sunset waters of Guatavita. But it was only hay dust they were washing off and the sting of a day's sweat in the fields.

Omagh had a hill and two towers soared up from it, a landmark for miles around. The two gigantic towers differed from each as was proper in a French Gothic church. This was the Catholic church, whose nave was high and narrow. Tall, narrow houses huddled about its foot, straggling down a narrow street, making an atmosphere so extraordinarily continental, that I could hardly believe I was not in France.

To walk from the hill by the church to Omagh's main street was to go from Normandy to Ireland in thirty seconds flat. Gone was the medieval gauntness and an imaginary smell of garlic and wine-sour cellars. Instead there was the broad homeliness of country Georgian, presided over by the Doric portico of the court house. The pigeons on its pediment had a view right down the high street. From their eyrie they could see Omagh's attempts to get-with-it architecturally, a Victorian bank with a Norman façade, another with echoes of *Art Nouveau* and a period piece cinema of the angular modernity of the 1930s, and, coming up to date, a smart post office with the smooth marble and metal and glass beloved of architects today.

The pigeons, however, had the sense to keep to Georgian architecture as did the pipe-smoking old men who sat on the court house steps, sagely and critically surveying the soldiers from the army camp walking into the town with their girls. Omagh had always been a khaki town for me, especially during the war. I went into the Bear's Paw for a pint of porter and was accosted by a small man who eyed me in a glazed way and introduced himself.

'I'm the regimental barber,' he said, and then, 'no harm done.'

'No,' I agreed, 'no harm done.' But I was not at all sure. Although the army has an unnatural horror of hair, it does grow, and at least one soldier, formerly stationed at Omagh, had forgiven past barbarisms. This was the barman in the Bear's Paw. After the war he left his native Glasgow and returned to the quiet of Omagh's trout streams.

The town stood alongside the Strule, a river noted for its salmon and trout. There were shops in Omagh too, which sold pearls taken from the Strule. Fishing, more than anything else, used to take me to Omagh. Apart from the main river, tributaries and minor streams were irresistible to anglers. Many of them had fine runs of salmon and sea-trout in the autumn. Routing Burn, Fairy Water, Owenreagh, Drumragh, Camowen, Cloughfin have been streams in the desert of army life for many friends of mine who were stationed at Omagh.

That evening of my arrival, there were few soldiers going after brown trout or to watch the swifts and swallows at their acrobatics. Most of the town's male population, as well as the barracks', had gone to watch another kind of swift—the Belfast football team of that name, playing against the Dublin Stars. Only the barmaid was left, with the television set and *Coronation Street*, when I booked into an hotel near the court house.

AMONG THE BUSHES

Later in the evening when the Dublin team and some of their fans decided to spend the night in makeshift beds all over the small hotel, the place was suddenly transformed into a Dublin bar, one of those where artists and writers are accused of loitering with intent to work. Young farm boys with virgin pay packets burning holes in their pockets and a group of Tank Regiment Cockneys being sentimental about the Old Kent Road, sat about in the hotel corridors. When the bar closed they opened a bottle of the 'Wee Bush' in my bedroom. The soldiers stopped singing *My old man says follow the van* and the two farm boys who had still to face a five-mile walk home to the farm where they worked, sang, solemnly and sadly:

> *Oh, from sweet Dungannon to Ballyshannon,*
> *From Cullyhanna to ould Arboe,*
> *I've roved and rambled, caroused and gambled*
> *Where songs did thunder and whiskey flow,*
> *It's light and airy I've tramped through Derry,*
> *And to Portaferry in the County Down,*
> *But with all my rakings and undertakings*
> *My heart was aching for sweet Omagh town.*

But it was my head which ached when I went down to breakfast later the same morning to my place under the picture of a boy eating soup, captioned with the cautionary words 'Some people are wonderful musicians with a soup spoon.'

Music of another sort was to preoccupy me for the following days which I spent at Fivemiletown. For me the term 'The General' means one person and although his name is Montgomery, it is not the hero of Alamein, but Major-General Hugh Montgomery. I remember the General from my boyhood, a strange figure on his bicycle, Boy Scout hat perched on his head, going off to see if the Wolf Cub camp had enough milk, or pedalling down to a village concert, or wandering up into the mountains to find a block of granite he could take home to sculpt. Unlike his brother Field-Marshal Sir Archibald Montgomery-Massingberd, General Hugh retired from the army and returned to Ireland to fight bigotry. He set up headquarters at Blessingbourne, a house which his father had built with Pepys Cockerell son of the great C. R. Cockerell.

AMONG THE BUSHES

Young Pepys Cockerell was an artist as well as an architect like the generation of great men before him—'The Giants', as Sir Albert Richardson called them. He probably sited the house and gave his knowledge of early Renaissance to the details of the house, which for a Victorian structure is remarkably devoid of ornamental clutter. Blessingbourne's beauty is in its landscape and the views afforded by its windows of the hills and woods beyond. Cockerell was also asked to design the village school on model lines for it was to serve a model purpose. Both Catholic and Protestant children were to use it together without restraint.

This Olympian independence of faction has been the strength of the Montgomery family for generations. They would wear neither the Orange nor the Green sash nor join any institution which might infringe on human rights. When the builder of Blessingbourne died in 1924—the Father of the Northern Ireland Senate—his son General Hugh carried on this humanitarian tradition and founded the Irish Association to bring North and South closer together.

I went to Blessingbourne and marvelled at its landscape setting of woods and lakes, and marvelled also at the inside which showed the family to have sensibilities in cultural matters as well as sense in political issues. The rooms were full of beautiful and intriguing things. One room still has an original William Morris wallpaper on which hangs a portrait of Cromwell glaring at the opposite wall where hangs Michelangelo's patron Pope Julius II. These extreme opposite poles of human nature were only two of Blessingbourne's whole collection of paintings which included many by Irish artists, Paul Henry, Æ, Derek Hill. Among more recent works was Cherith McKinstry's *Joseph of Arimathaea*, a most moving and beautiful painting.

I could have spent hours just going through the collections of portfolios and letters. There were scrapbooks with rhymes and their illustrations, a game in which Edward Lear joined when he was on holiday with the family, leaving his own drawings of the Owl and the Pussy Cat behind. There were mementoes of Charles Darwin and china by Josiah Wedgwood both of whom were family ancestors. Among the letters were some from Voltaire to a previous generation of the family and more up-to-date letters from Bishop

MacNeice to the General. One family letter, dated September 11th 1855, written in the Crimean War in the camp before Sevastopol, ran 'My dearest Mother, do not be alarmed about little Robin and myself,' and the mother at home in Ulster need not have worried, for little Robin lived to win the V.C. and become yet another general in the family.

The letters which most interested Blessingbourne's present owner, Peter Montgomery, and myself were those from his kinsman Ralph Vaughan Williams. 'I have such delightful remembrance of my visit to you,' the composer wrote after staying with Peter Montgomery. And so indeed, have I, for more than anything Blessingbourne seemed to be music since Peter Montgomery himself is known as a conductor.

A story that both Thomas Beecham and Vaughan Williams loved to tell concerned the owner of Blessingbourne. A B.B.C. orchestra conducted by Peter Montgomery was to broadcast Mozart's *Jupiter* symphony from Belfast. Vaughan Williams saw this in the *Radio Times* and switched the programme on, unfortunately missing the first movement. However, he heard sufficient to form an opinion on Peter's progress as a conductor. While listening he jotted down copious notes as to tempo and rhythm and tonal balance. These criticisms would both help and encourage the young cousin whose conducting had certainly improved since Vaughan Williams last heard him. The symphony came to an end, and the announcer apologized again to listeners for the technical hitch. Instead of the *Jupiter* from Belfast it had been the *Jupiter* from Beecham, on a recording of the Royal Philharmonic. Nothing daunted, Vaughan Williams sent off the criticism intended for Peter Montgomery to Beecham, who was highly amused, enough in fact to tell the story himself many times.

Peter Montgomery was lucky to grow up in a house like Blessingbourne where there was always a family quartet and an atmosphere which Stanford and Harty and Vaughan Williams loved so much, and where young people from the locality were always welcome to the piano with its ever-open lid. On the first evening of my own visit we rose from the table so that Peter Montgomery could accompany Leo McCaffrey.

AMONG THE BUSHES

This young singer, once a policeman, had travelled a long way since he went round Ireland collecting folk songs to sing to Peter Montgomery's accompaniment or arrangement. Leo had just come back from recording some of these songs in America and I listened while he rehearsed songs for a Carnegie Hall concert in New York. I recalled that Gervase Elwes, the great tenor, would never have become a professional musician if he had not been encouraged by Peter's mother in her drawing-room.

It would be natural to assume that the Fivemiletown Choral Society was a parochial affair at which old ladies sang *Home Sweet Home*. But this would be a wrong assumption for under Peter Montgomery's expert baton this group has become the most interesting musical society in the western counties. Covent Garden stars were always pleased to be asked to one of Fivemiletown's venturesome festivals, such as the Handel-Purcell one of 1959 held in Enniskillen.

My evening at Blessingbourne fled too quickly. It was late when Leo McCaffrey came to his last song, another by Stanford *A Soft Day*, to words by Winifred Letts. But although it was not raining, the same scents the song awakes so evocatively were rising heavily into the sweet evening air. I took a last walk through Blessingbourne's woods and along one of the lakes which the family had fitted up as a swimming pool for people from the town.

Bright is the ring of words was one of R. L. Stevenson's poems which Vaughan Williams set to music. It became a kind of theme song for me, and whenever I hear it Blessingbourne and its garden and lakes and the lyrical landscape will come before me like the vision they are. Peter played the simple moving tune as a voluntary at Sunday morning service on the organ which Stanford had chosen for the church. The ring of words, the fragrant memories of Hamilton Harty and Herbert Hughes will always wake echoes in me of Fivemiletown.

The trains of the Clogher Valley Railway used to force their way through the market crowds and herds of cattle in the middle of Fivemiletown's main street. Like Fintona's horse tram these trains can now only be seen on postcards, so I was glad to accept a lift in a car from another house-guest at Blessingbourne. Clogher was the first town we drove through. The town could not lay claims to any particular architectural distinction in spite of being a bishopric founded by St. Patrick. On a hilltop beyond the town, however, stood an extraordinary folly, built in the last century, as an eccentric mausoleum for the eccentric George Brackenridge.

The folly is a three-tiered tower of such a curious form that strangers always ask what it is, so fulfilling its builder's obvious desire to be remembered by posterity. The tower's three stepped blocks were built well in time for his decease; thirty years, in fact, before he died in 1877. At four o'clock in the morning he was interred in his mausoleum, but buried in a standing position. Some say this unusual verticality was the result of Brackenridge's belief that the magnetic poles would be reversed by the swift flight of the Lord's return and he wanted to be the right way up to greet his Saviour. Local people, however, who talked to me about it, held that the eccentric landlord arranged such a burial in such a monument in order to spite his neighbours.

Brackenridge came to the district a mystery man with no known ancestry or baptismal record. The mystery man did not make himself any more popular with his county neighbours when he fell in love with Sir John Bunbury's beautiful daughter who married him in the face of fierce opposition. The eccentric Brackenridge made sure, by his tower mausoleum, that his irate neighbours would never be free of him. And as though to underline this, his ghost, in frock coat and top hat, haunts the gorse up on Tower Hill. But this is hardly surprising for the poor man's bodily remains were disturbed after the vertical interment, by people who could bear the suspense no longer, wanting to see for themselves if he *was* upright. Souvenir hunters have scattered the bones until only the skull remained, and this was recently taken.

One of the first people to write about Brackenridge was his friend William Carleton, who made the odd landlord into Councillor Crackenfudge in *The Black Baronet*. Carleton was born in this district at the parish of Prillisk in 1794. His parents had fourteen acres and fourteen children. Amongst themselves they spoke Irish, but William wrote in English and, in the words of Yeats, became 'The greatest novelist of Ireland by right of the most Celtic eyes that ever gazed under the brow of storyteller'.

AMONG THE BUSHES

Carleton was educated in a hedge-school under three tyrannical masters, and his experiences there later appeared in his book *The Hedge School*. From the fourteen acres of the Clogher Valley and the valley's music fired by poteen drunk from eggshells the young William started on his travels, getting a lift in a hearse as far as Drogheda.

He reached Dublin in 1818 and was obliged to seek a bed in a cellar occupied by beggars and tinkers who had hung up their wooden legs, crutches, artificial cancers, wens and sores and were merrily drinking away the day's profits. Carleton tried to get into the army by writing a letter in Latin to the colonel of a regiment. He did odd teaching jobs, and finally met the Reverend Caesar Otway who asked Carleton to write for *The Christian Examiner*. Remembering the Clogher Valley people setting out for the pilgrimage to Lough Derg, Carleton wrote about them and so *The Christian Examiner* saw his début in print. And after the pilgrims, Carleton recalled other characters from his youth—his friend George Brackenridge, his schoolmasters, and fiddlers and rogues and a host of others who were to make this Irish Dickens stand up like 'Slieve Donard over his contemporaries'.

I left the Clogher Valley and went north of County Tyrone to have another look at Cookstown, that Ulster market town which shows *par excellence* the influence of the Classical grand manner in town layout with its mile-long, forty-yard wide straight-as-a-ramrod main street driven, like one of Le Nôtre's axial avenues, through the Tyrone landscape.

I wondered if the eighteenth-century planners of settlements like Cookstown were fully aware, as Haussmann was in Paris, of the military usefulness of such wide long streets down which cannons could be fired at rebellious inhabitants. But if ulterior motives originally lay behind the layout of places like Cookstown, certainly their architectural merit had long survived them. Cookstown is a model of what might be aimed at in the untidy, suburb-riddled landscape of England.

It was a Saturday and a market day when I arrived, and the sun was out and all the country people had come in for their shopping and to meet their friends and to taste the fine summer morning's news and gossip, and to wander at leisure amongst the market's treasury of stalls and second-hand booths set out gaily in the open. There was something for everybody, from violins to double beds, from grandfather clocks to gramophones with horns, from paper parasols to paper-backs. The double beds were a great attraction to the children who jumped up and down on them like trampolinists. And the bed sellers, far from objecting, seemed to regard this as a good advertisement for the bedsprings' sleep-worthiness. Perhaps the most significant for Cookstown was the Bible stall, since the town's literary fame rests squarely on a gentleman who spent thirty years translating the Bible back into Hebrew!

The market stalls, however, did not have it all their own way and the shops along the wide sunny street determined to rival the stalls by setting out their goods along the pavements—bales of curtaining, racks of trousers, festoons of blankets hanging from the walls, crockery and bread tins, though not even the whitest of white soap powders and detergents stacked dazzling in the grocers' windows could rival the dazzling white sunshine dancing on the smart white paint of the neat houses set side by side.

I had other prey in mind than bargain hunting among the market bookstalls. The day's weather was auspicious for a walk out of Cookstown past its Lutyensesque war memorial and American-looking toy church, down the far end of the mile-long street and deep into the countryside to the castle of Killymoon, hiding among its trees except for battlements and towers peeping above them.

Killymoon never heard the clash of arms or watched its knights riding off to the Crusades. In fact, only two battles were ever fought over it. The first was in a gaming room when the Prince Regent won Killymoon from one of the Stewart family who had built the castle in 1803, and the second was hardly a battle at all and took place a few years ago when the present owner bought Killymoon for £100— almost as a throw-away in a bargain he was striking for some of the land.

For his £100, the farmer who lives in Killymoon today got one of John Nash's masterpieces. He also saved the house from destruction —a fate which was meted to another of Nash's castles at Kilwaughter in County Antrim where the roof was stripped and the building allowed to fall into ruins as a shell in 1951.

AMONG THE BUSHES

Colonel William Stewart got John Nash to design Killymoon. This architect, later to be the darling of the Prince Regent and London Society and to amass fame and fortune, fell in with the growing penchant for the Romantic and designed Killymoon in the Gothic taste. The irregular arrangement of the rooms which he used here for the first time became a type of house plan which persisted in various forms right through the nineteenth century. Nash had flair and Killymoon was one of his finest works. Already Killymoon showed the fanciful and masterful manipulation of detail which he was to use later with breathtaking brilliance at Brighton for the Prince Regent's seaside Pavilion.

Like Sir John Soane, Nash was conscious of each room being a spatial entity, and he modelled Killymoon's ceilings with domes and pendentives. Over the graceful, divided staircase at Killymoon, Nash placed a lantern light supported on a series of ingeniously vaulted brackets. The narrow flight of steps leading from the entrance to the staircase hall also had a flat vault whose delicate ribs were gilded. The dining-room was an oval, and the drawing-room an elongated octagon—and one of the finest rooms I had ever seen. Nash's flair was seen in this magnificent room, for the short corner walls of the octagon were filled with gigantic mirrors, increasing the room's apparent extent almost infinitely.

The farmer's dog was fascinated by the mirrors, for the drawing-room was normally out of bounds to him. He barked and tried to get behind the glass to deal with the impudent intruder. In a quiet voice the farmer's son told me how he and his brother had been born in Killymoon and how they loved the place and estate with its woods and rivers. They treated the building almost with reverence, for it was only after buying it their father realized it was a building of special and rare interest.

I thought their care of it was remarkable and said so, for Ireland, once rich in great architecture, is now dotted with ruins, most of which could have been saved from the greed of demolition contractors if only enough people had been aware of the destruction threatened. We wandered through Killymoon's rooms, whose paintwork had been carefully redecorated by a local Cookstown man the farmer had brought in. Then we stood outside on the terrace, beneath the smooth, massive walls, looking over the park and the river.

Farmer Coulter could only afford to buy part of the land in 1922 when Irish estates were in the doldrums. The previous owner had decimated the woods by cutting and converting it all to timber. Then there was a mighty fire which destroyed it, but his claim to the insurance was foiled by his cap found lying there, giving away his grand scheme of arson. He never received a penny and the estate was sold in lots and Nash's castle was put up for sale as nothing more than £100 worth of scrap.

Although Farmer Coulter and his family do not live in a grand or sophisticated fashion, Killymoon is their home. The old man stood outside talking about his strange stroke of luck. He pointed with his blackthorn stick at the trout river. They were waiting for it to swell so that the salmon could come up. Beyond were the woods, thick again with trees, the rape of the previous owner forgotten. And in the fields pheasants ran to and fro, pheasants which the Coulters had reared to fill the valley with the birds' strident Oriental crowing.

The house itself, with its rounded towers and high *porte cochère* in an attenuated Norman style, had considerable outbuildings, and as I left Killymoon, walking along the quiet sunlit drive, I looked back at the £100 miracle. Even in Nash's time Killymoon had cost £80,000. 'And in those days,' Farmer Coulter had said, smiling secretly to himself, 'they only paid a mason sixpence an hour.'

It was a perfect day for walking and perfect country, God's own, for walking in. My first port-of-call was Pomeroy, the highest town in Tyrone, but as it lay some miles from Killymoon I eventually capitulated and got a lift with a young man in the skin trade— rabbits, hares, foxes, badgers. Having known so many farm labourers in my youth who had found employers at Pomeroy's 'hiring fairs' I wanted to see this eyrie town, though when we got there after grinding up the hills, my skin-trader friend arranged with a builder to take me on to Sixmilecross, as I wanted to reach Omagh again by nightfall.

Perched on a pile of bricks I felt the wind rushing through my hair and I had before me, spread out like the map I had pored over in London, all the kingdoms of the earth. At least, Tyrone seemed like it that afternoon, as we rushed along by stone walls and hanging woods and hay-fields and green knolls, and whitewashed farms with barking dogs, running now under a tunnel of trees, now breasting a hill to see the chequerboard of fields and the blue-green hills ranged in infinite succession in the distance.

Then, farther on, this garden-like intimacy and greenness changed to the larger expanses and the more sombre colours of the moors. The country now looked deserted, hardly a house or a tree interrupted the stretches of wild cotton moors and bogs which were on the point of heathering.

Tyrone, above all others, is the county of the 'wee people', which is not surprising for the wee people have an eye for beauty as well as a love of secret, lonely places. They could not do better than Tyrone which has just the right mixture of beauty and loneliness. Part of the moors reminded me of similar landscapes I had seen in Iceland, where long stretches of country are lonely and weird and isolated, utterly silent except for the scrape of the pony's hooves over bare rock.

The sombre aspect of Tyrone's moors was intensified by recalling that during the Great Hunger, caused in 1845 when the potato blight first appeared, thousands of men, women and children crowded the country roads in abortive attempts to reach the soup-kitchens in the towns. They died of hunger by the roadside, their mouths filled with grass.

I bought some oranges at Sixmilecross Co-op and sat to eat them on a bench outside one of the little houses in the main street which was a miniature version of Cookstown. Swallows dive-bombed among the network of television aerials, narrowly avoiding head-on collisions with each other and with the walls and roofs of the houses.

A bus soon left for Omagh where I was glad of a week-end's humble roach-fishing in the Strule. And the modest catch was once again the cause of controversy with the local fishermen who held that my roach was in fact only a new-fangled name for rudd. With so many trout and salmon runs on their doorsteps, Ulster anglers adopt a superior attitude to coarse fishing. 'Vermin' is their comment, and many the curse there is to be heard when the delightful little perch is taken on flies by those fishing in the gloaming for trout.

Perhaps I regard pike fishing so highly because the record catch of my own youthful fishing days was taken in Lower Lough Erne, though this success of mine was a mere shadow compared with the local sixty-five pounder taken in the same waters many years before.

Hamilton Harty was one of those who loved Ulster's lakes and rivers. Nearly all his letters home mentioned fishing incidents. In July 1935 he wrote to Peter Montgomery 'Godfrey Brown is coming to fish for a couple of days. I am not deterred by the fear that the train I travelled by last evening became derailed near Dromore Road and tore up most of the already very un-permanent way. I was taking a 4½ lb trout back to England when the smash came. My only thought was whether the fish would be spoiled. Strange how one's mind works.'

On Monday morning I continued my journey but did not desert the beautiful Strule River for I followed its banks to Newtown-stewart. Again, I walked part of the way and then was given a lift by James Fulton who could still drive even though he had lost one arm in a threshing machine. His home was called Camp Hill Farm because James II and his army camped there on their way to the Siege of Derry in 1689.

'That's Bessy Bell and Mary Gray,' said James Fulton in a rich and musical brogue when he saw my interest in two mountains standing sentinel beyond the road. Then the farmer repeated a jingle he had learnt as a boy:

> *Bessy Bell and Mary Gray*
> *Were two lovely lassies*
> *They built their house upon the lea*
> *And covered it with rushes.*

Behind the woods on the other side of Bessy Bell lay the fine Georgian home of the Duke of Abercorn, Baronscourt, a house famous for its collection of old masters and the splendour of a room designed by Sir John Soane. The proximity of the ducal demesne could be seen in the town of Newtownstewart by the Abercorn Arms Hotel.

Newtownstewart's great glory was the river, which skirted the town. At one period the river must have been overlooked and guarded by the Scottish-looking castle which still stands at the end of the main street, though now a ruin with little more than a high stepped gable remaining, the rest of it being used to store 'Layer's Mash' and 'Pig Fattening Meal'. Part of the great fireplace was also left and a boy was burning Daz and Tide boxes in it, much to the irritation of the castle's last remaining occupants, the pigeons.

From the castle I could see the river, crossed just beyond the tiny town by a magnificent stone bridge, arching gracefully in noble strides across the Strule that had joined up with the Mourne River. The bridge rose in a beautiful arc and the water played musically round the stout buttresses and ran swirling through its six arches. I sat on the parapet for an hour or so basking like a lizard, and then strolled through the town again to try for another lift on to Strabane which an Omagh man finally gave me.

His mission that day was to attend the court proceedings against a woman customer who had bought a gas-cooker from him on hire purchase, and then had sold it and cleared off to England, from whence she had been brought to appear in court for her sins. The Omagh man said hire purchase firms rarely prosecuted though he supposed they had to make a stand occasionally. I said I supposed they did.

We passed through Sion Mills, which was nothing to do with those of God, but with spinning, for whose workers some high-minded person had constructed rows of Gothic cottages which were not without charm and reminded me of Christian IV's model housing at Copenhagen, built in the seventeenth century for his sailors. Sion Mills also boasted a new Roman Catholic church which was modern but church-like nevertheless and had an external mural of the Last Supper routed out in slabs of Westmorland slate. The workmen were giving the church its finishing touches.

The broad waters of the Mourne River that tumbled and rushed through the rocks at Sion Mills became the border between Strabane on one bank and Lifford, capital of County Donegal in the Republic on the other. I left the gas-cooker magnate beside another bridge and after a convoy of armoured cars passed over it, stood to admire its eight arches and the fast moving waters which were a most beautiful transparent dark amber. Houses clustered along the high bank and behind rose the massive forms of the hills of Donegal.

AMONG THE BUSHES

It seemed to me to be peculiarly perverse that Strabane grocers were selling tins of salmon and trout from Peru when the town is surrounded with rivers famous for their trout and salmon, and even the novice to the rod can be certain of a brown trout in Lough Allen. But equally odd were the Spanish plums and Guernsey tomatoes for sale in the heart of this rich farmland. Perhaps extra sales appeal was necessary. The local people may have been bored by the wonderful things around them. They certainly were in the past, for servants and farmworkers stipulated in their contracts that fresh salmon should be served at only a limited number of meals in the week.

However, this was the silly season and the shops were in the throes of their Summer Sales. Because on that day at least, I was not in need of any 'Blanket Ends' or long woollen drawers 'for cooler days' I went into the McHugh Himself Bar for a sandwich lunch. I did not know whether to be flattered or not when they mistook me for an American tourist. I must, they said, see the press inside Gray's printing works where John Dunlop had been apprenticed—the man who later printed America's Declaration of Independence, and who had also been the first man to have a daily newspaper in the States. But I knew all about John Dunlop and about Charles Thomson too, who had first written the Declaration in long hand.

History is absorbing, but so is human nature for it changes little from one century to the next, as attendance at any law court will show. I went out of Strabane duly fortified by McHugh Himself, passing the public weighbridge where little girls were trying to weigh their ponies. I was side-tracked by the irresistible smell of the oatmeal and maize mills of Robert Smyth and Sons and emerged just in time to see the gas-cooker man about to enter the court house opposite.

Petty Sessions in Ireland make even more amusing entertainment than their reportage in the local press. The gas-cooker runaway was not being heard for several hours because a long and complicated case was going on about a fight in which a series of wounds had been inflicted. The whole affair, it appeared, had started over some men in a pub who insisted on singing. I was dying to jump up and ask the court if it was because the television was on, that the land-lord seized a hammer and smashed four glasses and various bottles in his attempt to stop the singing men from breaking them.

The landlord was in the witness box and did not look the least like the hammer and glass sort. He was the most composed witness I had ever seen.

The lawyer—'Don't you think that these men seeing you coming armed with a hammer and baton might have thought they were going to be assaulted?'

The landlord—'They would not have been touched, Mister Solicitor.'

The doctor went into the box to give unbiased medical evidence about bruises and the length of cuts and the number of stitches put into the various pates involved.

I could not stay long enough to hear the outcome of these sorry events—which had befallen the publican and his singing customers on a beautiful summer evening in Sion Mills, which was, after all, supposed to be a *model* village.

7

Airs and Graces

—❦—

As though by poetry rather than geography, the Mourne River became the Foyle. But this river's geography *is* poetry—and music too, for few Irish rivers are more sung about than the beautiful Foyle. There is in its beauty something so innocent and lyrical, so sweet and gentle, something so fresh and shining as if the world had only just been made that morning and the first dew of the first day ever still lay about its meadows.

The River Foyle flows through North Tyrone and into Londonderry on one side and meanders tranquilly about the foothills of Donegal. It is impossible not to admire this land and want to cross the border into the Republican county of the old province of Ulster, whose business centre was once Strabane. Usually, the visitor to Strabane finds himself in Donegal in any case, drawn by the mystical beauty of the valleys and hills opening before him. He goes as though a spell were put on him, and as though protected by this spell he crosses the border without attracting the notice of the Customs Officers who, often as not, do not even stop the buses.

I was in the bus to Londonderry from Strabane and like a sort of Ulysses I allowed myself to be bound, metaphorically, to the bus seat so that the sirens singing from across the Foyle River should not lure me from my purpose of going to Derry. So for this journey I stayed on the Northern Ireland side of the river. This had the advantage of displaying the river and the range of distant country beyond in a long, sweeping panorama. The beautiful Plain of Raphoe lay across the river, a pastoral landscape with trees and bright green water-meadows and isolated Georgian houses with white cottages dotted on the hill-slopes rising gently from the river and the wide belt of meadow-land. In gaps between these nearer hills were the shadowed blue profiles, rounded and bold of the hills of Donegal. The noble hills receded, plane behind plane, into the distance. One sweeping, tree-dotted valley floor went for miles towards this distance, a mythical magical land indeed. Both sides of the river were well-farmed and presented a picture something like the road to Camelot:

> *On either side the river lie*
> *Long fields of barley and of rye,*
> *That clothe the wold and meet the sky;*
> *And thro' the field the road runs by*
> *To many-towered Camelot.*

Bearded barley *did* run for miles alongside the road and Tennyson seemed the right description for this scene of fields and thatched cottages out of picture postcards with buddleia in bloom over the hedges.

Other people saw the beauty and riches of Derry Vale long before I did, and these were the Guilds of London. They appropriated the whole lot in 1613 and parcelled the land out to its Grocers, Mercers, Fishmongers, Drapers, Skinners, Goldsmiths, Merchant Tailors, Tallow Chandlers, Haberdashers, Salters, Ironmongers, Vintonners and Cloth Workers. The settlers from England who moved in hailed mostly from around London. It was in this way that 'London' was added to 'Derry' making Londonderry, although, like the bishop who is still called simply the Bishop of Derry, even after three centuries most people still refer to the town as 'Derry'.

When the Guilds appropriated all this and put their own people in, the native Irish were either driven off the land or retained on the payroll of the settlers. These were called Servitors and for a time were placed under soldiers who had served the English cause against Ireland. The Livery Companies abused their supremacy and much ill-used the Irish. So bad in fact was their interpretation of the Plantation obligations that a Sir Thomas Phillips led a twenty-five-year long struggle against the City of London. Charles I allowed his advisers to take up Phillips's claim and at the Court of the Star Chamber the Settlers were fined £70,000 and much of their land forfeited. The City smarted under this royal disapproval of its deeds in Ireland and waited for an opportunity of revenge. Tension increased between the Court and the City, and when the Civil War finally broke, the City gladly went over to the Parliamentarian side.

It was Charles's son James II who rested near the farm at Camp Hill, which the farmer James Fulton had pointed out to me the previous day, while leading his men to the Siege of Derry. To the advancing armies the walled city must have looked much the same as it did when I saw it from the top of the bus from Strabane—except for the 'Ulster Fertilizer' factory on its waste ground full of gulls.

Derry is clustered round a hill rising above the River Foyle, which soon broadens into a lough to meet the sea. Beneath the walls of Derry the Foyle changes from a sweet country river and becomes a thoroughfare for ships, though it has none of the ugly excrescences and effluents which have ruined the approaches of most great rivers in England. From the opposite bank, Derry can be viewed complete before the bus turns sharply and runs across the long bridge over the Foyle, finally darting into the city's narrow streets.

Like most cities once small enough to be contained within an encircling wall, Derry has since spread beyond its earlier confines. But the wall itself, artillery-proof and wide enough to drive a carriage round, remains complete to this day. I found a small hotel on the east wall, and before lunch did the grand tour. I went up to the top of the wall by Coward's Bastion, buying the day's edition of *The Londonderry Sentinel* on my way. The front page headline was 'NEW BRA. FACTORY OPENS IN DERRY, *City chosen because female skills are renowned.*'

From the elevation of the city walls I could see that the ladies of Derry were skilled, for women sat busy at their sewing machines next door to McGinley's Ladies' Hairdressing Salon. What, I wondered, passed through the minds of the mums and big sisters as they sat under the plastic beehive hair-driers looking out at the seven great cannons? The guns were given to the city by the London Guilds in 1641, and which still stand on the wall built twenty years earlier—for only £8,357.

The day when Derry's apprentice boys closed the gates in the city wall in the face of James II's army still seems more real in Derry than the Great War of 1914. Derry was the nut James II had to crack if England was to become a Roman Catholic kingdom again. And the one hundred and five days of siege which began that day in 1689 still seem to be nearer in time than even the last war.

Lundy, Derry's governor, decided to get out while the going was good. He climbed over the city wall, making his way down by an old pear tree, and fled to the enemy's lines. His flight has earned him a dubious place in Derry's story and notoriety with posterity, for at the ceremonial closing of the gates, which is still done every year, Lundy, like Guy Fawkes, is burnt in effigy.

When Lundy deserted to the Jacobites, command of Derry's defence was taken over by George Walker. This fighting parson earned himself a more distinguished memorial than Lundy—a tall stone column topped by a statue of himself. I stood by the Royal Bastion craning my neck to see the Reverend Governor Walker. Rumour has it that the sword fell from the statue's hand on the very day that the Act of Catholic Emancipation was passed.

Derry cathedral stands within the walls and it was at this building, only completed some fifty years before the siege, that the besiegers fired a cannon ball bearing their terms of armistice. And it was in reply to this cannon ball that James II's army got the admirably worded reply—NO SURRENDER. Their reply has been the watchword of the Orange Order ever since.

No matter what happened, the Derry men would not give in, and so began what Macaulay called 'The most memorable siege in the annals of the British Isles', which was a polite way of describing the horrors of starvation and disease which ravaged the beleaguered city. Seven thousand inhabitants were dead, mainly from hunger, when the siege ended. During the siege, a handful of chickweed had cost a penny, a quart of horse blood a shilling, and the same price for a rat fattened on corpses. But at last, on 28th July, three relieving ships got through the vast boom of floating beams roped across the Foyle River. On 1st August, James II's army struck camp and marched away. Derry had come through the siege with no surrender.

The cannons, after their glory, still poke menacingly through the unbreachable walls. But now that the smoke of battles long-ago has cleared what is revealed beyond the old city? I walked on top of the walls peering over at rubbish-strewn waste sites and rows of shabby, decrepit houses. Acres of slate roofs finally made their way via the cemetery to the surrounding hills.

Compared with previous visits I had made, few political slogans were scrawled on Derry's walls and gables. I only saw the occasional 'Release the Prisoners' (a reference to political prisoners then held in Belfast's Crumlin Road jail). In several places people had written in white paint 'Give us a university'—a decided improvement on the old type of slogan of disparaging remarks about the Pope or the Queen.

While jotting a few observations down in my notebook by the famous Roaring Meg cannon a 5-year-old boy stood to watch me.

'What are ya writin', mister?'

'A story,' I said.

'What story?'

'A story about soldiers,' I answered.

My new friend paused. He pulled a face, as though he did not think much of stories about soldiers. Then he said 'My da's a *sailor*. See that boat down there?'

I saw it. It was a white one with a red and black funnel, lying below us in the harbour.

'That's my da's ship.'

His da's ship was one of many in Derry's harbour that day. Four Canadian warships were also tied up there, trim and clean in their coats of light grey paint. Canadian sailors swarmed through the town to the delight of young boys for whom the sailors never failed to 'put 'em up' when the children shot at them from the walls. The sailors had returned to the city because one of their shipmates had to face a murder attempt charge against a woman he had met on a previous visit. But not even the fact that the sailors were standing-by in case they were called as witnesses could keep the women from responding to the flashing eye and homely charm of the New World.

I had left my camera, I thought, on the bus from Strabane. But it had not been handed in at the bus depot and I was taken to read the notice-boards outside the police station where there were lists of lost property given in to the authorities. My camera was not amongst the 'screw drivers, babies' panties, spare wheels, rosary beads, ladies' dressing gowns' that crowded the lists. Fortunately, I found the camera later back in Omagh where I had left it.

A lady who I am sure never lost her dressing gown in a public place was Princess Macha of the Golden Hair, whom I much admired. Holding a bird, she sat in state in front of Altnagelvin Hospital outside the town. The fine bronze statue depicted this legendary princess who gained her reputation by reputedly being the first person to establish a hospital in Ireland at some time around 300 B.C.

Her hospital, I am sure, had nothing in common with the cloud-capped towers of the new Altnagelvin building. I much preferred the sculpture to the architecture. The princess was made by F. E. McWilliam, the distinguished Ulster sculptor. He is only known in Northern Ireland for this Princess Macha and a recent work at Queen's University. The Princess of the Golden Hair is very upright and very formal as befits a royal lady who is only a legendary one. She is also in a highly-stylized form which probably has caused eyebrows to be raised at the hospital by people who may well have preferred a conventional, realistic statue of Florence Nightingale and her lamp rather than the princess with her bird.

Still, the girl of the golden hair is there now and those responsible should be congratulated. Official taste in Ulster is not always so enlightened. Belfast Art Museum has another work of McWilliam's, the second copy of his bronze bust of the Ulster painter William Scott. The first copy of this is in the Tate Gallery, London, where it is paired with Scott's wife. To have the one bust without its mate seemed to me to be a curious acquisition for Belfast to have made.

Cathedral bells were ringing the hour when I woke next morning and looked from my hotel window at the broad walk along the top of the east wall. As I sat down in the dining-room to my snap-crackle-pop, I could not help thinking about the beleaguered citizens of 1689. What would they have said, on sitting down to their dinners of horse blood and boiled rat, if they had known that in three centuries' time the bells of their own Protestant cathedral would sound across the city with those of the Catholic one?

In view of the good round oaths and curses in which people of those days were expert, it did not bear thinking about. However, both sets of bells *were* ringing, advising me that if I was to catch the early bus along to Limavady I would have to hurry. Ulster food is not the sort which can be hurried, nevertheless by dint of gobbling and gulping I was away out in record time. Workmen were coming down the wall carrying their midday 'piece' and whistling. The milk-boy was doing his best to whistle in tune (it wasn't the *Londonderry Air* or anything sentimental like that, but *Come on, let's twist again like we did last summer*). The verger in the cathedral was a whistler also, as I had heard, but admittedly he kept to hymn tunes.

I had to do something of the twist myself in order to catch the bus but I caught it just in time and sat upstairs again, watching the River Foyle give way to the lough as the bus crossed a bridge, leaving Derry to lose itself behind bends in the road.

The sea adds an extraordinary dimension to landscape and an extraordinary range of colouring. The scrappy ugliness of new industrial development settled beyond Derry's walls like another besieging army, was swallowed whole in the immensity of white clouds reflected in the lough waters and the sight of blue hills across the water, silhouetted like sitting lions.

The London Grocers' Society gave charm to the village of Eglinton, the first one the bus from Derry passed through, and a former Lord Lieutenant gave it his name. Previously the place had been called Muff for the village stood at one end of Muff Glen. The North Irish Brigade was in residence at the local army camp and the tethered alsatian dogs looked as if they were expecting ban-the-bombers.

Ballykelly Forest covered the next mile or so and there were no further eye-sores until an R.A.F. camp came into view the other side of the woods. The R.A.F. boys were lying out in singlets taking advantage of the sun, while the cattle were doing exactly the opposite by standing in pools of shade beneath the chestnuts to escape the biting clegs, their tails going to and fro like punkahs pulled by invisible strings.

As a special claim to distinction Ballykelly boasts a fine church

spire built under the patronage of Earl Bishop Hervey. It intrigued
me to know what little Ballykelly did to merit this mark of favour
from the extraordinary father-in-God whose name is still known
across Europe by the Bristol Hotels where he stayed. But perhaps
the rector of Ballykelly had merely been in one of the athletic events
which his lordship held for his clergy. The Bishop made vast ban-
quets to which he invited gout-ridden archdeacons and doddery
deans. When they were glutted and dizzy with the choicest malmsey
he made them run races, competing with younger and longer-legged
curates.

The races, however, were of considerable interest, for the
winners always received substantial prizes, either in the form of
promotion within the ranks of the church, or in the equally tangible
form of a new rectory or church spire. The episcopal grace and
favour might, on the other hand, have been won by a mere whim.
One curate, on raising his glass of Madeira to propose 'a rot amongst
the rectors' was immediately made a rector by the eccentric Bishop.

Another scorching day had set in and the oven-like top of the
bus was decidedly less pleasing than the River Roe where I went
swimming as soon as we got to Limavady. There was a warm breeze
which, together with the sun, were sufficient to dry me on coming
out of the river. Some American anglers who espied me among the
bulrushes like an overgrown Moses, complained they had walked
for six miles up the river's tidal stretches and had not got a strong
enough wind for taking trout with fly, though they had waited all
day to catch the favourable ebb tide.

Limavady was lively, unlike some other of the dreamy country
towns, and surprisingly, in a way which reminded me of Omagh's
hilltop, its main street had a strong French quality though perhaps
this atmosphere of the *place* in a French town was created simply by
the trees planted in rows down the street. Thomas Sandby did a
pen drawing of Nottingham's market square in the eighteenth
century, and Limavady reminded me of this drawing. Limavady had
the flat archways leading through to yards behind which are common
in all small Ulster towns. The town also seemed to have almost
entirely escaped any vulgar improvements and additions, the notable
exception being the new Post Office. I cannot imagine why the

Post Office architect thought 1930-Brewer's-Dutch was suitable for this almost perfect Georgian town or, indeed, any other town. Apart from this blemish, Limavady more than any other place in Ulster, except possibly Armagh, gives the best idea of what Irish towns must have looked like in Georgian times.

Limavady boasts a fine collection of Georgian wooden doorcases, each with a fanlight different in design from the next. The two most interesting houses were the police barracks and the war memorial house across the road. Sir Thomas Phillips once lived in Limavady, the man who led the fight in the Star Chamber against the London Guilds. He was given the lands around the town for a 'cabbage garden'.

The parish church was locked but the churchyard was not and I was able to see some beautifully carved slate tombstones, splendidly decorated with the flowing calligraphy peculiar to that medium. Two old men leaning by the gate followed my progress. Their amazement was evident that so young a man should be so occupied with something which would soon, in the inevitable nature of things, occupy them.

'What's that called?' I asked them, on my way out. They looked to the headlands jutting out into the sea.

'The proper name is Benevenagh,' the two old men said in chorus, 'but we call it Magilligan's Point, for short.'

Although trains no longer run to Limavady the railway station is used for buses and I boarded one going along the coast to Downhill, by way of Benevenagh and the fantastic basalt escarpment which runs for miles, rising from the coastal land for all the world like the inaccessible castles of the Assassins in Persia.

Suddenly I saw the sea. It appeared unexpectedly, immediately ahead of the bus, breaking in long white crests over the flat sands with the cliffs rising, grass-tufted, just behind. This was Downhill, a haphazard hamlet of a few scattered houses. I got off the bus and marvelled again at Ulster's seashores, sandy without pebbles or tar deposits, perfect for a family seaside holiday, but almost always deserted. On a headland just beyond the bay stood Mussenden temple, an eighteenth-century monument, haloed with circling gulls. From the sea beneath the temple rose a pinnacle of rock like a pharos, and beyond that, in the recesses of distance, more headlands with barely discernible white breakers at their feet.

I went into the bar of the Downhill Hotel which shelters immediately beneath the cliffs and echoes with the soft, continual roar of the sea. I took my drink across the road on to the sands again, tasting the fine salt spray on my lips and breathing in deeply the fresh sweet sharpness of ozone.

Down to these sands Frederick Augustus Hervey, Earl of Bristol, Bishop of Derry had brought his clergy for donkey races against the Presbyterian ministers. His episcopal paunch would have quivered with mirth as he watched clerics even fatter than himself thrown off their donkeys one by one along the course.

It was from Downhill that the Earl Bishop rode out in 1783 to attend the Convention of Volunteers in Dublin. He sat in an open landau robed in purple, and his knee and shoe buckles were of diamonds, while his white gloves were gold laced. His nephew, the wild and notorious George Robert Fitzgerald went as companion, similarly attired for this almost royal progress to Dublin. The six horses drawing the carriage were caparisoned with purple trappings, and in addition to a troop of servants and lackeys a whole troop of dragoons in full dress uniforms was in attendance on his lordship.

The Bishop, however, had things other than silk and lace up his sleeve. He had given a great deal of money to the Volunteer movement as well as a battery of guns engraved 'Open Thou our lips O Lord, and our mouths shall show forth Thy praise'. His regal appearance and large entourage was meant to impress the Volunteer Convention with his power and wealth. Probably it did but, much to his lordship's disappointment, the Volunteers did not elect him as their president, so depriving the Earl Bishop of this first step on the way to getting the crown of an independent Irish kingdom.

But Hervey was not the man to sulk. If he could not actually *be* a king, at least he could live like one. In the Earl's day, great men expressed their greatness in buildings, and Hervey himself set to, building so many edifices that he became known as the Edifying Bishop.

After an excellent lunch I climbed up the steep road behind the hotel to find Downhill Palace itself. Although the lodges to the

Lion Gates were lived in, a shadow of ruin fell over the approach to the palace, even among the bright glory of the barley fields. But the Lion Gates were a taste of beauty to come, even though one of the lions had lost its tail and looked like a Manx cat. The gateposts had niches flanked by delicately proportioned Doric columns and a frieze above enriched with reliefs of ox-skulls and garlands.

Beyond the gates, rising above the barley, stood the mansion itself, roofless and gutted on a ridge.

Writing from his palace the Bishop invited a friend to 'Come and imbibe some fix'd or unfix'd air at Downhill where a tree is no longer a rarity since about 200,000 have this winter been planted in my glens round the house. Come and enjoy the rapidity and the success with which I have converted sixty acres of moor by the medium of two hundred spades into a green carpet sprinkled with white clover. . . .'

Not a grove of this forest remains today, and I walked up to the shell of the palace through nothing but rolling barley. Gone also are the thousands of pictures and statues which had made Lord Bristol the delight of French and Italian artists. Only a herd of bullocks wandered through the great rooms, under the open sky. Nothing filled the windows except the sky. The scrolls carved along the main frieze stopped against nothing but sky. Weeds, knowing no better, had sprouted from the tops of walls. Lichens had added their rich patina to the pilasters of the upper floors. Behind rusticated walls at ground level, a quiet disintegration was going on in the vaulted chambers supporting the floors of the *piano nòbile* above. Some of these vaulted chambers had collapsed already into heaps of rubble. Others were green-stained with damp and water dripping from them had formed long stalactites hanging from the vaults.

The Bishop of Derry went to Rome for two years in 1777 because his son had inclinations towards architecture. When the Bishop returned he found that he had succeeded to the earldom of Bristol, with another £20,000 a year to his already large fortune. Downhill was one of the results of the Bishop's travels and wealth. Much taste and much skill went into the making of this building, whose two wings extended towards the sea, and which could have been such an adornment in modern Ulster. But alas, in Ulster as elsewhere, wealth and power are divorced from culture, a sad fact which the Earl Bishop would not have understood.

Still less would he have understood had he been alive a few years ago to watch his great and beautiful house having its roof removed for scrap. With the roof gone, the winter gales sweeping across the headlands from the Atlantic will soon make short work of what few fragments still remain of fantastic plasterwork and exquisite examples of the mason's art such as the wafer-thin helical staircase I found. As I picked my way among the pathetic heaps of fallen stones, I thought again of Farmer Coulter who had bought John Nash's Killymoon as £100 worth of scrap but had saved the building.

Downhill's magnificence must have had few rivals during its hey-day. Yet the Earl Bishop was far from being the quiet-living prelate and connoisseur. One of his favourite tricks was to scatter flour on the floors in the servants' quarters after dark so that by the tell-tale footprints he could see which pantry-boy went to bed with which kitchen-maid. The Bishop himself was not above such *affaires*. One of his most long-lasting liaisons, still going strong in his old age, was with the mistress of Frederick William II of Prussia, the Countess Lichtenau. Hervey wrote frequently and copiously to this lady, pouring out his passion for her not only in terms which could leave no doubt in her mind about his feelings, but with an intimacy which would have been a scandal coming from any pen, let alone a bishop's.

Hervey, however, was a man of parts. He was mean in nothing he did. His fleshly passion was matched by prodigality, and the greatness of his ambition by equally great affection for those around him. To complete the wonder of his palace at Downhill, the Bishop built a Temple of the Winds right on the cliff edge, lying on the centre axis of the great house itself which was built farther back from the cliffs. He dedicated this circular, domed temple to his cousin Mrs. Frideswide Mussenden.

By good fortune this superb building has escaped the palace's fate by falling into the National Trust's hands rather than into ruin. The temple is certainly one of Ireland's most beautiful eighteenth-century buildings and its cliff-top site, commanding wide sweeps of the Atlantic and the bluffs and headlands of the coast and the shadow of the Scottish mountains on the horizon, is without parallel. Michael Shanahan is thought to have been the architect, using Tivoli's Temple of Vesta as a model.

The approach to the temple from the house was down a path leading straight to the cliff edge between two fields of barley where only the gulls and faint sea sounds disturbed the afternoon. The temple was quite circular with tall sash windows lighting the single room which had a coffered ceiling and was big enough to be used as the library for the palace. This beautiful room, like those in the house was supported on ingenious vaulting in the chamber below. And the temple, like the palace, had a sensitive use of Classical motifs. The frieze reliefs were of exquisitely carved drapery caught by rings on the underside of the entablature, interspersed with bronze letters quoting from Lucretius, which might be rendered:

> *It is pleasant to see from the safe shore*
> *The pitching of ships and hear the storms' roar.*

The Bishop sat in this room with all the winds of the four quarters caressing and battering its stones. He would have sat over his books and drawings in a gaudy robe of crimson silk with purple stockings, or perhaps in green satin with a silver-spangled sash while writing one of his passionate letters to Countess Lichtenau, or addresses to the 'Freeholders and Inhabitants of Maghera' or the 'Volunteer Corps of the Province of Connaught' or inviting a 'black Indian preacher from New England' to tour the country.

Until 1786 his frequent companion was the disreputable nephew, George Robert Fitzgerald. But only three years after this curiously assorted pair made their spectacular journey to the Dublin convention, George was hanged on the gallows. The Bishop could hardly have been in ignorance of the young man's escapades. Kidnapping was a favourite sport and George's own father fell victim to it. One thing led to another, however, and George was found guilty of murder and executed at Castlebar in 1786. I wondered if the Bishop assumed one of the disguises he used on his visits to fortune-tellers and witches, and travelled incognito through the night to attend his nephew's midnight interment in the family tomb.

Even if he did, the Bishop survived his good-for-nothing relative by almost two decades, years crammed with a frenzy of art collecting. In 1798 the French authorities arrested the Earl Bishop in Italy and his vast collection of antiques was seized. He was imprisoned in a castle in Milan. But three hundred and forty-five artists of different nations signed and gave the French a petition which secured the collection on payment of £10,000. But a week later this valuable collection destined for Downhill was plundered and none of it ever reached the Bishop's cliff-top palace.

After his release from prison the Bishop wrote home to his diocese about the injustice of Presbyterians having to pay a preacher they did not want to hear, and on 3rd May 1799 he wrote to Nelson about his 'nine months confinement' in Milan and the discontented French officers he met—'one the chief engineer to Bonaparte whose avarice led him to employ this man in composing an atlas in 30 sheets'. Hervey turned war correspondent and reported one battle to the great admiral as 'a *fleur d'eau*, laying the town in ashes, burning the arse'.

Then on a hot summer's day in 1803, while riding outside Rome, the Earl Bishop had a severe attack of gout and was taken to a peasant's house. But the owners recognized the great traveller and were too frightened to have a heretic prelate die in their house. For fear of priestly or divine retribution, the stricken Bishop of Derry was carried to an outbuilding and there the builder of palaces died.

The irony of his death was not simply that the lordly man died in a shed but also that Catholics had been responsible for this. In parliament Hervey had championed the relaxation of the penal laws in Ireland. His efforts were principally responsible for the passing of the act which relieved Roman Catholics from the oath of supremacy.

But Italian peasants could hardly be expected to know the subtler points of Irish politics and so their superstitions, not surprisingly, got the better of them. Superstition also terrified the sailors who were to carry Hervey's body back home. In the end his corpse was put in a crate labelled ANTIQUE STATUE.

In Derry, however, the peasants' and sailors' attitude to the great man was offset to some extent by contributions made towards his memorial both by the Roman Catholic clergy and the non-Conformist ministers. Frederick Augustus Hervey had many sides to his nature and even in his lifetime became a legend in the land of legends. John Wesley had spent a Sunday with him in 1775 and was deeply moved by the 'admirable solemnity' with which the Bishop celebrated Holy Communion.

Lord Charlemont, however, who had years of experience in which to judge the builder of Downhill described him as 'a bad father, a worse husband, a determined deist, very blasphemous in his conversation, and greatly addicted to intrigue and gallantry'. Boswell wrote of him as 'the learned and ingenious Hervey'. Voltaire said, 'The Bishop of Derry has as much brilliance as Lord Chesterfield and more of the solid.' But perhaps Hervey is best summed up by a contemporary who wrote of him as a student going to the Inns of Court 'but his Parts were too lively for the plodding Gravity of that profession and he then turned his thoughts to the Church'.

At the time it was said that 'This world consists of men, women, and Herveys'. But of course, the Earl of Bristol could not know that though he fancied himself as an ambassador or viceroy, to posterity he would be simply the Bishop of Derry and founder of Hervey's sauce and the man behind the name of the Continent's numerous Bristol hotels.

No doubt the Earl Bishop experienced some regret in his last hours at not seeing his beautiful palaces in Ireland again. The regret he would experience on seeing them today would be keener still. I left his Downhill estate by another way and found the twentieth century clamouring at his gates. A swarm of labourers and machines were there engaged on a road-widening operation. The road was one which the Earl Bishop had originally caused to be laid by his 'medium of two hundred spades'. I hoped that his own gates would not be destroyed in the improvements.

The Cantrell and Cochrane mineral water representative pulled up and offered me a lift to Coleraine. Downhill Palace and the beautiful Temple of the Winds stood out clearly on their headland as we dropped down to the coast again, passing through Castlerock. This was a tiny settlement consisting almost entirely of summer houses. Yet it had a large golf course and clubhouse. I asked my mineral water friend if, as certainly seemed, every village had a golf course. He laughed and said almost every village. He knew that Castlerock collected a large week-end crowd. And later I was told that in the Six Counties there were sixty full-blown golf courses.

'Something to do with Ulster's fine green turf,' I suggested, trying to hide my ignorance about golf. The game was a newcomer to the town since the days of the beautiful *Kitty of Coleraine*, justly celebrated in the famous song, ignorance of which would be quite inexcusable in an Ulsterman.

The song, published anonymously in 1810, gave Coleraine greater fame than even St. Patrick gave it by calling the place 'The Corner of the Ferns' in the fifth century, or by St. Bernard of Clairvaux calling it 'a city' in the twelfth century. In more recent times Coleraine also enjoyed fame because of the H.C. Whisky made there, which had so amused the Japanese visitors on the train to Portrush. *Kitty of Coleraine* is still well known but another song about the town I knew in childhood is seldom heard now:

> *Cleopatra once gave a great banquet,*
> *And sent for her wines off to Spain,*
> *But knowing Mark Antony's weakness*
> *She smuggled a cask of Coleraine.*

For me, however, Coleraine needed no more than just its situation on the banks of the wide and beautiful River Bann to be worthy of notice—the 'fishy fruitfull Bann' as Edmund Spencer termed it in the sixteenth century. The river is deep enough here for biggish ships to come up from the coast and use its quays. With its meadow-flanked lands, its salmon-passes and eel-weirs, the gulls following the ships, the town is as beautiful as St. Patrick's name 'Corner of the Ferns' suggests and as fishy as Spencer thought it.

I walked over the bridge and followed the river out of the town. The local handbook said that twenty-five million elvers went up the river in the annual ascent. The book failed to say what percentage of the eelfares descended the river again, for eels constitute an enormous industry at Coleraine. It was St. Patrick who taught the Bann Valley people how to fish by day, doubtless to keep them from poaching by night. But it is certain that the saint did *not* teach his young converts how to convert the river algae into explosives.

The River Bann's marginal ooze consists of billions of diatoms which the microscope reveals as exquisitely formed cells of geometrical design. They have shells in two halves fitting precisely like a box and its lid. When the living algae die a siliceous deposit is left and there are sufficient quantities of this to be used commercially in the manufacture of explosives—and confectionery.

Also going in the up-river direction apart from eelfares, were six dead sheep in the van of John McKay, the local butcher of Garvagh, or rather, as butchers still term themselves in much of Ulster, the 'flesher' of Garvagh.

Irish signposts and Irish miles are traditionally a source of amusement although having once arrived at a destination there could be no surer guide to local history than the pub signs. Garvagh was no exception to this rule for the Canning Arms pub was evidence of that family's influence in the district. To some extent Garvagh had moved with progress and the village could now boast a 'Sally's Hair Stylist'. George Canning, the British Prime Minister of the early nineteenth century, would probably have had distinct opinions about his village's progress, though he did claim to have 'called the New World into existence, to redress the balance of the Old'.

From Flesher McKay's van of six dead sheep I transferred to a lorry-load of sixty very-much-alive, 4-month-old pigs on their way to be fattened at Castledawson. But when we got to Maghera—The Field of the Solemn Vespers—I thought it time to consider the problem of a bed for the night and so I left the porkers to finish their journey and the last eight weeks of their lives.

I bought a new pair of sandals at Maghera's Trustworthy Boot Store and crossed the road to McMaster's thatched pub in order to christen my purchase. It was, by the time I had finished, more of a launching than a christening. Three young plasterers were celebrating the end of their week's work on some new houses in the town before driving to their homes in Magherafelt, and soon included me in the rounds of Guinness. We moved into the farm kitchen behind the bar, for although this was a pub in the middle of the town, calves were crying up the yard, waiting to be fed.

Sitting by the open hearth was a big farmer who looked as if he might have come down from winning hay in the mountains. And this was exactly what he had been doing. He was proud of belonging to the mountains and of having 'to lift the cow subsidy'.

When I asked him what Slaghtneill, his farm's name, meant, he laughed. Why would I want to know a thing like that? But it was an Irish name and the local expert on such matters was the solicitor up the road. His office hours were over but nevertheless the publican's wife or sister went to find him and get a translation.

'I could take you out to see it,' offered the farmer by the fire, 'but there's nothing yonder but Her,' he added insisting I had a whisky to support my pints of Guinness.

While the young woman was gone to consult the law, one of the plasterers asked, on account of my interest in names, if I had ever heard a Christian name like his own before—Celestine. Had I, he said, as though I were some sort of oracle, any idea where it came from. But the mountain farmer got the answer in before me.

'I'll tell you who Celestine was,' he said with a glint in his eye. 'He was the Pope that allowed the English to come here, may God forgive him.'

The girl returned then just in time to save a dispute about Pope Celestine's merits or demerits, bearing a typewritten note from the lawyer's office. The note explained that the name Slaghtneill derived from the pile of stones beneath which Nial the Black-kneed was interred. Since they had put themselves to so much trouble in order to oblige me, I did not like to disagree with this explanation. However, I thought it much more probable that it was only the place where the famous Nial Glundubh, the tenth-century King of Ireland had fallen in battle, for I well knew the slope of Tibraddan mountain near Dublin where the popular king is in fact buried.

I kept this to myself but pleased the mountain farmer by telling him that a proud family heirloom of the Macleod of Macleod in Dunvegan Castle on the Isle of Skye, was King Nial's communion cup. The farmer of Slaghtneill was highly delighted at the attention I was paying to his little mountain farm and wanted me to go up there with him and stay the night. However, the three plasterers had already offered to put me up in Magherafelt for the night, and they were anxious to get home, eat a meal and be away out for the night's bingo session.

Magherafelt—The Plain of the Rushes—had a spacious market-place arranged, rather unusually at a crossroads, built in Georgian times under the influence of the Salters' Company of London. An electric cross burnt before a Sacred Heart as we sat in the kitchen eating our high tea in a house opposite the police barracks. And although there was potato bread, as elsewhere in Ulster including Belfast's hotels, there was no boxty. To be a good boxty baker, using grated raw potatoes mixed with flour, was the sign of a good housewife when I was a boy. The girls used to have a rhyme:

> *Boxty on the griddle, boxty on the pan,*
> *If you can't bake boxty, you'll never get a man.*

My friends were anxious to get away in good time for the drive of fifteen miles or so to the evening's bingo down across the Tyrone border. They would take me to Arboe on Lough Neagh's western shore where for centuries a famous high cross had stood, one of the finest specimens of this kind of cross in Ireland. Unlike English roads, those in Ulster, wherever the terrain permits, go straight for long stretches, so that it is possible to drive very fast. My plaster friends did just this, with speedometer needle hovering uncertainly between sixty and seventy. Clouds of midges dancing in the roads told us that Lough Neagh was not far away.

In no time I found myself sitting in Devlin's Bar at Arboe, talking to the fishermen while waiting for the landlord's daughter who would take me down to the lough shore to see the high cross and the ruined abbey. The fishermen wore cloth caps, for all the world like men in a back-street pub in the north of England. The peculiar pollan fish they caught in Lough Neagh, a type of freshwater herring, did in fact go off to cloth-capped Manchester, just as their crates of live eels were sent to Billingsgate.

Anne Devlin kindly responded to her father's phone call and came across from their house and walked with me down the midge-clouded lane to the old high cross. The stone carvings, arranged in twenty-two panels on both sides of the cross, showed a remarkable kind of discipline in the way they were designed, though there was no trace I could discern of Roman Classical carving. In Ireland in the A.D. 900s perhaps ancient Rome was all but forgotten. The cross, however, 'did' the Bible rather like an American tourist 'doing' Europe—from Adam and Eve under a tree in Eden to Christ coming in judgement, in twenty-two scenes! Anne did not know the biblical story which all the panels illustrated though there was a local man called Isaac who could still translate the whole cross. In the eight-eenth century, pilgrims came to Arboe Cross and while praying walked round it on their knees.

Such excesses of pious penance were no doubt an excellent and harmless way of letting off masochistic steam—certainly the rounded stones of Lough Neagh's shores must have given some delicious pain, particularly as the water's edge, in those days, was much nearer than it is today. To supervise the delights of self-inflicted pain, an abbey stood near by, probably founded by St. Colman Macaidhe towards the end of the sixth century. An enemy clan, however, from across the other side of Lough Neagh, raided and destroyed the abbey three years before the first Anglo-Norman landing in Ireland.

The abbey has been a ruin ever since, and a well-preserved one too. It says much for the skill of those early masons that the exposed walls have withstood the wind and weather for eight centuries. Part of the reason for this long survival is ascribed to the strong milk of a large cow which came out of Lough Neagh. This cow's milk was used to mix the mortar of the abbey stones and the mythical-magical cow even gave the place its name, for Arboe means 'The Hill of the Cow'.

Anne Devlin thought 'High Cow' was a more attractive transla-tion, useful for describing things other than Arboe! She took me to a corner of the ruined abbey's churchyard to the Wishing Tree. This churchyard beech was so stabbed and embedded with pins and pennies and even army trouser buttons, that the tree had died, no doubt from copper poisoning. Its trunk looked like an old ship covered with barnacles. Sticking a penny edge-wise into the tree trunk was supposed to bring luck.

Late evening haymaking was going on in the field beyond the abbey ruins, though it was no Pre-Raphaelite scene but the petrol-smelling process of mechanical baling. My own quarrel with haymaking by machine was that it affected the bird life of the meadows. My boyhood summers were filled with the *crek crek* of the male corncrake. The sound was everywhere, at night as well as by day, coming from the meadows and pastures. But nowadays with machines repeatedly cutting the after-grass in the fields for silage throughout the summer months, the corncrakes have nowhere to breed in the secrecy so essential to their nature. Their penetrating and persistent call has almost disappeared from many districts.

Going back along the lane towards her father's bar, Anne pointed to an elderly man working in a field. 'That's Isaac, holding the lamb by the lugs,' she said.

I looked at the old man who could translate the high cross panels. Tired though I was at one in the morning when I got back to Magherafelt I did not need Isaac to translate the printing on the converted millers' sack sheets which said 'Turkey Starter'.

This turkey did not start too early next morning. With the pressing generosity which was more typical of Ulster than either its brogue or its landscape, I had an invitation to stay at Dunadry, the County Antrim home of Paddy Falloon. This was across the other side of Lough Neagh from Arboe and I went there, already prepared to some extent for what I was to find, since Paddy Falloon was famous for his taste and works as an amateur architect. Louis MacNeice had first told me about Dunadry and had planned to stay there the very week of his death.

Dunadry is one of the most beautiful houses in the county. It was nothing more than a rural slum when Paddy Falloon found it, and began, with his peculiar genius to give the place a new beauty. Dunadry was never a country house, but originally a paper mill built by William and Daniel Blow, court printers to William III. Later, until 1936, Dunadry was used for linen bleaching and by the American Army during the last war from whom Paddy Falloon took it over—a two-acre scab on the Antrim countryside.

Paddy, a maker of bricks much admired by practising architects in Ulster, and his wife Helen set out to work on Dunadry. Down came the hundred-foot chimney stack. In went a water-garden to one mill dam, and in went a swimming-pool to the other. The factory yards became walled gardens with clematis and wistaria around Oxford-smooth lawns. The twenty derelict village cottages were rebuilt to make an hotel of thirty self-contained suites.

And in the middle of all this was the factory itself, now transformed into a beautiful house, the Georgian industrial architecture glorified far beyond its humble original purpose. The floors were of Oriental woods, and between the deep-set windows hung paintings by modern artists including Cherith McKinstry and George MacCann. There were also some works of Paul Nietzsche, the Russian who became one of Belfast's most spectacular figures.

Jack Loudan has written a play *Trouble in the Square* about the Belfast people who tried to have Paul Nietzsche removed during the last war because he was an alien and indulged in the highly-suspect and dangerous practice of painting still-lifes and flowers. A self portrait by him hangs at Dunadry showing the high forehead and noble face framed by long white hair and the distinctive-looking goatee beard. I preferred Mercy Hunter's quick sketch of this remarkable man, for it showed the Russian painter in the patriarchal splendour of old age, the beard full and flowing by this time, the eyes penetrating in the way I remembered them from my own earlier years in Belfast.

I used to see this striking, most un-Ulster figure, striding through Belfast like a prophet—though he was probably prophesying nothing more than a few hours' enjoyment at Mercy Hunter's where he could speak Russian with her and devour one of her enormous goulashes.

Paul Nietzsche loved Ulster and Ulster people, even after the 'trouble in the square' when some were playing at Holy Inquisition about resident foreigners during the war. I was glad to see the canvas of himself by himself in the drawing-room at Dunadry. He looked like a Russian priest or mystic. And perhaps it was an element of mysticism that haunts Ulster life which kept this strange, gifted man captive in Belfast rather than Paris or London.

8

Another Road in Time

When I was at street-urchin age, rather than go to Saturday morning cinema, I rode out of Belfast on the backs of lorries. Cowboys and Indians were all right, but not so all right as the cold country lanes of a February day when I could see the barren strawberry bloom. And summer days spent on the sands of County Down cutting biblical texts in the sand for the design competitions were a poor substitute for being up on the mountain with ring-ouzel and my own secret dreams of the moors.

I cannot remember my first Charlie Chaplin film. This is a serious forgetfulness in these sophisticated times. But what were films to me? I could remember the first, thrilling sight of peregrine falcon, the rapid flight and sudden, vertical drop on unsuspecting waders.

I was born and grew up in Belfast but from the beginning I disliked its streets and longed for the country. Perhaps the most exciting day in my life, either before or since, was when our school-teacher told us we were going to be evacuees. The German air-raids were going to send us not merely to the country, but to County Fermanagh, the magical county in the west.

This was the county that, unlike the other five counties of Northern Ireland, had no need of Lough Neagh's shores because it had a huge lough all its own—Lough Erne, crowded with islands, surrounded by mountains, haunted by legends, garlanded by purple loosestrife, the secret waters of common scoter and home of golden-eye.

It does not do to break the spell of childhood magic. It is wrong to trample on the gossamer memories with grown-up's shoes. Too often, the once-wonderful place looks small or tawdry when revisited, or the favourite hideouts vanished or the old friends gone. It does not do to destroy our past.

But it was always right for me to go back to Fermanagh afterwards. Each return still excites me as much as that very first day in the war when, along with hundreds of other evacuees, I climbed out of the train at Enniskillen station, gas-mask in one hand, borrowed suitcase in the other. My later travels around the world only made my home-comings sweeter and more poignant.

Two years had passed since my previous visit to Fermanagh and I knew the countryside would be changed, but I also knew it would not be changed beyond recognition. The biggest change, of course, was that for years now there has been no railway to Enniskillen beyond Omagh. But although sad, this is no problem transport-wise. Within minutes of leaving Omagh station I got a lift with a family going on a pilgrimage to Lough Derg where, on an island, St. Patrick had a vision of Purgatory. Thousands of people pass through County Fermanagh every year on such pilgrimages, as thousands from all over Europe have done for centuries.

Lough Derg's fame today is overshadowed by other shrines. But in the Middle Ages it had few rivals. The story of Knight Owen going there as a pilgrim in 1147 gave the world an early best seller, with seventy-four Latin versions of the story in circulation by 1500, as well as translations into almost every European language. Pope Alexander VI, pausing in the midst of his Roman orgies, decreed in 1497 that the Lough Derg pilgrims' excesses had gone far enough and he ordered the Purgatory on the island to be destroyed. However, Pope Pius III revoked this seal of the Fisherman's Ring and by the seventeenth century Pedro Calderón de la Barca, the famous Spanish poet, was writing a play about Lough Derg. It had also appeared in an earlier poem by Ludovico Ariosto, though the point remains debatable as to whether Shakespeare or Dante got their ideas of Purgatory from the pilgrim stories of Lough Derg.

The twentieth-century pilgrims who gave me a lift in their car had been twice before to Lough Derg. They were making their third trip because they believed that if they could withstand the rigours of its penance and fasting three times they would be certain of heaven. 'In any case,' the comfortable wife assured me, 'even if I don't get as far as heaven, it is the only way I can take dieting seriously.'

I left the pilgrim band in order to get to Irvinestown where I had been before, though not during its Sunday morning sleep. It is difficult to believe that this small, sleepy market town is the second largest town in County Fermanagh. But Fermanagh, like other places in Ireland, has suffered from the decimation of its people during the past hundred years. Before the Great Famine of 1846 more than 150,000 people lived in County Fermanagh. Only 51,000 were left in the county at the census taken two years ago. There are even fewer people today in the county than in 1940 when I drove into Irvinestown on a farm cart with a sow which was to be mated.

But although a lot of people have gone, I was pleased to see one well-known man who had not. I found him sitting in the same doorway I had known twenty years before. Matt Valentine, the horse dealer in Sabbath boots and best cap, scarcely looked any older in that Sunday sun pouring through the windows on to saddles and breeching, winkers and bits. His legs were not as nimble as they used to be in the days of Irvinestown's fairs that I remembered, yet because it was such a fine warm Sunday he offered to take me out to see his new Arab mare and foal.

'I've got a grand wee tub-trap for sale,' Matt added after I excused myself by saying I must get some lunch first. I knew horses of old, one led to another, and Sunday went in no time. Matt did not let me go, however, without making me a parting gift for luck and this was an old horse-brass for me to take back to England.

My boyhood years in Fermanagh had brought me into contact with many men like Matt Valentine. They were shrewd and knowledgeable and knew a good horse when they saw one. Horses were in their blood. Nowadays most of the horses have gone and most of the fairs too. It does not need so much experience or character to sell tractors.

But Irvinestown still has its market as I saw on the notice of the town's market trustees who made the following charges to traders on market days, 'Timber and Rope £1, Boots and Shoes £1, Second-hand Clothes 5/-, Farm Produce 2/6.'

It was Sunday and no pubs were open. I joined some children in thirst-quenching at the village pump and went in search of a place to stay. I certainly did not expect something so fine behind the modest façade of Mahon's Hotel. The airy and light, almost Scandinavian atmosphere about the place appealed to me immediately. I was given a comfortable, bright bedroom and a lunch which kings would not have complained about. Through my bedroom window I could see the stone tower of an old chapel of ease. Although centuries old this tower was a newcomer to the district compared with the ancient ruins on an island in Lough Erne I saw in the afternoon.

After lunch I walked in almost tropical heat to Castle Archdale. Fermanagh's summer days of twenty years ago had been like that when many wells and sheughs dried up and cattle stood panting in any shade they could find.

Fermanagh's countryside had been full of soldiers and airmen in those war-time days. Not only was the county Britain's most westerly territory but the lough provided excellent bases for seaplanes on U-boat patrols. The great *Bismarck* was finally tracked down by one of the planes from the lough, so leading to the sinking of the enormous battleship.

Castle Archdale was an R.A.F. camp and I had friends there who liked to cycle with me round the countryside or fish in the lough. There was hardly a lane, or a part of the shore good for fishing, where a figure in blue or khaki could not be found, wondering how to fill off-duty hours, how to kill the tedious and dangerous days that must pass before the end of the war.

As I walked through the new forestry plantation in Castle Archdale along lonely, densely green paths, I wondered how many of those servicemen remembered County Fermanagh. Perhaps most of them had been bored by the woods and pheasants, by the beauty of Lough Erne and its water, and fretted for bright lights and noise, like city people often do when away from home. They would hardly know Castle Archdale today. The R.A.F. moved away a few years ago, and now even the eighteenth-century mansion itself is as silent as the ruin of the Plantation castle down the road.

I threaded my way along overgrown paths to look again at the fragment of Jacobean wall which is all that remains of the first castle, an Aztec-like ruin standing mysteriously in a jungle of shoulder-high nettles.

I had seen neither of the estate's castles in the full spate of life, as I had done another great house, Riversdale, the home of Sir Edward Archdale. Even during the war, the twentieth century had hardly touched this house. Six months of my life as an evacuee were spent on the banks of the Ballinamallard River. I lived in a cottage on the Riversdale estate with an under-gardener and his sister who worked in the kitchens during pheasant shootings.

Riversdale seems like a dream, looking back now. The estate was beautiful and beautifully kept. Carters used to lead their harvest-loaded horses past our cottage door. Byremen used to drive me away from teasing the great bull. After gales and storms the woodmen used to give us a tree felled by the winds, so that we could cut from it as much firing as we needed. The gamekeepers used to be as wary of city evacuees as they were of genuine poachers, though they were always glad of extra beaters at the shootings. The water-bailiffs used to guard their rivers jealously, but never carefully enough, for I was often up and out at dawn with a rod. And in the musty potting sheds old gardeners used to sit and eat the 'piece' I took them, and tell me stories of years ago, of years before even my own dream years at Riversdale. Things, declared these old men sitting in the cobwebby sheds which belonged perfectly to the nineteenth century, were not what they were in *their* young days.

Nor were they indeed, for all this beauty, this quiet tenor of life, the solemn beauty of woods and rivers and smoke going up with still evening air as peacefully from cottage chimneys as the chimneys of the great house itself, these days were lived under a cloud. And this was because of the Master himself. Sir Edward was old and bent over two sticks, so old and bent that he could hardly climb into his private box-pew in church on Sunday. When I went up the long drive at night to meet the kitchen-maid after the Master's mysterious ceremony of late dinner, I always looked up at his room to see if the light was on. Its dimness or brightness told us whether the Master was in good health or ill, for we well knew that should he die our world of Riversdale would change. Luckily for us we did not guess the end. Two years later Sir Edward *did* die, and the mansion was left to desolation. Fungus was growing on its walls when the demolition men drove up the drive years later and razed it to the ground. The walled gardens went back to pasture, and the estate was taken over by the government for artificial insemination. Gone indeed was our little world!

But at least the ruins of the original Archdale house built in 1615, are being protected as an ancient monument—not that there is much of them to see. During the three centuries since Plantation times, estates and fortunes and ruins have come and gone. The passing of Riversdale was significant, mostly perhaps, because I saw a way of life much unchanged for hundreds of years being cut down for ever by modern life. What I saw happen at Riversdale had happened to English estates and country houses thirty years earlier, at the Great War.

Yet, for all this transitory life, Fermanagh itself and the vast gleaming stretches of Lower Lough Erne could have changed only little. Up on a high point of the road running past Castle Archdale, I met old Jack Armstrong. He was standing by the roadside hedge surveying one of the world's most spectacular scenes. Before us was spread, not only the lovely farm by the shore where Jack lived and worked, but the whole wonder of his own world. For me the view from that hilltop revealed a sudden, unexpected landscape, as though I was looking at the heart of Finland or the west coast of British Columbia. The water of the island-studded lake was liquid gold in the brilliant afternoon. The lakes appeared, laid out like an elaborate landscaped garden, at the foot of the hills which receded into a blue distance to meet even further-distant blue mountains. Where the sun glinted on the lake the water was transformed into elaborately worked silver. From the boldly curving shores, the banks rose up wooded and rounded. And then there were the islands, green and humped, or flat and brown, Heron Island, Scattered Rocks, Water Horse, Tully Point, Owl Island. There was Goat Island too covered in spring with the olive-shelled gulls' eggs, and Kinnausy covered with domestic goats gone back to nature like so much farmland that used, once upon a time, to be sown and reaped on the islands.

And more important than any of the islands, there was Devenish, with its round tower and ruined abbey founded by St. Molaisse in the year 600. But the tower and the abbey are mere modern innovations for according to tradition it is here, amid the waters of Lough Erne, that the prophet Jeremiah lies buried. Jeremiah was in Ireland visiting his daughter who married the son of Ireland's High King. She took Jacob's Pillow, the Stone of Destiny (now the Stone of Scone), with her as a dowry. Irish kings sat upon this stone for their coronation for nearly a thousand years before Fergus took it to Scotland. St. Molaisse's ruined abbey is a far cry from Westminster's glory where the stone now rests.

Far out on the water little boats, looking even smaller than water-boatmen on a pond, plied over the silver water and laid arrow-headed tracks between the islands, islands as small as kitchen gardens or as large as the Archdale estates, islands varying from a few yards to several miles in length. At the end of Lough Erne a new hydro-electric scheme has been built, and Farmer Armstrong complained that it kept the water level 'too high for the comfort of the boats'.

He knew because he had a boat himself. He said I could use it for rowing across the lough to an island immediately below us. This was White Island and the farmer pointed out some of his nephew's Black Angus cattle. Jack Armstrong seemed to be quite lost in this world of lakes and islands and sky. He stood looking at it all as though it were a book he could read.

After twenty minutes of lazy rowing I tied the painter to White Island's tiny wooden landing stage among the reeds. Trees ringed the island, as though to hide it. Many trees stood half in the water, like cattle in the amber shallows, revealing how the level of the lake had risen. White Island lay silent and shimmering, soaking in the sun. I walked through the screen of water's-edge trees and came upon a rounded hill. The grass was speckled like a Donegal tweed. Flecks of red and white clover showed in it, as well as bugle ranging in colour from green dyed with pale violet to the darkest blue.

I suddenly had the feeling of being watched, though I had supposed I was alone on the island since mine was the only boat at the little landing stage. Then, with shock, I saw the eyes looking at me. I had walked up the grassy slope and through the doorway of a roofless church. Against the far wall were the figures, impassive, mysterious, watching.

The seven stone figures were not unfamiliar but I had not expected to find them *there* like *that*, nor to find them so inexplicably uncanny. It may have been the loneliness of the place, but the seven figures seemed to have an extraordinary presence. A pagan air clung about them, as though their dead stone eyes had looked on human sacrifice. Although the largest was no more than four feet high, they were awesome.

The figures are said to date from the eighth century, five hundred years before the island's church was rebuilt in the twelfth century in the Irish version of Romanesque. Old superstitions say that the figures could produce fertility in humans and animals. Veneration for them in past ages was also linked with fear. Even in the hot sun of mid-afternoon there was something sinister about them. The Church was so embarrassed by the statues that for centuries they were kept concealed. The wonder is that they were not destroyed as idols.

I put such supernatural nonsense out of my head and tried to tell myself that the statues could have been Barbara Hepworth *maquettes*, or that the seven figures were like kings and queens and jacks in a pack of playing cards. I wandered round the church and looked at its yard-thick walls and its carved round-headed doorway. I lay down in the scorching sun to sunbathe, and heard no sounds louder than the ticking of my watch, and bumble-bees busy-bodying too close to my ear, and the distant hum of motor-boats with youngsters water-ski-ing on the lake. But every now and again I peeped at the pagan idols. There was no use arguing with myself. They *were* uncanny.

Plashing through the lough in my lazy boat again, I felt the old, deep beauty of the place, a lonely, haunted beauty. What would Vaughan Williams or Sibelius have produced, I wondered, if they had grown up among these lakes and islands of ruins and romances that were already ancient by the Middle Ages?

Fermanagh had one musician, at least, who has captured the ghostly beauty. Joan Trimble, and her sister Valerie, made themselves famous during the war by their playing of music for two pianos. Their deft and lyrical touch made the radio programme *Tuesday Serenade* one of the B.B.C.'s most successful musical undertakings. Joan and Valerie Trimble's pianos sing. Professional duos of this kind and quality are rare. Yet Joan Trimble is rare in another way, too, for she composes piano music of an extraordinary, moving and evocative power. This music is rare also because Joan Trimble is one of the few composers who can use the style devised by Vaughan Williams without either copying or debasing it.

She makes the modal harmonies and the flattened seventh serve her flowing melodies, whether in original pieces or in her arrange-ment of traditonal airs such as *Gartan Mother's Lullaby* and *The Cows are a-milking*. Her own compositions are in the same *genre*, fresh and alive, with original melodies which might, for all one knows, be as old as the hills. It is a pity that lovely things like *The Green Bough* and *The Bard of Lisgoole* or the happy jig *Buttermilk Point* are almost unknown. But then, so is Fermanagh itself.

Irvinestown was an ideal place to stay for both the lough and the countryside were accessible. And Mahon's Hotel was also ideal, neither too formal for relaxation nor too lax for comfort and good fare. In short, the little town was a fine place for indulging in the eighth deadly sin—the love of being spoilt. But I wanted to follow Lower Lough Erne's shores and so next day boarded the Belleek bus.

It trundled along the main county roads which, though now newly made-up were as unfrequented as country lanes. The only traffic which slowed the bus was reaping machines and balers going from one field gate to the next. Occasionally the bus driver pulled up while the conductor threw out bundles of the day's newspapers at the end of farm lanes. Trees in the full heaviness of high summer hung in clouds over the roads, then opened out to views of the lough, sleek in the morning sun, still hazy with enough morning mist to make the islands mysterious and luring.

We passed a hillside of donkeys which belonged perhaps to Matt Valentine. We passed one part of the lough opening like an inlet from the sea, where so many small islands crowded together that they looked like a fleet at anchor. Before running into Pettigo we passed a stretch of Lough Erne with hills on the farther side. The morning light and haze played curious tricks with colour, the hills were a deep, unreal blue, and the sky-horizon immediately above them, brightened into an unreal yellow, so that the landscape here looked momentarily like a Victorian oleograph.

We stopped at Pettigo, a town famous for centuries as the starting and ending for pilgrims going to and from Lough Derg. In spite of its Walls Ice Cream and Coca-Cola signs, Pettigo remains a country town, still with more tractors than Cadillacs in its streets.

The border between Northern Ireland and the Irish Republic neatly cuts Pettigo in two. The border, however, is not an affair of barbed wire, anti-tank emplacements and machine-gun nests. The schoolboy who described the Equator as a menagerie lion running round the middle of the earth, would probably describe this border as a menagerie donkey. Off-duty policemen sat under a chestnut tree like great blond Danes in Copenhagen's deer forest. Without examination or even having to stop, the bus passed the Customs Post and we went over into the Republic.

It is difficult to imagine, in the general run of things, gold nuggets or hashish being run as contraband through the Customs Post. During the war, smuggling was common. Many of my Fermanagh days were enlivened by smuggling runs, taking tea into the Republic and bringing back sugar. To my regret ever since, I never took part in those mock funerals whose coffins contained rationed goods.

Today, the greatest traffic, apart from farmers who drive cattle over the border to get the Northern Government subsidy, is in plastic or plaster Madonnas and medallions, rosaries, prayer cards and lives of the saints being brought by pilgrims from Lough Derg as mementoes of their three days and nights penance and fasting.

The pilgrims had not always been so well behaved during Pettigo's long connection with Lough Derg. Long after Pope Alexander VI closed the lough down as a place of pilgrimage because of wild excesses of behaviour, it was opened up again. Fighting celebrations often occurred to mark the end of the holy exercises. When the remarkable Philip Skelton was Protestant rector in the eighteenth century he engaged a boxer called Jonas Good to protect him from 'so rough, disorderly, drunken and quarrelsome pilgrims'.

But the clergyman was good with his own fists when the occasion arose. When he was curate Skelton had given a rude churchwarden a sound thrashing during a vestry meeting.

Like the great Bishop of Derry who chose him as his chaplain, Skelton was full of contradictions. He was in no way sentimental about defending himself. Yet his care for the poverty-stricken made him the most charitable and diligent divine in the Church of Ireland before its disestablishment. Born in County Antrim in 1707 Skelton's boyhood was such that even candles were a luxury. After dark he had to throw dry furze on the fire and study by its blaze. Yet he achieved a high level of literacy. Some of his early writings were, at one time, erroneously supposed to be by Swift.

Skelton never forgot the conditions which the poor struggled against. Soon after arriving in Fermanagh as a curate he tore off his shirt to dress the wounds of a child in a burnt cottage. His generosity was unlimited. He sold his library and put the proceeds in the poor box. Four times famine struck his people and four times he got rid of his personal possessions in order to feed them.

The good parson must have been highly strung for, like Dr. Johnson, he suffered from hypochondriasis. Occasionally, he assembled his congregation to witness his death. This particular quirk was cured when one parishioner said, 'Make a day, sir, and keep it, and don't be always disappointing us thus.'

When he went to the wild moorland parish around Lough Derg, he took Jonas the ex-boxer with him. While Jonas was helping to keep the pilgrim wolves from his door, Parson Skelton was laying down the law to the Presbyterians who went so far as to charge the rector with being a Sabbath breaker, for they discovered that he shaved on Sunday!

This part of Lough Erne is frequented not only by pilgrims bent on pain but by people seeking pleasure on Bundoran's seafront. Bundoran is for Fermanagh what Brighton is for London, and the county people feel, in any case, a great affinity with County Donegal.

The border is difficult to define around Pettigo and after the bus left the town we whisked in and out of Northern Ireland and the Republic as quick as pixies jumping on a milk churn. At one moment we passed an ordinary Post Office standard issue red telephone kiosk and the next moment a green one with ᴛeᴌeꝓon over the door.

Now the road ran for miles by the lough and the mountains came down like sea cliffs. And well they might at this point, for the sea lay only five miles beyond this northern tip of the lough, the narrow neck of land which joins County Donegal to the rest of the Irish Republic. The countryside changed from verdant pasture and soft woods to stark mountains and wild cotton moors exactly like Paul Henry's tourist posters of the 1930s with their piles of cumulus cloud, dry-stone walls, thatched cottages and turf stacks.

At the entrance to Castle Caldwell we passed a huge violin carved out of stone erected 'To the memory of Dennis McCabe, fiddler, who fell out of St. Patrick's Barge belonging to Sir James Caldwell, Bart. and Count of Milan, and was drowned . . . August 1770.' The epitaph added a warning to other fiddlers to keep away from water:

> *On firm land only exercise your skill,*
> *There you may play and safely drink your fill.*

The craftsmen at Belleek were exercising *their* skill on firm land when I went into this world-famous pottery. In fact, there were over a hundred of them working in the gaunt grey building outside the diminutive town. With a finger nimbleness no less enviable than the fiddlers', they were making angels and roses, cake-stands and ash-trays, using fine strands of china-clay which are one of the distinguishing marks of Belleek china. Somehow, this craftsmanship struck me as being offbeat in the modern world where such clever fingers are usually found assembling transistor radio parts in Japanese factories or in Swiss farmhouses on long winter nights where the farmers put together the tiny wheels and cogs of Swiss watches.

Apart from the cups and saucers, jugs and bowls decorated with harps and shamrocks there were some large figure pieces. The design of these 'Prisoner of Love' or 'International Centre Piece' was High Victoriana, and there were other things of this kind, notably girls with water pitchers such as may be seen in any sentimental Victorian picture of the simple life. Visitors to the pottery are numerous and little parties of them are steered around the building to see in turn each process. Most of the sightseers were Americans and Germans and they admired it all immensely and queued up to buy souvenirs.

I went back into the town and saw a real girl from the Belleek China Showroom with a pitcher drawing water from the village pump, a difference in detail being that *her* pitcher was an electric kettle. From the vicinity of the Provincial Bank in the parlour of one house (opened on Thursday from 11 a.m. to 1 p.m. and every third Friday) came the sound of bantams crowing. Holidaymakers complete with their own boats on trailers or on the top of their cars were driving through the town and I had no difficulty once again in getting a lift, this time to Garrison.

Here is the shrine of pilgrimage for the disciples of Izaak Walton. Lough Melvin is surrounded by woods and mountains and its waters are sacred to fishermen. Garrison itself is in Northern Ireland but the highly-prized waters are shared by both North and South and Green Parson and Orange Grouie are much recommended flies for those anglers after salmon.

Many people come here to fish for sonaghan which, like the handsome gillaroo, is indigenous to Lough Melvin. Sonaghan are deep-coloured trout, and though seldom weighing more than a pound, they are renowned for their bold rising and hard fighting. Gillaroo—the red serving boy—is a larger trout with a bright golden sheen, and is, without doubt, superior eating to any of its salmon relatives.

A Swiss or French *chef de cuisine* would disagree, however, about the gillaroo, because Lough Melvin teems with their *omble chevalier* —the char which is taken, like the ferox, by trolling. Although I had caught and eaten char as a boy, it was not until years later when I lived in Zürich that I understood why this fish is so revered on the Continent, even to the extent of being protected by a special licence in France.

Forest stretched for many miles along the road to Enniskillen. When I got off the bus in Fermanagh's county town, I knew once more I was 'home', a delectable feeling of ease I had known each time in my life I returned to Enniskillen, that pleasant town pleasantly islanded between Upper and Lower Lough Erne. I had more in common with the local lads out after perch with worm than with the business executives after the lordly gillaroo at Lough Melvin.

I sat in the broad meadow. It was evening. The meadow lay beside the lough, though here the water is a mere neck, a river, at this point, making a beautiful park for the town. Youths were spinning stones across the millpond surface of the water. Their dogs, as well as nobody's dogs, chased up and down the bank barking with the excitement, yet not daring to jump in after the stones. The plumbers' mates had rolled off their dungarees and joined the young cattle-drovers in sweaty singlets for the day's last bout of football. In the narrow channel, the rich sped by in boats with out-board motors and the not-so-rich passed more slowly, plying their oars through the reedy river to the wider horizons of the lakelands. And the gregarious swallows, the gliding swifts, and the fluttering house-martins drifted and darted about black against a sky draining slowly of light, as they high-tea'd on the wing.

Nostalgia rose out of this landscape like the evening scents of honeysuckle that presently would rise out of the hedgerows. Straight across the water from where I sat in broad meadow was the red shed once owned by Ovens the cattle-drover where I bought my first dropped calf. And there also was the Scotch store which cattle, then driven on the hoof, did not like to pass on their way to the fair because of the smell of pigs being slaughtered. And I could not quite see Gracey's store where, once upon a day, I cycled into the town every morning with my harvest of rabbits from trapping and snaring strung proudly over the handlebars.

Enniskillen's main, winding street had changed little over the years, little indeed since Georgian times except for the addition of another cathedral and a Victorian town hall. From the broad meadow by the river the Catholic cathedral dominated the scene, rising up above the slate roofs in much the same way as St. Philip Neri commands the roofs and sweeping wooded downland at Arundel in Sussex.

However, this cathedral—like another Sussex building, the splendid chapel of Lancing College—never had its tower built, so that from the main street it is the Planters' Gothic church, now the

Protestant cathedral, which catches the eye. Its chief glory lies in its links with the military exploits of the two regiments associated with the town, the Inniskilling Dragoons and the Royal Inniskilling Fusiliers, whose fading and disintegrating colours hang in state from the cathedral walls.

In the days when battles were thought to be much more fun than they are generally now regarded, Enniskillen's name was one of glory all over the world. But the town did more than merely lend its name to fame—it had its share in Ulster's own battles. With Derry, Aughrim and the Boyne, Enniskillen enjoys special mention in Orange songs. But perhaps none of this valour ought to surprise for the old name of the island town was Innis Cethlen—after Cethlen, wife of Balor of the Mighty Blows.

Unlike Derry with its still-complete walls, Enniskillen today shows little signs of its own battle scars. Almost the only remnant of its fighting days is the old castle water-gate, a two-turreted stone gateway separated from the lough by the meadows.

Enniskillen, however, has something immensely superior to this ruin from a crude and brutal age. Not a mile from the town's outskirts a drive wends its way between overhanging trees and between summer meadows, and curving round a gentle rise leads to the magnificent Castle Coole, a masterpiece of James Wyatt, designed in the late eighteenth century and already exhibiting the eschewing of elegance which distinguished the work of the nineteenth-century Classical architects. Refined taste was already out of fashion, largely due to the influence of contemporary French architects. Solidity, massiveness, even a certain degree of coarseness were introduced, and Wyatt, knowingly or not, built Castle Coole along these lines.

The great square blocks of the house and its superbly impressive giant Ionic portico rise abruptly from the meadows around it, for formal gardens had here gone out with elegance. As Wyatt himself said, he wanted to design a house where it was possible to 'step from a hayfield into a mansion'—perhaps not such a strange conceit as might at first appear. It was a form of reality, expressive of the different world which had come into being since such frivolities as the Queen's pretty Dairy at Versailles had been built before the Revolution.

ANOTHER ROAD IN TIME

Castle Coole is as solid as rock and has been kept in perfect condition through the years. Although the property is now in National Trust hands, the family still lives in a part of the house. The Earls of Belmore have always taken an interest in their seat and this has saved the building from the fate of so many great houses in Ulster.

Even as late as 1949, a horse-drawn carriage used to go up and down the long winding drive, under the storm-scarred oaks and past the misty meadows, taking the Earl of Belmore into town. A liveried coachman sat on the dickey while the old lord sat behind in his straw boater looking at the girls going by. And why not, indeed, for the girls of Enniskillen with their buttermilk skins and fine-gold hair and green eyes are worth looking at.

It was the first Lord Belmore himself who, having commissioned James Wyatt to make the design, acted as the contractor and supervised the erection of the mansion. The Earl could have had no easy task for Castle Coole is a large house with a great central block and two lower side wings terminating in pavilions. The style is plain yet enriched with Classical motifs. The central block has the enormous and stately Ionic portico and the wings have Doric porticoes. On the other side, the building breaks into a bow which makes a splendid shape for the rooms behind it.

The interior is well preserved and sumptuous, each great saloon opening into the next. A double staircase leads to an upper hall which has a gallery running behind truncated columns, designed with the curious clumsiness which was deliberately contrived and much in vogue in France at the time. With an almost modern sense of ingenuity the stoves in this upper hall were set into niches and disguised as column stumps serving as the base for busts of Greek poets, resulting in a composition most markedly French.

Outside, the day was simmering in a humid, high summer heat. The air was heavy with the smell of hay. I was glad to sit outside in the cool shade of a portico. The present Earl, a red-headed schoolboy, was home with some of his friends. The young Earl's mother recalled her first meeting with me twelve years previously—when, as she put it, I was a wild young poet with curly hair. Those were the days, I reflected sipping gin, realizing I was no longer wild, young or curly-headed.

The boys, though spending their holidays at Castle Coole, were not at Portora, the public school founded in 1608 by James I, which stands on a hill at the other end of Enniskillen. I walked out to the school after lunch, and was able to see it all since the boys were away. I was, however, disappointed in not meeting the school's music master, Anthony Smith, who has been St. Cecilia's devotee for many years in County Fermanagh. However, I did see, in the list of royal scholars, against the year 1871, the name, Oscar Wilde. Perhaps it was at Portora Oscar Wilde decided that '. . . examinations are of no value whatsoever. If a man is a gentleman he knows quite enough, and if he is not a gentleman, whatever he knows is bad for him.'

Wilde himself must have known the wonderful landscapes seen from the school's hilltop. Spread before Portora are the loughs and islands and Enniskillen and Mount Belmore to the right. Portora could, in such a position, hardly be anything else but a 'rowing' school, but more importantly the boys are encouraged during their free time to go cycling or boating in exploration of the rivers and lakes and mountains which make Fermanagh a paradise.

I continued my own exploration of the county, principally by the bus which delivered and collected mail. Upper Lough Erne is different from the Lower Lough in that its islands are so crowded that little water is left between. A map of the lough looks like a partially completed jig-saw puzzle. Tenuous peninsulas snake for miles into the water like islands. Many have their own, lesser lakes within them, as some of the islands themselves have also, such as Cleenish which has two lakes. The shore line is so corrugated and indented that hundreds of bridges and causeways would be needed for a road to follow the lough's edge. First thoughts might suggest that this absence of a water's-edge road is a disadvantage, but the lough shore and islands remain in their natural state, a perfect place for escape from a noisy world which is too much with us.

Conscious of, but not always in sight of the Upper Lough, I went in the mail bus from Enniskillen and our first stop was at Lisbellaw, a small town which I associate with my own growing up, for it was from there that I had my first long-trousered suit of Lisbellaw tweed. Then I set off north away from the main waters to Lough Eyes and its crannoges. But these lake dwellings did not detain me as did the manor dwelling at Tempo, farther north still. The lake here, and the surrounding gardens are reminiscent of Hokusai and the serenity of the wood engravings done in his old age, such as *The Gatherer of Rushes*. Like Japanese gardens, Tempo's landscape is intellectualized, and not merely because of its Japanese maples and flowers. The whole layout and design of these fabulous gardens resembled the illustrations of a poem by Abe Nakamaro.

But as I walked round the lake it was a D. H. Lawrence poem which seemed most apt, for I saw the deepest blue willow gentians:

> *black lamps from the halls of Dis, burning dark blue,*
> *giving off darkness, blue darkness, as Demeter's pale lamps give*
> *off light.*

My eyes darted from magnolia and camellia to red and pink, white and lemon lilies scattered like confetti over the placid water gardens. And as though to carry my Japanese impression even further Sir John Langham took me into his study and showed me more wonders of drawing than even Hokusai attempted, for Sir John's painted studies of flowers were not the odd individual one but whole sets. He worked at these paintings with consummate skill and he had so far recorded over four thousand sets of flowers in this way with a precision and detail beyond the powers of the camera. He had also begun to record fungi in the same fashion. He told me that so far he had found one hundred and seventy-seven different kinds of fungi around Tempo.

Lady Langham said I must see the stables before leaving for they had a story, somewhat gruesome, but sufficient to add an air of mystery to Tempo's romance—a romantic story, I told my hostess, at least on a par with the romance of her father's home in Cornwall—Menabilly, which Daphne du Maurier made famous as Manderley in *Rebecca*.

Like Enniskillen, Tempo was once the property of the Maguires, Fermanagh's chieftains before the reign of James I. One of the Maguire stable-boys was brutally murdered and buried under the stable step at Tempo Manor. Thirty years ago, Sir John's father dug up this grave and took the skull into the house, which is crammed with scholarly objects of research. Immediately afterwards, a series of accidents to the occupants began, so markedly connected with the skull being brought indoors, that it was taken out of the house again, whereupon the accidents stopped.

Auto-suggestion? Deep psychological anxiety about the skull's presence? Nobody, of course, will ever know. But psychology cannot explain why curious things also happened in the stables. These had been disused until recently. The present owners, not being given to superstitions, decided to open the stables up again and use them for rearing calves. But not one calf was reared. All died violent deaths, by going berserk or dashing through windows, Lady Langham told me as we came out of the stables, which are now empty and disused again.

Skulls also figured in the next country house I saw, Colebrooke. The late Duke of Abercorn used to call its dining-room Golgotha. Hundreds of animal horns complete with skulls hung there on each wall. The *pièce de résistance* was the centre lamp-fitting, a pyramid of antlers and light bulbs. But this Landseer graveyard quite belies Colebrooke's elegance and proportions, and above all the beauty of its setting. The parkland is perfect. It is neither too wild nor too tame with the hoary oaks, trout stream and cattle sleek with summer grasses.

Colebrooke is the home of Northern Ireland's former Prime Minister, Lord Brookeborough, who is a born countryman, happy at last to be free of office so that he can devote his time to these ancestral acres. Lady Brookeborough put down her scythe from cutting grass and took me to the river where her husband was talking with a farmer. Trout broke the still waters and grey wagtails bobbed about the weirs. This scene, with Lady Brookeborough in old gardening trousers, calling her husband home to tea, might have been the scene on any Fermanagh farm. I had tea with this man and his wife whose talk was country talk about fairs and farmers and that year's scarcity of kingfishers.

Going back towards Upper Lough Erne I came to Maguiresbridge on the Colebrooke River. The weather was still hot, and the farmer were going about in shirt-sleeves and waistcoats. Dragonflies glided along the riverbanks, clad in jewels and veils like Oriental princesses. Maguiresbridge is quiet enough today, but it perpetuates the memory of the Maguires who, in common with their age, seem to have been a bloodthirsty crew. Aghalurcher church, beyond Lisnaskea, was the scene of another Maguire murder, an even more dramatic one than the unfortunate stable-boy's. Here, according to the *Annals of Ulster*, Thomas Maguire, Junior, put a 'French roof' on the church in 1447. The tree-shaded graveyard is both now a ruin and an ancient monument in state care. It is a monument, however, generally avoided by local people, like Tempo's stables, for on the altar itself, in 1484, another Maguire killed a kinsman in a tribal feud.

The Maguires' name peculiarly persists in these parts for besides Aghalurcher—The Field of the Foal—Lisnaskea is also associated with the family. Lisnaskea means The Fort of the Whitethorn Tree and it was under this tree that the Maguires were inaugurated as the local princelings. Fortunately for me, nothing more murderous than Lisnaskea's housewives were out, sitting under the trees of a new housing estate, busily knitting, hoping to win their crown in the '£50 Knitting Competition' advertised on all the posters.

The Maguires' bloody history put me in mind of *Hamlet* and especially of Ophelia as I went across the Upper Lough to the island of Inish Rath, for the island's outer fringe was a water garden of Shakespeare's long purples and reeds. The purple loosestrife which garlands so many of these islands is what Millais put in his painting of Ophelia. But although long purples is probably the best known name today for purple loosestrife, Shakespeare probably meant the bawdy *Orchis mascula,*

> *That liberal shepherds give a grosser name,*
> *But our cold maids do dead men's fingers call them.*

The early purple orchid was the principal source of aphrodisiac mixtures even in Dioscorides's day. He records how the Thessalian women served its roots. The liberal (free-spoken) shepherds of Shakespeare's day had a more straightforward not-quite-polite name for early purple orchids as people in the north of England still do. One old charmer I knew in boyhood in Fermanagh had all the recipes of the Thessalian women for exciting desire.

But the long purples were as genuine on Inish Rath as the land-scapes by Matthew Smith and Victor Vignon I saw in a house on the island. Without ever doing much about it, I have often contemplated taking to the simple life. One of Fermanagh's islands would be ideal for this purpose, provided of course that the simple life could be rendered comfortable with such things as central heating, long-play records, paintings and a library.

This happy, almost unbelievable combination was what Konstanty Scheunert and his wife Ruth have built for themselves. Konstanty came like some medieval hermit or pilgrim to the islands and made a refuge from the horrors of the war's barracks and prison-camps and the rape of his native Poland.

Inish Rath is an island of twenty acres, cloistered by old woods of oak and beech, and as though drawn by Russalka, the water-sprite of Slavonic legend, Konstanty settled here when his misfortunes of war turned to the fortunes of peace. Now, the lawns of his house ring to the playing of children and the frolicking of whippets. Fantastic peaches hung velvety on the walls, ripening beside Egyptian moon-flowers, and along the woodland paths Himalayan honeysuckle was no stranger to the simple birch knolls carpeted with montbretia.

Konstanty and Ruth have their farm on another island, Derenish, where only a fisherman lives and the herds. Here on Inish Rath there is only their own house. They have no television in the house but through the windows there are the beauties and wonders, seen in gaps cut in the encircling ring of trees, of the view across the lake to Derenish and its sister islands.

I sat in the log-warmed hall with Konstanty looking down to his sheep and cattle grazing on the next island, watching the mystery of water changing mood and colour under a tortured Vlaminck sky. And when the curtains were finally drawn, and everybody else had gone to bed, and Konstanty sat talking to me, I watched the log-flames leaping in the fireplace and over the walls, unable to tell quite which were the colours and flicker of the fire and which were the similar things glowing and warming the young flesh of a Matthew Smith nude hanging on the wall.

This was the ideal way to farm, but few of Lough Erne's islands are as carefully husbanded. Many are tangled woods of spindle-tree and guelder-rose or wild gardens choked with milkwort and creeping-jenny, occupied only by wren and willow-warbler. The purring sound of sewing machines breaking the stillness of the gathering night was not from any engine. It was the churring nocturnal song of nightjar, going about its business of hunting the tiger and the fox or any other moth which came within the range of its direct, deliberate flight.

James Fraser, the Dublin landscape gardener, made a number of visits to this part of Fermanagh. In his book, *Guide through Ireland* published in 1838, he wrote, 'It is only those who have sailed through this labyrinth of little lakes can form a correct idea of their devious wanderings—their endlessly varied creeks and bays—or the numerous pretty islets they contain.' This, however, was before the Great Famine when so many people lived on the islands. Fraser also wrote, 'And it adds not a little to the interest of the scenery to see the peasantry who are located on the islands, rowing their little home-made skiffs over the smooth waters from isle to isle, at which men and women, young and old are equally expert.'

The lough's smooth waters have claimed the skiffs and most traces of the cottages have been swallowed up by holly and hawthorn, weeping ash and the ubiquitous rush. Life has left most of the islands, but still thrives on the main shores. But another kind of remote life goes on in the cottages nestling against the roots of the mountains. It is almost secret, so far removed is it from the noisy, hurrying, luxurious and protected life of the affluent society which is becoming normal in England. What goes on in these cottages when the long winter nights descend and storms race in from the Atlantic and the woods roar and the mountains moan in the gales? Do the people still leave a cup of water on the dresser for the fairies? Do they put a saucer of milk-sops on the hearth for the crickets, which tumble out of their crevices behind the fire when the last rosary is said and the oil lamp extinguished? How many remember the Irish grace for light on taking their candle to bed, 'O Redeemer, grant the light of heaven to every poor soul who has left this world, and to all souls whom we wish to pray for'?

Mount Belmore is the peak of the bleak plateau west of Enniskillen. It is a poor mountain region where the old system of herding is carried on by labourers who run the farms for absentee landlords of whom many are shopkeepers in Enniskillen. To reach this country the Scillies River has to be crossed, and before this there is Glencunny Wood, and I once lived there when I was a boy for four months.

Not everybody took kindly to Belfast evacuees and to me, but the herdsman of Glencunny Wood did. He had already seen life, for he had been away from Ireland for many years, trapping in the North of Canada. He knew what it was like to be alone. What heavenly days I had in that little house among the trees, getting up to go through the pre-dawn forest to fish in the Scillies.

When the doubtless well-meaning education authorities decided that fishing and rabbit-snaring and all the thousand busy moments of a free life along the river and in the woods were not as good as blackboards and exercise books, for which I displayed a strong dislike, they whisked me away to another billet. And this was on a farm in the wide valley between Battery Fort and the hills of Nixon Hall.

The ruins of Nixon Hall are now used as the shed for an Enniskillen butcher's cattle. His herdsman was a school friend of mine and every time I go back to the farm now he comes down the hill to call on me in the valley where, by strange good fortune, the despairing authorities billeted me in 1941.

Stones from old Nixon Hall went to the making of the farmhouse's whitewashed walls. It stands, on a slight rise, at the end of a long, crooked lane which passes bog-banks and overgrown orchards. This lane and the little house at its head, and the fire still burning on the open hearth and the welcome I know is always there, is the reason why my pulse quickens when I get as far west as Enniskillen and then leave the town for the last miles—home.

More than twenty years have gone by since the elderly brother and sister took the wild Belfast boy into their home. And they are still there, running the farm of thirty-five acres. In all the terrible frosts and deep snows of the 1962–3 winter, Christy went out to cut wood from the hedges to keep the open fire going, for the fire is not only the place where all the food for both humans and animals is cooked, it is also the soul of the house.

ANOTHER ROAD IN TIME

Christy's sister, Maggie, goes half a mile through rushy pastures every time a bucket of water from the spring is needed. These people are the granite stock of Ulster, people who have made Ulster, people who are the image of Ulster, whose hayseeds are the ones that drop out in the streets of Belfast, and, for that matter, all over the world.

Neither Maggie nor Christy has ever been to a doctor or a hospital in their long lives. When a cow put its horn through Christy's eye he accepted the resulting blindness as oncoming old age. When Maggie slipped on the winter's ice coming from the well she went up to see the man with the charms for sprains at Five Points.

So from Enniskillen and the lough and its islands and the great country houses and the lesser country houses, I walked once more up the happy lane of my home. The house, I was sure, would be full of people come in for a *ceili*. Their talk would be about everyday life as woodmen or byremen, farmers and roadmenders. And since few people in country districts are bitter, there would be sad songs of sad happenings in troubled, rebel times, and, almost in the same breath, rousing Orange battle tunes. And afterwards there would be the sound of hobnailed boots flying in two-hand reels—the sweetest of all the sounds I had heard on my journey through the Six Counties.

I lifted the latch at the back door beside the dairy where the pet pigs were now kept because they had outgrown their box by the kitchen fire. Voices came from within. Hughie's would be surely one of them. Shortly he would break into one of his strange Irish songs, sung in the age-old traditional way, full of strange quarter-tones and nasal sounds, and odd rhythms, the melodies from which Stanford and Harty and Joan Trimble drew their fluid, easy music.

Hughie was one of the last mummers. Like his singing, this local tradition also came down from immemorial ages. The mummers went from farm to farm at Christmas time. Dressed in their weird straw costumes they danced and sang and performed outrageous impersonations of women or Beelzebub, Devil Doubt, Doctor Bighead, Oliver Cromwell or Prince George. After the Christmas mummers, other 'Straw Boys' used to call at Maggie's and Christy's farm. These were the Wren Hunters complete with holly bushes and dead birds. They would cry and wail like the banshee as they went through the rites of hunting the little wren whose ancestors had spied on Christ in Gethsemane. Wild reels and hornpipes were then danced by the Wren Boys to shouts of:

> *The Wren, the Wren, the king of all birds,*
> *Was caught on Stephen's Day in the furze,*
> *Among all birds the wren is great,*
> *So rise up young master and give us a treat,*
> *Up with the kettle and down with the pan*
> *Give us a ransom and let us be gone.*

The traditional handing-round of funeral clay pipes and tobacco was performed for the last time in this district at Hughie's father's funeral. But others of Fermanagh's old ways do not pass so easily, and I wondered if Tom's voice was among those I heard round Maggie's kitchen fire. He often came down from Garrison to spend a day cutting wood for the old people. Tom could lead a child to water to cure the mumps, muttering his secret charm which he inherited from his father. 'He let the last wee girl fall into the river' Maggie assured me adding, with a glint in her eye, 'He'd had a wee glass taken.'

Next morning when the kid goats had perched up on the window-sill to put their heads through my open window, I got up and took a basin down the lane to the bog to wash and shave in its soft, amber water. I passed the corner of a field where a penny hedge-school once stood. When I was a boy of 12 and Christy told me of this primitive country school, I thought it such a strange, old fashioned thing. Christy told me also how some local boys pulled away the wooden prop which held the hedge-school up, so that the place collapsed and afterwards fell into disuse.

But who was I to laugh at old fashioned things? Already, a mere twenty years later, the mill at Florencecourt where I used to take Christy's corn for grinding, has become a museum-piece in Belfast. A horse-drawn van once carried us boys up and down the Fermanagh hills to Master Sullivan's school at Lisgoole. It was like something out of a Wild West film. To the boys of today who go to Lisgoole in a special bus, the horse van would seem as antiquated as Christy's propped-up hedge-school did to me.

ANOTHER ROAD IN TIME

I finished my shaving in the rare luxury of the marvellously soft and fragrant bog water and went off down the road to borrow a bicycle to ride in to Enniskillen. I went by Gransha Orange Hall where I once put by the gate a bootbox full of straw tied in knots for some innocent passer-by to pick up and unwittingly buy my warts. Then I saw two boys coming sheepishly out from raiding an orchard. This was an orchard I had plundered many times myself.

An idea came to me, welling up like a spring, running like a stream. I cycled into Enniskillen, careering wildly along, trying to identify the idea. And at last, the rushing river inside of me got its name—it was the river of re-generation, of re-birth, and recurrence of life itself, which even here, in this place I have loved more than any other on earth, goes on from season to season, spring following spring, and . . . apple-stealing boys following apple-stealing boys. . . .

Yes, I thought, walking about Enniskillen trying to recognize the farm-tanned faces of old friends going to the cattle market, a lot has changed since the gangling Belfast evacuee tumbled out of the train at Enniskillen with his borrowed suitcase on a summer's evening in 1940.

But, beneath, it is the same. Nor was this a crank idea of mine alone for the Ulster poet John Hewitt knew it also.

His verse is the voice of Ulster's soil, the mood of its harvest fields and harvest songs, the voice of walks through the timelessness of the Mourne mountains, of the reed-ruffled surface of Erne's lakes, and even of the lanes such as my herdsman friend from Nixon Hall and I went as we plundered orchards on our way home from Lisgoole school whence the horse-drawn van had brought us—

> . . . *The boys I met*
> *munching their windfalls, coming late from school*
> *are like that boy a hundred years ago,*
> *the same bare kibes, the same drab heirloom rags,*
> *but they must take another road in time.*

Index

INDEX

INDEX

INDEX

INDEX

INDEX

INDEX

INDEX

OTHER BLACKSTAFF PRESS TITLES
by

ROBERT HARBINSON
(ROBIN BRYANS)

NO SURRENDER
ROBERT HARBINSON

'The event was spectacular. Nearly eleven pounds I weighed. "Ya've the muscles of a man," said the district nurse when she congratulated Big 'Ina on having such a brute. My mother never forgot the nurse's remark. The years that followed were to prove that only those muscles would ensure our survival.'

Robert Harbinson's famous account of his Belfast boyhood – the devastating shock of his window-cleaner father's early death, his mother Big 'Ina's unending battles against poverty and tuberculosis ('It' to the little family), his first rapturous encounters with nature, circumscribed as it was by 'the Bog Meadows' marshy steppes' – was enthusiastically received when it was first published in 1960.

'A tough, but never a hard-luck tale Mr Harbinson manages to make his; full of pathos and pride and fresh, hot anger. . . [he] makes us believe in the passions of his childhood.'
Guardian

'He is on all planes at once; humorous, detailed and objective as a Brueghel village scene; quietly indignant over injustices practised by the toffs; puzzled, exploratory, expectant, as a growing boy. . . He writes as one with a true sense of poetry.'
The Times

'. . . crammed with the stuff of life. The raucous cobbled streets, the grimy mission halls and the evening mists that made the Bog Meadows a place of mystery, the bitterness and the passion of the religious and political background – Robert Harbinson conjures them up out of his memory with a sureness of touch that gives authority to every page.'
Irish Independent

First paperback edition

198 x 129 mm; 224 pp; 0 85640 383 0; pb
£4.50

SONG OF ERNE
ROBERT HARBINSON

'My mother's last words, flung through the window as the bus gathered speed, were – "An' keep yer snout clean up there." For her, the country was always "up there", and she was anxious I should forsake the evil ways I had picked up in the city. She wanted me to come back sobered and settled, prepared to face a steady life in the docks. Wild escapades must be at an end, new leaves must be turned, my snout, in fact, kept in an impeccable condition.'

Leaving the tough Belfast life, Robert Harbinson continues his successful autobiographical sequence with the story of his stormy time as a World War II evacuee in the woods, fields and lakes of County Fermanagh. Suspicious, scruffy, sectarian, belligerent, the twelve-year-old Robbie is a terror to the county, rampaging in quick succession through a rectory, a workhouse and a liberal sprinkling of large farms and small cottages before finding at last the perfect 'billet' with Christy and his sister Maggie. The profound joy of his life with them, helping with the farm work, enjoying their kitchen ceilidhs, basking in their uncomplicated love for him – their 'wee cub' – reverberates through these pages, making this book truly a 'Song of Erne'.

'What a gloriously nostalgic picture this is: what a delightful book to read and read again!'
British Books

'a delightful pastoral, timeless, and smelling richly of the deep country: truthful and genuine'
Tablet

First paperback edition

198 x 129 mm; 244 pp; 0 85640 394 6; pb
£4.50

UP SPAKE THE CABIN BOY
ROBERT HARBINSON

'We walked as though through a forest whose trees were made of steel, harshly etched against the morning sky. Instead of leaf-laden branches stretching out to catch the sun's rays, I saw a multitude of cranes, swinging poles and a phalanx of gantries. . . A rush of loneliness caught me and I felt dreadfully homesick for the farm.'

After his idyllic life as an evacuee in wartime Fermanagh, Robert Harbinson is back to the city with a vengeance, as a cabin boy on a dredger on Belfast Lough. This oddly circumscribed maritime life, with the salty characters and the tough 'man's work' holds him for a while, but Fermanagh's lure is stronger and he jumps ship.

A turbulent, shifting adolescence follows, with jobs in drapery and hardware shops, falling in love with one 'saved' girl and having his first sexual encounter with another one in a County Antrim hayshed, preaching in mission halls and eventually leaving Ireland for missionary training in response to the calls of the sea, adventure and religion.

'Robust, amusing, very descriptive, down to earth and down to gutter, truthful, and authentic.'
Belfast News-Letter

First paperback edition
198 x 129 mm; 256 pp; 0 85640 400 4; pb
£4.50

THE PROTÉGÉ
ROBERT HARBINSON

Full of Protestant missionary zeal and other less respectable passions, Robert Harbinson crosses the water from Ireland to wartime Britain. By turns he becomes the protégé of committed evangelicals, rich old ladies, an exotic mystical group and other, more eccentric, protectors.

'God is good, and the devil isn't bad thank God, so the boy quickly climbs into the grace and favour of an England which we know all too little about. . . With the help of pulpit-piton, Biblical axe, and ropes of charm, young Mr Harbinson at length reaches the refined and rarefied air of upper-class English society, is welcomed at great houses, and meets many rewarding and worldly people.

'He accomplishes his climb with such candour, innocence and desperation of poverty, that one feels he was really a climber on the level, and a youth with unusual gifts of hope, humour and charity.'

W.R. Rodgers, *Sunday Times*

First paperback edition

198 x 129 mm; 208 pp; 0 85640 413 6; pb
£4.50

ORDERING
BLACKSTAFF BOOKS

All Blackstaff Press books are available through bookshops. In the case of difficulty, however, orders can be made directly to the publisher. Indicate clearly the title and number of copies required and send order with your name and address to:

Cash Sales
Blackstaff Press Limited
3 Galway Park
Dundonald
Belfast BT16 0AN
Northern Ireland

Please enclose a remittance to the value of the cover price plus: 60p for the first book plus 30p per copy for each additional book ordered to cover postage and packing. Payment should be made in sterling by UK personal cheque, postal order, sterling draft or international money order, made payable to Blackstaff Press Limited.

Applicable only in the UK and Republic of Ireland